Economic and Natural Disasters since 1900

Economic and Natural Disasters since 1900

A Comparative History

John Singleton

Sheffield Hallam University, UK

EE Edward Elgar
PUBLISHING

Cheltenham, UK • Northampton, MA, USA

Published by
Edward Elgar Publishing Limited
The Lypiatts
15 Lansdown Road
Cheltenham
Glos GL50 2JA
UK

Edward Elgar Publishing, Inc.
William Pratt House
9 Dewey Court
Northampton
Massachusetts 01060
USA

A catalogue record for this book
is available from the British Library

Library of Congress Control Number: 2015954317

This book is available electronically in the **Elgar**online
Economics subject collection
DOI 10.4337/9781782547358

ISBN 978 1 78254 734 1 (cased)
ISBN 978 1 78254 735 8 (eBook)

Typeset by Columns Design XML Ltd, Reading
Printed and bound by CPI Group (UK) Ltd, Croydon, CR0 4YY

Contents

Acknowledgements

I am grateful to Edward Elgar Publishing for commissioning this book, especially Alex Pettifer my initial contact with the book proposal, and John-Paul McDonald my commissioning editor and Bob Pickens, my desk editor. I also thank everyone who has been involved at the production stage. In the History Group at Sheffield Hallam University, Joanne Laycock commented on the first draft of Chapter 1, and Melodee Beals (now at Loughborough University) drew my attention to a conference on 'Coping with Crisis' at Durham University in 2013, which proved an excellent testing ground for my early thoughts on disasters. The Durham conference also led to invitations to write chapters in two edited volumes, forcing me to clarify my thoughts as I worked on the monograph. I am grateful to all at the 'Coping with Crisis' conference who commented on my paper either on the day or later. Other papers related to the disasters project were presented at the Sheffield Political Economy Research Institute (SPERI) conference at the University of Sheffield (2013), the business history workshop at the University of York (2013), the Management History Research Group annual meeting at Institute of Financial Services (IFS) University College in London (2014), and a staff seminar at China Foreign Affairs University in Beijing (2015). I send my thanks to everyone who took part in those events. Sheffield Hallam University's Strategic Research Investment Fund kindly paid for background research relating to Chapter 5, and Chris Corker provided efficient research assistance. Teaching a final-year module on economic disasters to history students at Sheffield Hallam also helped me to focus my thinking.

1. The disaster cycle

There are disasters almost everywhere we look. England's disappointing performance at the 2015 Cricket World Cup was depicted as a 'disaster' in the British media. Team management promised to 'look at the data' in an effort to discover what had gone so badly wrong (Ashdown 2015). Few of us, however, would regard the failure of a cricket team as a disaster when set alongside an earthquake that kills 50 000, an underground explosion that results in the death of many coal miners, or an economic depression such as in the early 1930s. Whether or not an adverse event qualifies as a disaster depends on its scale and the perspective of the observer. Australians, for example, do not regard England's cricketing fiascos as disasters, even from a sporting angle. The purpose of this book is to investigate the extent to which large-scale disasters in different spheres of human activity, as well as the people and organizations caught up in them, follow the same or at least a similar script. The investigative framework is provided by the 'disaster cycle', a device that was developed by social scientists and disaster management practitioners in the twentieth century.

Every scholar comes to their subject from a certain background and perspective, and my origins are in economic and business history. The analysis of disasters has not been a major theme in economic or business history, and the disaster cycle is relatively unknown in those disciplines. Indeed, Adam Tooze (2007, 671) confesses that 'economic historians have a way of making disasters ... disappear from the long-run trajectory of economic growth'. Larry Neal, in a presidential address to the Economic History Association, makes a similar point, and urges economic historians to focus 'an increasing share of [their] research efforts on shocks ... [including] wars, epidemics, famines, natural disasters, or depressions' (Neal 2000, 332). Economic historians do investigate some disasters, not least economic depressions and financial collapses, as will be seen in later chapters, and in consequence their neglect of the area is relative rather than absolute.[1] Nevertheless, I approach the theme of disasters as something of an outsider, or at least as someone with different intellectual baggage. Before starting work on the current project, I published two books on the history of central banking (Singleton et al.

2006; Singleton 2011). The writing of the second of those books overlapped with the economic disaster commonly known as the 'Global Financial Crisis' (GFC). The hypothesis that there might be parallels between financial disasters and other types of disaster intrigued me as the second of those projects approached completion, and inspired research for the current volume.[2]

This introductory chapter begins with a section discussing the concept of disaster and how it should be defined. In the second section, the potential for making comparisons between different sorts of disaster is explored. The third section distinguishes between crisis and disaster, terms that are often used interchangeably and in a way that sows confusion. The measurement of disasters is discussed in the fourth section. In the fifth section the origins of the disaster cycle are examined. Some modifications to the disaster cycle framework are introduced in the sixth section. The seventh section concerns the drivers of the cycle: they are to be found in aspects of individual and group behaviour.

The approach taken in this volume is positive rather than normative. The objective is to show how people and organizations (firms and governments) behave at different stages of a disaster. No specific policy recommendations are made. Faced with similar dilemmas and incentives, people and organizations are likely to make the same or similar errors over and over again. This rather pessimistic conclusion does not, however, make the book useless for practical purposes. Actors who find themselves in the disaster cycle may benefit from knowing where they stand, and from observing mistakes made in the past, not only in their own area of endeavour but also in quite different ones.

WHAT IS A DISASTER?

Defining the concept of disaster is by no means a straightforward task even for specialists in the field (Quarantelli 1998). There is consensus, however, that all disasters are to some extent social phenomena, and that they are very costly, whether or not that cost is measurable. An earthquake only matters if there are people who, for whatever reason, are in harm's way.[3] The authors of the Old Testament understood that many disasters involve a complex interplay between human behaviour and natural – or in this case divine – forces. In Genesis, a mighty flood wiped out the human and animal population of the world, except for Noah and the other passengers on his ark. Rather than an exogenous event, however, the flood was the result of human disregard of God's laws that provoked divine wrath.[4] Noah, incidentally, was an effective crisis manager. He listened attentively to God's warnings, prepared for the flood by building an ark, and did not panic when the deluge began. Later, in Exodus, Egypt was devastated by a series of horrible plagues. Pharaoh, unlike Noah, proved to be a hopeless disaster manager, principally because God had hardened his heart. Pharaoh refused to let the people of Israel go, despite being warned that there was no other remedy.[5] In modern terminology we might say that Pharaoh was in denial. We will meet other Pharaohs in later chapters.

The study of disasters may be approached from several angles. The least sophisticated, a legacy of Cold War social science, treats disaster as an external attack, whether from nature, disease or an enemy force, which must be repelled. A second approach regards a disaster as an event that either stems from or exposes existing social vulnerabilities. The flooding of communities along the Mississippi River, for example, demonstrates their vulnerability in brutal fashion. A third approach focuses on disasters as radically disruptive events that create uncertainty and confusion, or a loss of society's bearings (Gilbert 1998). All three perspectives are useful. Disasters often involve an external shock, reveal weaknesses in individuals and organizations, and induce states of uncertainty and confusion. The Mann Gulch disaster, which claimed the lives of 13 firefighters in Montana in 1949, provides an effective illustration of those points. A team of smokejumpers parachuted into a remote area to combat a forest fire. The team expected to find a routine fire and to extinguish it without too much trouble, but the threat confronting them after landing was far more serious. Weaknesses within the team, including distrust of an unfamiliar leader, Wag Dodge, soon came to the fore. Most of the smokejumpers became disoriented. They ignored Dodge's advice about how to extricate themselves from danger. Unable to make any sense of the situation, they panicked, and most paid with their lives (Weick 1993).

Shock and incomprehension are standard human responses to disaster. The great flood of Paris in 1910 brought much of the city to a standstill, and called into question the belief of many Parisians that their city, reputedly the best planned and most modern in the world, was immune to the hazards of previous ages (Jackson 2011). To Arthur Pigou, the Professor of Political Economy at Cambridge University, the First World War involved the senseless rupture of a regime in which households, firms and nations went about their business harmoniously, a successful regime that generated a slow but inexorable improvement in living standards. He could not comprehend the reasons why, between 1914 and 1918, 'the unconscious processes of normal life were abandoned … [and] Europe swung reeling to the conscious agony of war' (Pigou 1921, 2).

The financial disaster of 2007–09 and the subsequent Eurozone disaster shattered the comfortable illusion that the developed world had entered an age of moderation in the 1990s, liberated at last from the old boom-and-bust cycle (Reinhart and Rogoff 2009). The situation was hard to fathom. By contrast, hardly anyone was shocked or bemused by England's failure at the 2015 Cricket World Cup, which rather confirms that it was not a genuine disaster after all.

HOW WIDELY SHOULD WE CAST OUR NET?

The disasters analysed in this book are extremely varied, and deliberately so. They consist of a classic 'natural' disaster, Hurricane Katrina; three economic disasters – the depression of the 1930s and the twin GFC and Eurozone disasters of the early twenty-first century; the First World War; two industrial disasters in the Welsh coalfields; and a health disaster – the deadly effects of tobacco smoking. The method is to put the disaster cycle to work in a variety of historical situations in order to see how well it works.

Traditionally, however, the term 'disaster' has been reserved for natural disasters and for man-made disasters such as industrial and transport accidents. In the International Disaster Database (em-dat), maintained by the Centre for Research in the Epidemiology of Disasters (CRED) at the Université Catholique de Louvain, Belgium, there are seven classes of disaster: biological, climatological, complex, geophysical, hydrological, meteorological and technological.[6] There is no place in the database for financial and macroeconomic disasters, wars or non-biological health disasters such as tobacco smoking. CRED's classification is therefore unduly restrictive, for it excludes many episodes, including some of those discussed in detail in later chapters, which were equally if not more costly and disruptive. Although the designation of systemic banking collapses or significant macroeconomic contractions as disasters is not unprecedented in the literature, it does not have universal acceptance; hence it deserves some justification.

Contemporaries often used metaphors relating to natural disasters, extreme weather events or industrial accidents to describe periods of actual or impending economic turmoil. 'It came upon us as a thunder-bolt,' wrote the financial journalist Hartley Withers (1917, 1, 3) of the financial upheaval at the start of the First World War, 'The fury of the tempest was such that no credit system could possibly have stood up against it.' In a survey of competing interpretations of the depression, Myron Watkins (1933, 504) discovered that for many authors, whether or not they were economists, the depression was 'the final eruption of social "faults" – a historical earthquake resulting from a tension produced by opposing tendencies or forces in society which could no longer be withstood'. The purple prose of the American agricultural economists G.F. Warren and F.A. Pearson (1932, 24) included metaphors of war and flood. 'We are like a gassed and wounded regiment in No-Man's-Land', they wrote of the USA in the early 1930s. 'After the deluge is over', it might be possible to fathom what had gone wrong, but for now everyone including the president 'was groping for light'.

After the catastrophic Indian Ocean tsunami of 2004, some economists adopted the tsunami metaphor when warning of impending financial doom: 'the next sovereign debt tsunami will crash on a foreign currency debt market that is by design more accident prone than its predecessors. Whether we will have adequate tools to handle the disaster remains to be seen' (Flandreau et al. 2009, 54). Criticizing delays in the implementation of measures to avert financial disaster in the USA in 2008, Luigi Zingales wondered, 'What would one say about a hurricane emergency plan that took two months after the calamity to start working?' (Stultz and Zingales 2009, 72). The nuclear metaphor was also deployed during the GFC: 'Deconstructing a mortgage meltdown' was the title of one article in this vein (Anderson et al. 2011). Each author probably reached for the most convenient and topical metaphor; if so, their choices are suggestive of the parallels that come spontaneously to mind.

Liaquat Ahamed (2010, 501) argues that, during the depression of the 1930s, earthquake, flood and storm metaphors were used strategically by those wishing to absolve either themselves or their allies for the economic collapse. During the GFC, the leaders of major financial institutions resorted to disaster metaphors in an effort to shift or minimize blame. In testimony before the Financial Crisis Inquiry Commission (FCIC), Loyd Blankfein, the chief executive officer (CEO) of the investment bank Goldman Sachs, mused that in 2007–08 the financial industry was the victim of a freak storm: 'After 10 benign years in the context where we were, look, how would you look at the risk of our hurricane?' (Financial Crisis Inquiry Commission 2010, 29; see also Rohrer and Vignone 2012). A former vice chairman of Goldman Sachs, Suzanne Nora Johnson (2010, 156, 157), opted for the language of medical disaster: 'The 2008–2009 financial crisis – arguably a disaster – was an economic cancer that metastatized.' The financial system was 'gravely ill', and presumably deserved sympathy rather than condemnation. When, however, the former leaders of the troubled British banks, Halifax Bank of Scotland (HBOS) and Royal Bank of Scotland (RBS), were questioned by members of parliament (MPs) on the Treasury

Committee in 2009, it was the politicians who referred to earthquakes, hurricanes and tsunamis, evidently in an attempt to goad their witnesses (House of Commons Treasury Committee 2009).

A few economists and non-economists have gone beyond metaphor, and grasped that severely adverse financial and macroeconomic events are in some objective respects similar to other types of disaster, and should be described in the same terms. According to Robert J. Barro (2006, 826), one of the most influential macroeconomists of the late twentieth and early twenty-first centuries: 'Actual and potential economic disasters could reflect economic events (the 1930s depression, financial crises), wartime destruction (world wars, nuclear conflicts), natural disasters (tsunamis, hurricanes, earthquakes, asteroid collisions), and epidemics of disease (Black Death, avian flu).' What matters to Barro when defining a disaster is purely the magnitude of the event's impact, an issue to which I return shortly. On a smaller scale, Emmanuel Skoufias (2003) shows how a financial collapse and a natural disaster require similar forms of mitigation and response from the perspective of house-holds in developing countries. Both pose threats to the prosperity and stability of the household. In *The Irrational Economist*, Erwann Michel-Kerjan (2010, 41) notes that the early twenty-first century has witnessed a spate of 'terrorist attacks, natural disasters, financial crises, to name a few', and suggests that their increasing frequency reflects a combination of myopia or complacency, the greater interconnectedness of the world, and the concentration of population and assets in risky locations. Seen from such perspectives, an economic disaster is simply another type of disaster. At the same time, all disasters have economic ramifications because they generate large losses.

Non-economists may also be aware of the parallels between financial and other disasters. At the beginning of a study of health and safety on British railways, Bridget Hutter (2001, 3) offers a list of disasters between the mid-1980s and mid-1990s. Within Britain there were 'health and safety' disasters such as the Piper Alpha oil rig explosion, and 'financial' disasters such as the collapse of Barings Bank. Overseas disasters included the Bhopal chemical plant tragedy in 1984, the nuclear accident at Chernobyl in 1986, and the Black Friday crash on Wall Street in 1987. We might question whether the failure of Barings was serious enough to qualify as a disaster. The point, though, is that Hutter recognizes that in practice a financial disaster is simply another type of disaster.

DISASTER OR CRISIS?

A recurring problem during the research for this volume, and in seminar presentations on the disasters theme, was the interchangeability of the words 'crisis' and 'disaster' in conversation and in the media, and even in some academic publications. To add to the confusion, certain conventions have arisen around the use of those words to describe phenomena in different domains, hence 'natural disaster' but not natural crisis, and 'economic crisis' but rarely economic disaster. In their influential survey of financial 'folly' over the past 800 years, Carmen Reinhart and Kenneth Rogoff (2009) follow convention, describing episodes that were nothing short of economically disastrous as crises. The word 'disaster' does not appear at all in their text.

The literature on the economics of natural disasters pays considerable attention to the impact on macroeconomic performance and financial stability (Cavallo and Noy 2011). For instance, the San Francisco earthquake and inferno of 1906 helped to cause the financial panic of 1907. Large payments were made by British insurance companies to policy holders in California, putting pressure on the British balance of payments. After interest rates were raised by the Bank of England, there occurred a severe recession in the USA, which destabilized some important financial institutions (Odell and Weidenmier 2004). Nevertheless, whilst the part of natural 'disasters' in causing some economic or financial 'crises' is acknowledged, the standard view is that they are conceptually different types of event.

Given the prevailing confusion over terminology, especially in economics, it is necessary to establish a new convention, at least for use in the current volume. The words crisis and disaster will be used in specific ways, even at the expense of some awkwardness. Crisis is defined here as a period of heightened danger that presents urgent challenges to decision makers. Disaster is defined as an event or process that generates heavy costs and severe disruption (Singleton 2015). Two caveats are unavoidable: firstly, when discussing the work of other authors it is not always possible to avoid acknowledging their terminology, especially in quotations; secondly, common phrases referring to particular episodes, such as Global Financial Crisis or GFC, cannot be excluded altogether.

Disasters usually occur within periods of crisis. Indeed, the crisis generally persists while emergency measures are being taken to alleviate or respond to the disaster. Crisis is not invariably accompanied by disaster, for a threat may be averted by good decision making or good luck. Most crises start before disaster actually strikes, although in some cases, such as earthquakes, they may arrive simultaneously. It is even possible for a disaster to begin before anyone has noticed that anything is wrong. Cigarette smoking began to affect smokers' health long before the rise of lung cancer attracted the interest of physicians in the 1920s. It was not until after the Second World War that the connection between smoking and lung cancer was grasped, and the existence of a crisis acknowledged (Bartrip 2013). For there to be a crisis, then, there must first be recognition that something is wrong.

The line taken here on disasters and crises is different from the approaches of some other authors. For example, the title of Michael Oliver's chapter, 'Financial crises', in a volume on *Economic Disasters of the Twentieth Century*, implies that a crisis is a type of disaster (Oliver 2007). Vincent Gawronski and Richard Olson (2013) argue that the 1976 earthquake, a natural disaster, triggered a political crisis in Guatemala: once again, their take on the relationship between crisis and disaster is different from the one pursued in this volume. The terms 'crisis' and 'disaster' also appear to be interchangeable in the work of some disaster studies experts (Boin 2009; Shaluf et al. 2003). Readers should be aware of the terminological imprecision in the literature, and bear in mind the solution offered above.

THE DIMENSIONS OF DISASTER

Disasters have several dimensions, depending on the size, scope and duration of the impact, and perhaps on the length of the forewarning (Kreps 1998, 34). We tend to think of disasters – floods, earthquakes, transport accidents – as happening very quickly. But some disasters seem to develop in slow motion, especially ones that affect health and the environment (Coppola 2011, 46, 645), such as tobacco smoking.

In everyday life the term 'disaster' is used far too loosely, to describe a missed train, a flood caused by a faulty washing machine, or a lost football match; events that on reflection are quite trivial. But it is not always so easy to determine the boundary between inconvenience and genuine disaster. Practitioners and scholars in disaster studies have devised a number of operational benchmarks, though no consensus has emerged. George Horwich, an economist, offers a very imprecise yard-stick: 'We take a disaster to be a loss of resource value beyond some socially specified level' (Horwich 1990, 532). The losses that Horwich has in mind are those to the stock of physical and human capital. In effect he argues that society must exercise a subjective choice (or perhaps a series of choices) over how much damage is required before an event qualifies as a disaster.

At the other end of the spectrum, CRED attempts to be precise: a natural or technological disaster is an event that meets at least one of these criteria: '10 or more people killed; 100 or more people affected; declaration of a state of emergency; call for international assistance'.[7] On CRED's definition, there were 18 000 disasters in the world between 1900 and 2013. Given that CRED's list is by no means exhaustive and, for example, fails to record many UK mining disasters, 18 000 is an underestimate. CRED's International Disasters Database also excludes financial and macroeconomic disasters. On the other hand, the criteria seem very generous. An episode that causes ten deaths would hardly constitute a disaster of national importance in most countries, unless there was something special about the people killed.

Robert Barro bases his definition of 'a rare economic disaster' on the extent of the interruption to the flow of income rather than the destruction of the stock of capital. A rare economic disaster is any event that causes real gross domestic product (GDP) per capita to fall by 15 per cent or more (Barro 2006, 828). Employing such a strict definition, Barro finds relatively few economic disasters in his sample of 20 developed countries in the twentieth century. There are in fact just 33 instances of disaster. The First World War accounts for eight, the depression eight more, and the Second World War ten. The Spanish Civil War and the aftermath of the world wars provide the seven remaining cases. Barro also provides results for a second sample of Asian and Latin American countries. World wars and economic depressions are responsible for all of the disasters in the sample of less-developed countries (Barro 2006, 828–9). No natural or technological dislocation was powerful enough to generate a rare economic disaster in either of Barro's groups of countries. Yet natural disasters do sometimes have a devastating impact on poor nations. The Lisbon earthquake of 1755 may have imposed direct costs of between 35 and 48 per cent of Portuguese GDP (Pereira 2009). The 2010 earthquake in Haiti is estimated to have cost a staggering 112 per cent of GDP (Cavallo et al. 2010, 4). Whereas CRED is too liberal, Barro's benchmark of 15 per cent of GDP per capita is too stringent. Barro, however, demonstrates convincingly that economic depressions are disasters.

Agreed definitions are equally elusive for specialists in financial crises, which as discussed above must be translated as financial disasters. Financial and macroeconomic disasters do not kill or maim directly, but are costly nonetheless. Carmen Reinhart and Kenneth Rogoff (2009, 3–14) list the various possible types of financial disaster. The first group of disasters includes inflation crises, currency crashes, currency debasement and the bursting of asset price bubbles. In each of the above cases it is possible to set a quantitative hurdle, such as a percentage fall in a stock market index, for an episode to count as a disaster. A second group is made up of banking crises, external debt crises and domestic debt crises, where disaster is defined not in quantitative terms but rather in terms of the occurrence of a specific type of event such as the declaration of a default. A financial disaster could start in any area of the financial system and then spread rapidly to other parts of the system. Banking disasters merit some additional comment, not least because their definition is so complicated. Type I banking crises involve 'bank runs that lead to the closure, merging or takeover by the public sector of one or more financial institutions'. Type II banking crises are somewhat milder: bank mergers, closures, takeovers or government bailouts occur pre-emptively before a run has started (Reinhart and Rogoff 2009, 11).

The cost of a financial disaster depends ultimately on its impact on depositors who in some circumstances may lose their deposits, on the taxpayers who bear the fiscal cost of bank rescues and depositor compensation, and on the nation as a whole because GDP will be affected through various channels including a sharp drop in the availability of credit, otherwise known as a credit crunch. The fiscal costs alone of banking bailouts may be large but difficult to pin down precisely. For example, the Argentinian bailouts of 1981 may have cost as much as 55.3 per cent of GDP, or as little as 4 per cent of GDP, depending on how the calculation is performed (Reinhart and Rogoff 2009, 164).

But Reinhart and Rogoff have no monopoly over their subject area, and there are other ways of approaching the identification of financial disasters. Luc Laeven and Fabián Valencia (2012, 4), for example, provide an alternative banking disaster database. They define a financial crisis or disaster in a way that combines cost thresholds with significant events. To qualify as a banking crisis, three out of the following six criteria must be met: the provision of liquidity above a specified threshold; bank restructuring costs of at least 3 per cent of GDP; bank nationalizations; the offer of guarantees; asset purchases by the authorities equivalent to at least 5 per cent of GDP; a deposit freeze and/or a bank holiday. They identify 147 systemic banking crises, 218 currency crises and 66 sovereign debt crises around the world between 1970 and 2011 (Laeven and Valencia 2012, 3). Once again, the reader should translate crisis as disaster.

To recapitulate, there are several ways of deciding what constitutes a disaster, but no consensus as to which is best. The issue of cost is crucial to the measurement of disasters, which may lead to a reduced flow of income, the destruction of capital (whether physical or human), a new fiscal burden on the taxpayer or some combination of the above. Cost itself is a tricky concept that generates debate. The value of life (and the cost of a life lost) continues to be a matter of controversy. Several methods are possible: estimating an individual's future earnings net of consumption, estimating their replacement cost (essentially the cost of bringing up a new person to adulthood) or deriving a capital value from the amount they would be prepared to pay to escape a one-off, low-probability risk of death (Viscusi 2008). Some costs are measurable, but others are not. Social disruption, confusion and anxiety do not lend themselves to measurement (Dynes 1998, 111–12). If one digs deep enough, moreover, the very concept of cost is revealed as subjective. An event such as a major flood will affect different groups in different ways. If property owners are well insured or compensated by the government, then from their perspective the disaster might not seem so bad. The cost has been shifted to others (Hallegatte and Przyluski 2010, 15–16).

No agreed test exists for determining what is and is not a disaster. Fortunately, however, the case studies in this volume do not lie close to the margins. All were unambiguously costly in lives, income or wealth, and some in all three.

THE DISASTER CYCLE

The Asian financial disaster of the late 1990s and the GFC encouraged specialists in economics and scientific disciplines to search for analogies between disruptive events or disasters in the financial system and in ecosystems. As ecosystems grow more complex they become increasingly vulnerable to the rapid spread of disruptive forces. Insofar as financial systems develop along similar lines to ecosystems, they are exposed to the same types of disruption (May et al. 2008; Haldane and May 2011; May 2013). Even before 2007–09 the pandemic analogy was popular amongst commentators on financial disasters. Health officials also studied the way in which economic and financial officials managed outbreaks of instability and contagion that crossed international boundaries, with a view to obtaining hints on how to contain the spread of disease (Peckham 2013).

Ecological and biological analogies for economic disasters are interesting, but the approach taken in this volume does not depend on such analogies. The disaster cycle, the conceptual tool employed below, is a social scientific framework that can be used to illuminate a wide range of disasters. The emphasis here is on recurring patterns of individual and group behaviour rather than on unconscious ecological processes. It is not contended that there is an analogy between an economic disaster such as the depression of the 1930s and, say, the First World War or Hurricane Katrina. Instead, it is argued that individual and organizational actors behaved in comparable ways at equivalent stages of each of those disasters.

The idea that disasters pass through a series of phases was suggested in the early twentieth century by sociologists. The possibility that in many, though not all, cases there is a disaster cycle was advanced by disaster researchers in the 1970s. When applied by practitioners, the disaster cycle became the disaster management cycle. A recent survey concludes that the 'disaster management cycle has … been influenced by many disciplines such as sociology, geography, psychology, civil defence, public administration and development studies' (Coetzee and van Niekerk 2012, 2). It is interesting to note that they make no mention of economics. Later in this chapter, however, it will be shown that certain economic ideas do help us to understand the disaster cycle and the forces that might propel it.

Samuel Henry Prince's doctoral dissertation on the great explosion at Halifax, Nova Scotia in 1917 was a pioneering effort to describe, step by step, the process by which a community was affected by, coped with and recovered from disaster (Prince 1920). The accidental explosion of a munitions ship, after a collision in Halifax harbour, wrecked much of the city and caused approximately 2000 deaths. Prince, an Anglican minister, was an eyewitness. Halifax had no contingency plan for responding to a catastrophe. At first, many citizens and officials were confused and did not know what to do. Although there was some looting of liquor supplies, people soon began to rally round. Neighbours helped each other. Troops from the citadel and firemen were amongst the first responders. Yet it was actors from the Academy theatre who, 'forsaking the school of Thespis for that of Esculapius', the god of medicine and healing, 'organized the first relief station' (Prince 1920, 60). The telegraph company restored a line to the outside world within an hour. In other words, the initial response was informal, relying on the bravery and resourcefulness of individuals and small groups. After several days, the city authorities, assisted by a disaster response team from Boston, began to coordinate relief measures through a Citizens' Committee. Aid, both financial and in kind, began to flow in from outside. The homeless and wounded were given food, medical treatment and temporary accommodation. After about a week there was a shift in focus towards rehabilitation, with the aim of returning the city and its inhabitants to normality. Victims of the explosion could eventually claim up to $5000 compensation for losses, though Prince (1920, 97) was uncomfortable with such munificence. Halifax was rebuilt and, according to Prince, substantially improved over the pre-disaster city. New regulations were introduced governing the transportation of explosives. Prince, a sociologist, concluded that the disaster resulted in social flux that had positive as well as negative features. Halifax, a rather sleepy place, was 'galvanized into life through the testing experience of a great catastrophe. She has undergone a civic transformation, such as could hardly otherwise have happened in fifty years' (Prince 1920, 139).

Lowell Carr (1932, 211–14), another sociologist, was more systematic in his delineation of the disaster phases. First came the 'preliminary or prodromal' period during which the forces that lead to catastrophe accumulate. The disaster itself – the 'precipitating event' – ushered in the second phase marked by 'dislocation and disorganization'. The third and final phase involved 'readjustment and reorganization' on the individual, interactive and cultural planes.

During and after the Second World War new disaster management legislation was passed, and responsible government agencies established, in a number of countries (Coppola 2011, 5). The US strategic bombing surveys of Germany and Japan in the mid-1940s gave further impetus to the emergence of disaster research as a discipline or quasi-discipline. Disaster studies centres for academics and practitioners were established, especially in the USA, and many new variants of the disaster phase framework emerged (Kreps 1998).

Disaster researchers at Bradford University have been credited with formulating the now familiar concept of the disaster cycle. Their interest was principally in natural disasters in poor countries, but their ideas have a much broader resonance. They noted that many disasters are preceded by warning phases. Relief, rehabilitation and reconstruction phases are observed as victims and the authorities respond to the disaster event. Finally, attempts are made to prevent or mitigate future disasters, and to strengthen relief services. The cycle is completed when new warnings foreshadow the next disaster (Baird et al. 1975, 42).

A simple disaster management cycle of four phases – mitigation, preparedness, response and recovery – was endorsed in the late 1970s by the US National Governors' Association (NGA). Mitigation involves taking measures to reduce the likelihood or severity of disasters, for instance by constructing levees along a river that is prone to flooding. Preparedness entails getting ready to respond to a disaster by accumulating emergency supplies and planning for the evacuation of communities at risk. The response phase includes attempts to contain and control the disaster and provide relief to victims. The recovery phase deals with the rebuilding and restoration to normality of the stricken area (National Governors' Association 1978). The types of disaster envisaged in the 1970s were natural and industrial. Since the September 11 attacks in 2001, terrorism has also become a major concern. Some modern textbooks on disaster management are organized around the concept of the disaster cycle (Coppola 2011).

The US Government Accountability Office applied a version of the disaster cycle when comparing four episodes of financial turmoil in the 1980s: the Mexican debt crisis, the Continental Illinois failure, the Ohio Savings and Loan meltdown and the 1987 Wall Street crash (Government Accountability Office 1997). In general, however, economists have tended to ignore the disaster cycle, and it does not figure in the collection of essays on *Economic Disasters of the Twentieth Century* edited by Michael Oliver and Derek Aldcroft (2007), or Cormac O'Gráda's (2009) history of famine, or the numerous studies of the depression and the financial disasters of 2007 onwards. Such neglect is a little odd, for economists and economic historians are well versed in cyclical phenomena, and to a lesser extent in stages models. For well over a century, cycles of varying length have been observed in a range of economic variables including prices and production. Such cycles are attributed to various factors including swings in innovation, profitability and investment, and changes in institutional arrangements (Lewis 1978, 17–31; de Groot and Franses 2012). Cycles of boom and bust in financial markets are also familiar to students of economic history (Kindleberger and Aliber 2011). The notion that certain economic processes unfold in stages is well known from the works of Adam Smith and Karl Marx, not to mention some later accounts of modernization (Rostow 1960; 1978). The financial boom-and-bust cycle, however, is the one that comes closest to the disaster cycle, and will be discussed later in this chapter. Unfortunately, there has been little conscious interchange of ideas between economics and disaster management studies. In fact the concept of the disaster cycle is not mentioned in a recent, authoritative survey of the economics of natural disasters (Cavallo and Noy 2011). Disciplinary and subdisciplinary boundaries are observed fairly rigidly within economics.

EXTENDING THE DISASTER CYCLE

The basic four-stage disaster cycle of the NGA does not adequately serve our purpose, which is analytical rather than practical. We examine the disaster cycle as a historical process. The requirements of disaster managers are of interest, but do not provide the rationale for this investigation.

As the work of early writers such as Prince and Carr established, the social and cultural aspects of disasters are important. Some variants of the cyclical framework make this explicit. Another sociologist, Barry Turner, argued that most disasters are preceded by an incubation phase during which there is an accumulation of anomalies that cannot be explained using conventional thinking. If, as is likely, those anomalies are ignored, the scene is set for disaster. A precipitating event then initiates a period of crisis. Those affected, including organizations, now begin to grasp that their precautions and ways of thinking have been defective. Disaster strikes, and there follows a rescue and salvage stage, which may involve some second thoughts, and then a more reflective period, including a thorough investigation of the errors made during the incubation period (Turner 1976, 381). Although Turner's framework is linear, it could easily be modified to follow a cycle. Already one begins to see how greater sophistication can be added, or perhaps restored, to the four-stage model.

Mark Stein offers a simplified version of Turner's periodization whilst retaining the emphasis on the social and cultural aspects of disaster. Stein's framework has an incubation period, a critical period and an aftermath. The critical period begins when a precipitating or triggering event occurs that 'in the absence of remedial action, almost invariably leads to disaster' (Stein 2004, 1244). Disaster may still be averted, but only if sense is made of the situation and correct decisions taken and implemented. The critical period continues until the immediate impact of the disaster is more or less complete. All actors during the critical period are challenged to make sense of what is happening and adapt their behaviour accordingly. They operate in an environment of uncertainty, ambiguity and pressure. If key decision makers panic or enter a state of denial then, as in the case of the Three Mile Island nuclear accident in 1979, only luck can save them (Stein 2004, 1251).

David Neal (1997, 259) concluded that 'the use of disaster periods provides a useful heuristic device for disaster researchers', but also expressed some reservations. In particular, he felt that it was not always clear whether the stages were meant to be temporal or functional. For Neal, a functional approach was preferable: phases such as mitigation and preparedness, or relief and reconstruction, tend to overlap. He also pointed out that different individuals or groups could experience the disaster phases in different ways, and pass through the cycle at varying speeds. During a natural disaster, for example, wealthier people may be better prepared, and able to extricate themselves faster, than people with fewer resources and less influence. A more recent article by David Neal

(2013) discusses how the concept of social time is germane to the analysis of disasters. Normal routines are disrupted by a disaster, and time takes on a different meaning for those affected. Time is measured not in hours, but in terms of events such as the rescue of victims, the restoration of water and electricity supplies, and the rebuilding of property. Social time may also be relevant to understanding financial disasters, the course of which is marked not by the passing of clock time but rather by the occurrence of key events such as the failure of a well-known bank, the intervention of the central bank as lender of last resort or the announcement of a rescue programme. A series of disasters – an earthquake, the economic collapse accompanying the end of the USSR, and the Nagorno-Karabakh war – in the late 1980s and early 1990s left many Armenians with 'the sensation that the present time had somehow been detached from the flow of historical, chronological time' (Platz 2000, 134). Time is different in a disaster.

An extended version of the disaster cycle is presented in Figure 1.1. Instead of the four stages of the NGA's cycle there are now eight, divided into two groups of four. There is a critical period of four stages, marked by great urgency and pressure, when time speeds up during many but not all disasters. Whilst the stages outside the critical period are no less important, they permit more time for reflection and, perhaps, procrastination. Particular attention will be given to sensemaking and blame, for they are the main additions to the standard framework.

It is convenient to start with mitigation and regulatory change. To an extent that varies from case to case, the environment in which each disaster happens is influenced by the response of people and organizations to a previous disaster, although not necessarily one in the same place or even of an identical type. After a disaster, the authorities may pass new legislation with a view to making future disasters less likely, and firms and households may change their behaviour with a similar end in mind. The appropriateness of the measures taken to avert or mitigate disaster is not the primary concern here. Even if they are half-hearted or ill-conceived, the disaster environment will still be affected in some way. Preparedness, as a separate stage, is dropped, and in effect incorporated into mitigation. Making preparations to cope with a future disaster is a form of mitigation.

The warning stage could be brief or protracted, depending on circumstances. Some organizations may choose to disregard warnings, while others actively seek out evidence of an emerging threat. During the Cold War, for example, intelligence agencies and specialists in the USA devoted a large amount of resources to monitoring and assessing Soviet

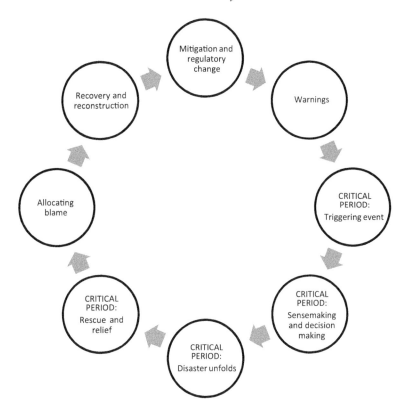

Figure 1.1   The disaster cycle

military intentions. The aim was to generate warnings of possible Soviet attack (Wirtz 2013).

The critical period or crisis is initiated by a triggering event. In the absence of a successful response to the triggering event the disaster will take place or, if unavoidable, be worse than it need be. Distinguishing the triggering event from a routine warning may be difficult at the time. Even with the benefit of hindsight it is not always easy to identify the key moment in a train of events. Historians, however, cannot avoid making judgements about which events are crucial, even if their choices are open to dispute. Sorting the past into important and unimportant events is self-evidently one of the key tasks of the historian. The triggering event is vital because it challenges individuals and organizations to think about a dangerous situation, and then act. Whether or not they actually do think and act is another matter. They could well fail to register the significance of the trigger, in which case the situation will soon run out of control.

The triggering event leads immediately into a stage described as sensemaking and decision making. The rudiments of sensemaking were introduced above in the discussion of the Mann Gulch forest fire (Weick 1993). The process of 'sensemaking begins with the basic question, is it still possible to take things for granted?' (Weick 1995, 14). After the discovery of an imminent threat, it becomes much harder to take things for granted unless one chooses to make light of the evidence. Sense-making is an active rather than a passive endeavour. It involves trying to understand a situation that on the face of it is surprising, confusing and possibly overwhelming (Maitlis and Sonenschein 2010). The situation demands a response of some sort, not only from individuals but perhaps more importantly from key groups. The more unfamiliar the circum-stances, and the bigger the threat, the greater is the pressure to reach an agreed interpretation and find a solution. A decision on how to manage the threat in order to avert or minimize disaster is required. Even denial constitutes a response, albeit not a constructive one. In *Wrong*, an analysis of nine economic policy disasters since the eighteenth century, Richard Grossman (2013) argues that poor decision making, based on misguided economic ideology, was a central factor in each policy disaster. Although Grossman does not use the concept of sensemaking, his work is essentially about the failure of sensemaking in crises and the disastrous consequences of that failure. Another point needs to be made about sensemaking: it is something that is happening all the time, although usually under less urgency than in the critical period of a disaster (Weick 1995, 43).

If poor choices are made in response to the triggering event, then disaster is unleashed in all its fury. Although some disasters, such as an earthquake or a hurricane strike, cannot be averted by human inter-vention, the damage to life and property may be reduced by effective sensemaking and timely decision making. The rescue and relief stage could well begin in advance of the disaster proper, as personnel and other assets are martialled and deployed. Nevertheless, much of the activity during this, the final stage, of the critical period will take place in the immediate aftermath of the event, whether it be a hurricane or a financial tsunami.

Once we pass beyond the critical period, if not before, the thoughts of many of those affected, as well as of interested observers, will turn to the apportionment of blame. Experts in disaster management are inclined to skate over, if not ignore, this stage (Coppola 2011). Disasters are always contentious because they impose significant losses on individuals, com-munities or society as a whole. Culprits are sought even when the disaster could not reasonably have been anticipated. A particularly striking example of scapegoating occurred after the L'Aquila earthquake in Italy in 2009 in which 309 people died. Four seismologists, two engineers and a government official were convicted of manslaughter and negligence. They were sent to jail in 2012 and ordered to pay compensation to survivors. The court found that they had failed in their duty to assess the risks to L'Aquila and warn the public. Predicting exactly where and when earthquakes will happen is effectively impossible (*Times Higher Education* Reporters 2013). Yet the court, and a section of the Italian public, demanded retribution. The reversal on appeal of most, but not all, of the L'Aquila convictions in 2014 was met with anger amongst some members of the public (Hooper 2014). Less dramatically, Thomas Birkland (2009) argues that official reports following disasters are often designed to protect powerful actors by deflecting blame elsewhere. Such reports, which he describes as 'fantasy documents', may also give the false impression that decisive action will be taken to prevent further catastrophe, when in fact the authorities have little intention of following up the recommendations. In order, then, to achieve a more rounded understanding of the disaster cycle it is necessary to find a place for blame. Birkland takes the concept of fantasy documents from the work of Lee Clarke (1999) who used it in the analysis of plans for averting or coping with possible future disasters. Both applications are equally relevant.

The next stage, recovery and reconstruction, is no less politicized. Interested parties argue over the most suitable recovery programme and over who should provide the funding. The disaster cycle ends and recommences with the implementation of new measures to avert or mitigate disaster. The content of such measures will be determined by negotiation rather than any dispassionate consideration of the alternatives.

DRIVERS OF THE DISASTER CYCLE

Although the disaster cycle was developed primarily as a guide for practitioners in disaster management, it is employed in a different way in the current volume. Each stage of the cycle is to a greater or lesser extent affected by the behaviour of individuals and organizations, as are the transitions between stages. Human and group behaviour drives the cycle and prevents it from becoming a series of self-contained boxes. This section examines the types of behaviour that set and keep the cycle in motion.

Disasters would be less frequent and less severe if mitigation was thorough, warnings heeded, sensemaking and decision making conducted calmly and effectively, relief and rescue operations carried out efficiently, disaster inquiries objective and reconstruction well planned. But several obstacles stand in the way of the smoothing of the disaster cycle. Those obstacles include conflicts of interest, such as over who should pay for mitigation or reconstruction programmes; the misperception of risk by individuals and groups; and inflexible thinking, especially at the group level.

Conflicts of interest are fairly obvious and need not detain us for long, though they will be visible at various points in later chapters. Whilst the outbreak of the First World War, for example, may have reflected the misperception of risk by the great powers of Europe, also involved were fundamental conflicts of interest over territory and relative power. On a smaller scale, individuals and agencies in control of supplies for the relief of disaster victims may have axes to grind, and discriminate against claimants on ethnic, religious or political grounds (Aldrich 2010). The US government, with an eye on the accumulation of votes, is more generous with the provision of disaster relief in election years (Michel-Kerjan 2010, 46). Charities and other non-government organizations have an interest in using the publicity generated by disasters to replenish their coffers and sustain their bureaucracies. They may even exaggerate disasters in order to achieve their own objectives, as Cormac O'Gráda (2009, 218–25) suggests happened in relation to famine appeals in the late twentieth century.

Building on the work of behavioural scientists, specialists in the economics of risk and uncertainty have devoted considerable effort to investigating how individuals and organizations assess the likelihood of disaster, whether natural or other. Experimental evidence suggests that humans are poor at estimating the probability of infrequent events such as disasters. Consequently, they may allocate too few resources to trying to prevent and mitigate them. The length of time since the last disaster of a similar nature also affects perceptions of risk. When calamity is fresh in the memory, mitigation and preparedness are taken very seriously. Once memories have faded, however, individuals and organizations, including firms, political parties and government agencies, may be inclined to discount the risk of recurrence, and to neglect precautions. Behavioural research also suggests that the probability of certain types of disaster will be overestimated relative to others. Particularly startling or horrifying events attract more attention than more mundane disasters. In the wake of the September 11, 2001 attacks on New York and Washington many individuals, as well as government agencies and airlines, overestimated the probability of future terrorist assaults. Resources were diverted from the mitigation and relief of other disasters, such as floods, to dealing with the perceived terrorist threat (Michel-Kerjan and Slovic 2010; Kunreuther and Useem 2010).

Research in political science suggests that the public only bothers about disasters when they are in the news. Strong public support exists for the US government to take the lead in rescue and relief efforts after a disaster, but there is far less support for spending taxpayers' funds on mitigation and preparedness, regardless of the fact that a dollar spent on mitigation and preparedness brings a much higher return than a dollar spent on rescue and relief. Natural and other disasters are news for a while, but the attention of the public soon moves on (Healy and Malhotra 2009).

Behavioural economists accept that humans are more than satisfaction-maximizing calculating machines, and that their actions are influenced by the narratives or stories they construct, often in conjunction with other people. At times they will be inclined to optimism, but at others to pessimism. When they believe that they have been treated unfairly they adhere to narratives based on the corruption of those in positions of economic or political power (Akerlof and Shiller 2009). The notion that confidence or emotions may have a significant economic impact has been endorsed by Alan Greenspan, chairman of the Federal Reserve Board from 1987 to 2006, and someone who could hardly be classified as a behavioural economist. According to Greenspan (2008, 17), 'Economists cannot avoid being students of human nature, particularly of exuberance and fear', emotions that sometimes cause markets to act apparently irrationally.

The financial instability hypothesis, developed by Hyman Minsky (1982; 2008), and applied to financial history by Charles Kindleberger and Robert Aliber (2011), shows in more detail how emotions may influence economic and financial behaviour. Minsky was concerned with the misperception of risk by borrowers and lenders. A cycle of boom and crash is set off by a positive exogenous event, such as the diffusion of a new technology, which prompts a perfectly reasonable increase in borrowing and lending. At some point, however, the expectations of borrowers and lenders about returns from new projects become detached from reality. Credit now expands at an accelerating pace, and the prices of the assets against which loans are made, including property and equities, begin to soar. Euphoria grips borrowers and lenders, and loans are extended to households and firms with no prospect of repaying unless asset prices continue to rise. After a while, however, borrowers and lenders become nervous, possibly when they observe that the boom has bid up interest rates (Minsky 1982, 33). The rate of credit expansion slows, and selling pressure halts the ascent of asset prices. If there is now an adverse shock, such as the failure of a big financial institution, asset prices may go into reverse, exposing both borrowers and lenders to ruin. The authorities must now step in to contain the disaster.

Kindleberger and Aliber (2011, 39–45) explain the changes in sentiment that drive the cycle by suggesting that rationality is an ideal that may not be achieved in practice. Human behaviour is influenced by feelings and hunches, and at times people may even be carried along by mob psychology. Even when attempting to calculate the best option, we are constrained by limitations in data availability and reasoning power. David Tuckett and Richard Taffler, a psychologist and a finance scholar respectively, employ psychoanalytic theory to analyse the dotcom bubble and collapse of 1998–2002. They argue that 'in the face of uncertainty', such as that routinely pervading financial markets, 'there is increased scope for emotional and unconscious phantasy to shape reactions to news' (Tuckett and Taffler 2008, 89). Financial assets, including internet stocks, become 'phantastic objects' representing the deepest desires of investors. In their 'paranoid-schizoid' state they suppress all doubt and make light of risk, but when the markets turn against them they resort 'to denial, to anger, and then to paranoid efforts to find scapegoats' (Tuckett and Taffler 2008, 404). Similarly, Mark Stein (2011) describes the culture of mania that gripped financial markets before 2007–09. Every setback was treated as a challenge to stake even bigger bets and prove the doubters wrong. It would appear, then, that the dynamics of the disaster cycle are at their most manic in the financial sphere. Similar frenzies are not evident in the world of natural or industrial disasters, although they might be in the realm of warfare. The reason for dwelling on the financial case is that the fluctuating emotions of greed, bravado, denial and panic, which to a greater or lesser extent saturate all disasters, are most transparent in the financial arena.

At the heart of the disaster cycle, however, is the need to identify and make sense of the triggering event. Sensemaking may be successful or it may fall flat. The Apollo 13 space mission in 1970 and the Three Mile Island nuclear accident in 1979 illustrate the contrast between successful and unsuccessful sensemaking. Despite a serious malfunction during the early stages of the Apollo 13 mission, Flight Control and the astronauts kept their heads, worked hard on containing the problems, and brought the craft back safely to earth. At Three Mile Island, however, the plant operators did not respond well to stress and chose to ignore inconvenient information. Persuading themselves that the problem with the reactor was under control, they dismissed new instrument readings that suggested it was still heading for complete meltdown, and assumed that the readings must be incorrect. It was by sheer luck that the plant avoided catastrophe.

Apollo 13, then, was an instance of creative sensemaking; Three Mile Island was the reverse. One team reacted creatively under stress, but the other went into denial, preferring not to contemplate the possibility of disaster (Stein 2004). Three Mile Island was the inspiration for Charles Perrow's theory of normal accidents. With technologies that are complex and tightly coupled, and have little inbuilt redundancy, unexpected combinations of malfunctions are bound to occur from time to time, and will be very difficult to understand and manage (Perrow 1984). Financial systems exhibit similar features of complexity and tight coupling.

Barry Eichengreen (2012) argues that in times of crisis, especially when information is scarce and misleading and there is no agreement on first principles, decision makers may reach for an analogy in order to frame the threat and devise a solution. Moreover, they are likely to grab the most obvious analogy – the 1930s depression in the case of the GFC in 2007–09 – whether or not it is the best one. Collective sensemaking is not necessarily a recipe for success. The outcome of a group discussion may be imposed by the most powerful member, or reflect a compromise between the competing views of members, as Mitchel Abolafia (2010), a sociologist, finds in a study of interest rate setting by the Federal Open Market Committee in the USA. 'Groupthink', the tendency for groups to reach a firm view, then ignore contradictory evidence and stifle dissent, is a concept that was first employed to explain US foreign policy and military mishaps, including the failure to anticipate the Japanese attack on Pearl Harbor in 1941 (Janis 1972).

Several types of crisis manager have been identified in the literature. Collectivists cooperate effectively with other crisis managers, delegate tasks and adapt their plans to the situation. Integrators are determined to follow best practice methods; although laudable in principle, in practice this may lead to delays until all assets are in place. Reactives lack a consistent strategy, fail to communicate effectively, and are inclined to autocracy. Finally, paralytics have no idea what to do or how to do it, and often lapse into passivity (Olejarski and Garnett 2010). Although developed in the context of natural disasters, this typology is potentially of far wider relevance. In practice, however, it has proven difficult to assign individuals and organizations to particular categories.

Whether or not a crisis leads to disaster, and whether or not the response to that disaster is effective, depends on the judgement and behaviour of human beings and organizations. Both judgement and behaviour may be clouded by favouritism, misperception and emotion, especially when crucial decisions have to be made at a time of extreme stress.

CONCLUSION

The central argument of the current volume is that disasters in different fields share many characteristics and pass, more or less, through the same phases. The unfolding of those phases is determined less by clock time than by the thought processes and actions of the individuals and groups experiencing and seeking to avert or minimize the disaster. Although a basic four-stage disaster cycle framework is preferred by many disaster management agencies, a more refined framework is needed for the purposes of historical analysis. The template developed above gives special attention to the distinction between those parts of the disaster cycle that lie within the critical period, when an urgent response is demanded, and those that lie outside the critical period. Emphasis is given to the phase of sensemaking and decision making that occurs in response to the triggering event. Much rests on the success or failure of sensemaking and decision making, which if done well may avert or at least lessen the impact of disaster. Prominence is also given to a stage in which blame for the disaster is determined and allocated. Inquests into disasters, whether in the financial, political or natural spheres, are invariably politicized. Our aim is not to offer practical advice on preventing or coping with disasters but rather to show how the same behaviour and mistakes recur across a range of disaster types.

The following chapters apply the modified version of the disaster cycle developed above to a variety of cases. Chapter 2 deals with a classic natural disaster, Hurricane Katrina, which inundated New Orleans in 2005. Hurricane Katrina is chosen as the first case study because the disaster cycle was designed with such events in mind, and it makes sense to move from the familiar to the unfamiliar. Chapter 3 discusses a particularly topical disaster, the First World War, which in many respects changed the course of European history 100 years ago. The challenge is to see to what extent the disaster cycle can help us understand a major war, and the behaviour of the people who started and attempted to manage it. Chapter 4 concerns the depression of the 1930s. It has already been established above that there is a financial disaster cycle, and Chapter 4 shows how it follows the essential contours of the broader disaster cycle. Chapter 5 investigates two disasters that are on a smaller scale to those discussed elsewhere in this volume, namely the Senghenydd and Aberfan mining disasters in Wales in 1913 and 1967, respectively. The objective here is to demonstrate the versatility of the disaster cycle framework. Chapter 6 is on the face of it the most problematical. Although the smoking of tobacco has hastened the death of millions of people over the past century, it has done so extremely slowly, so that each stage of the disaster has stretched out to years or even decades. If we remember, however, that some disasters are slow onset, and that the disaster cycle is about social time rather than clock time, the inclusion of the smoking case study is fully justified. Chapter 7 brings us up to date with an analysis of the Global Financial Crisis and the Eurozone episode.

Some time ago I contributed a chapter on the First World War to a volume on *Economic Disasters of the Twentieth Century* (Oliver and Aldcroft 2007). Chapters in that collection ranged over a wide area from global war to depression to financial crisis to economic decline in post-independence Africa and the failure of the Soviet Union. As one reviewer pointed out, however, neither the editors nor the contributors attempted to draw comparisons between those disasters (Jacks 2008). Nor were readers offered any conceptual framework that would let them make their own comparisons. The purpose of the current volume is to supply a conceptual framework that will be useful when comparing historical disasters of all sorts.

NOTES

1. Cormac O'Gráda's research on the history of famine is another important exception (O'Gráda 2009).
2. Whilst working on the present volume I completed chapters on the theme of comparative disaster for two collected volumes (Singleton 2015; 2016).
3. For 17 years I accepted the risks associated with living in Wellington, New Zealand, a city built on top of several earthquake faults.
4. Genesis, Chapters 6–8.
5. Exodus, Chapters 7–11.
6. The database may be found at www.em-dat.be.
7. www.emdat.be/frequently-asked-questions (accessed 30 September 2013).

2. Hurricane Katrina: a classic natural disaster

The control of the Mississippi River floods is now more than ever before
our greatest domestic problem.
(United States Chamber of Commerce Committee on Mississippi Flood Control
quoted in Delano 1928, 33)

One year before the onset of The Depression, which was the most
devastating macroeconomic disaster of the twentieth century, the US
Chamber of Commerce claimed that too much water was the most
serious threat to the safety and prosperity of American business and the
American people. The Chamber's comments were made in response to
the devastating Mississippi floods of 1927, which cost hundreds of lives
and severely disrupted the economy of a region that was already one of
the poorest in the USA. Notwithstanding the Chamber's hyperbole,
flooding along the Mississippi River, caused by persistent rain or
hurricanes, has been a recurring problem over the past two centuries.
New Orleans, a city that rests partially below sea level, is particularly
vulnerable to flooding, and in 2005 its defences were overwhelmed by
Hurricane Katrina. About 80 per cent of New Orleans was inundated.
Had the eye of the storm passed through the centre of the city rather than
to the east, the damage and loss of life would have been far worse.

The disaster management cycle was developed with natural catastrophes in mind. Consequently, Hurricane Katrina is a fitting subject for
this book's first application of the disaster cycle framework. The main
purpose is not to identify what could have been done better, although
some critical assessment is unavoidable, but rather to observe how
decision makers and organizations behaved at different stages of the
disaster. Much of the behaviour encountered in the study of Katrina and
other natural disasters will be familiar to students of financial disasters:
the misperception of risk, opportunism, denial, panic, coordination failure, and the politicization of regulatory reform.

Coming just four years after the terrorist attacks on September 11,
2001, Hurricane Katrina was the second defining catastrophe in early
twenty-first-century US history. The Global Financial crisis (GFC) in
2007–09 would be the third. Whereas September 11 demonstrated

America's vulnerability to an imaginative and carefully planned terrorist assault, Katrina showed that the world's largest and most sophisticated economy was still at the mercy of the elements. Both were shocking events that unsettled American society.

The GFC spawned numerous comparisons with the depression of the 1930s. Katrina also had a notable interwar precedent in the form of the Mississippi floods of 1927 (Barry 1997). The two disasters were by no means identical: in 1927 the source of the problem was heavy rain over an extended period and not a hurricane, and the city of New Orleans was spared the worst of the disaster. Although there were other major floods along the Mississippi in the 1920s and 1930s (Welky 2011), it was those of 1927 that attracted comparison with 2005, partly because of the way in which they were handled by the authorities. In 1927 President Calvin Coolidge put Herbert Hoover, the Secretary of Commerce, in charge of coordinating the response to the floods. Hoover's disaster management skills won high praise at the time. Although Hoover's presidency, in 1929–33, would be wrecked by the Depression, he continued to be admired for humanitarian work during the First World War and in the 1920s. Hoover's success in 1927, however exaggerated in the telling, was contrasted with the response of the authorities to Katrina which seemed tentative if not chaotic. Andrew Rojecki (2009) suggests that the bickering and defeatism that accompanied Hurricane Katrina reflected a loss of solidarity and self-confidence in American culture since the 1920s, when every challenge had seemed surmountable. The following sections examine Hurricane Katrina with the help of the disaster cycle, drawing comparisons, where useful, to other flood events.

MITIGATION AND REGULATORY CHANGE

The Mississippi River collects vast quantities of rainwater from as far north as Canada and flushes it into the Gulf of Mexico. Severe flooding occurs every few years. For millennia, storms and floods were attributed to divine anger with humankind. By the eighteenth century, however, they were increasingly viewed as natural phenomena which could and should be mitigated by acts of civil engineering (Allemeyer 2012). Over more than two centuries, the occupants of land near the Mississippi have constructed flood defences, including levees (earth or stone embankments or dykes), floodwalls, gates, canals, spillways and reservoirs to protect their communities, and speed the flow of water to the sea (Rogers 2008).

During the nineteenth century the profits generated by agriculture and trade appeared to justify the risks of settling the Mississippi Valley and

New Orleans. Until the growing railroad system linked the Midwest and South direct to the East Coast, the great river and its tributaries were critical transport arteries. Optimism about the capacity of engineers to tame nature was at its height in the early twentieth century, and was not seriously dented by the 1927 and 1937 floods. In each case the response of the authorities was to strengthen the levees. Additional investment in flood control was approved in 1928, albeit after considerable wrangling over who should pay (Pearcy 2002).

Over in Europe, the Dutch authorities responded to the devastating 1953 flood with the Delta Plan, which aimed at making the south-west Netherlands secure against a one in 10 000-year flood (Gerritsen 2005, 1286). It is worth commenting briefly on the differences between American and Dutch approaches to flood and coastal defence. The Dutch aimed for a foolproof system, whereas the Americans were willing to accept greater risks in order to save on capital expenditure. The Americans did, however, respond aggressively when disaster struck. Wiebe Bijker (2007) suggests that differences in political culture and attitudes to risk may explain those contrasting strategies. The Dutch are more risk-averse than the Americans and more willing to put up with large-scale government intervention. At the same time, however, the Dutch have far more at stake: their national survival depends on holding back the sea and mistakes cannot be tolerated, whereas only some parts of the USA are in danger.

The Mississippi flows through the centre of New Orleans. As well as flooding caused by bad weather to the north, New Orleans and its residents are exposed to hurricanes coming inland from the Gulf of Mexico to the south. The canals that serve the port of New Orleans and, under normal circumstances, drain the Mississippi into the sea, may reverse direction during a hurricane and propel a surge of water back into the city. The only certain way to eliminate the risk of flooding is to avoid living in vulnerable locations such as New Orleans and the Gulf Coast. For existing residents of New Orleans, however, many of whom are relatively poor, moving is a costly option that involves taking on new risks and uncertainties. During the late twentieth century, the Gulf Coast experienced an influx of families from other parts of the USA. They valued the amenity of living near the sea, and relegated the hurricane threat to the back of their minds.

Each meteorological disaster prompted new efforts to strengthen flood defences along the Mississippi. Hurricane Betsy in 1965 was in some respects a precedent for Hurricane Katrina. Betsy came ashore near New Orleans, overcame the flood defences, and inundated 5000 square miles. Eighty-one people lost their lives, 17 600 were injured and several hundred thousand temporarily displaced. The federal government responded by passing new legislation. The Flood Control Act 1965 promised to mitigate the threat to New Orleans. New flood defences – the Lake Pontchartrain and Vicinity Protection Project – were to be built by the United States Army Corps of Engineers (USACE), and the cost of construction shared by federal and lower-level authorities. Completed stretches of levee and other defences would be handed over to local levee boards, and they would be responsible for operation and maintenance (Mittal 2005). In practice, however, levee boards differed both in competence and in ability to pay for levee maintenance. The reliability of the system was determined by the weakest link. The USACE believed that the structures built as part of the Lake Pontchartrain Project would withstand a 'standard project hurricane', though not necessarily one on the scale of Betsy or Katrina (United States Senate, Committee on Homeland Security and Governmental Affairs 2006, 77–8). Paradox-ically, the greater sense of security offered by the Lake Pontchartrain Project encouraged further residential and business development in low-lying areas of New Orleans, exposing even more people to risk, albeit a somewhat reduced risk (Parker et al. 2009, 209). In the long run, moreover, levees are not a panacea because the land behind them dries out and sinks, a process that to a large extent explains why much of New Orleans was below sea level by 2005 (Congleton 2006, 10). Should the levees then fail, the consequences are bound to be even more devastating. Work to bolster the levee system was offset by the continual erosion of the coastal wetlands which to some extent had shielded New Orleans from hurricanes. In fact the loss of wetlands was caused in part by levee and canal building, working in a vicious cycle (Rooney 1989). By the time of Hurricane Katrina, almost exactly 40 years after Hurricane Betsy, considerable progress had been made with the Lake Pontchartrain Project, but construction was not yet complete. The public and their elected representatives gradually lose interest in expensive disaster miti-gation works, particularly when memories of the last disaster fade, the cost of construction rises and seemingly more pressing priorities emerge (Meyer 2010, 126).

Hurricane Betsy also prompted the establishment of the National Flood Insurance Program (NFIP). Set up in 1968, the aim of the NFIP was to encourage residents of vulnerable areas to purchase flood insurance, a type of cover that many private insurers were not interested in providing. Insurance was available at subsidized rates though the NFIP. Although some homeowners were compelled to take out flood insurance when they bought their properties, they were not forced to renew their policies. Demand for insurance tended to rise after a flood but then fade away.

Even in the most flood-prone states, Louisiana and Florida, only a minority of property owners took out policies (Michel-Kerjan 2010). Low take-up rates were not simply a reflection of moral hazard, or house-holders' calculation that for reasons of political expediency the govern-ment would have to bail them out whether or not they were insured. Many residents of areas at risk from earthquakes or flooding do not automatically assume that the government will save their bacon. Rather, they may be unable to imagine or estimate the probability of compara-tively rare events. For example, those who have not experienced a flood tend to underestimate the chance of being flooded in the future. In essence they put disaster risk out of their minds (Kunreuther and Pauly 2006).

During the 1960s and 1970s, new emergency response organizations were established by the authorities at the national, state and local levels. The most prominent of the disaster management bureaucracies was the Federal Emergency Management Agency (FEMA). Set up by President Jimmy Carter in 1979, FEMA amalgamated a number of existing disaster management schemes. Its functions were to oversee mitigation, prepared-ness and disaster response, and provide resources to state and local disaster agencies when required. But FEMA had a low status within the governmental hierarchy and struggled to attract suitably qualified person-nel. The federal government was refocusing FEMA on civil defence and counter-terrorism even before the attacks of September 11, 2001 (Bea 2007, 3). After September 11, FEMA was absorbed into the newly formed Department of Homeland Security (DHS) which made disaster preparedness and response a lower priority than in the past. Con-sequently, FEMA's effectiveness in its traditional sphere of activity was compromised in the years preceding Katrina (Perrow 2007, 48–67).

The measures taken to mitigate flooding along the Mississippi, espe-cially around New Orleans, were substantial but not comprehensive. Not only were the flood defences incomplete in 2005, but their maintenance was left to the vagaries of local politics. Public interest in flood protection varied inversely with the interval since the last disaster. Levee building generated a false sense of security, prompting further residential construction in low-lying areas. The take-up of flood insurance was low, multiplying the likely burden on taxpayers in the event of disaster. Risk was underestimated by many of those living along the Mississippi or near the Gulf Coast. Similar phenomena may be observed in other spheres. In the financial and macroeconomic fields, for example, interest in mitiga-tion is greatest in the aftermath of a disaster, such as the depression or the GFC, but wanes over time. There may also be a tendency to underestimate or ignore risk, especially if it is a long time since the last financial crash.

WARNINGS

One of the main purposes of weather forecasting is to provide advance warning of potentially disastrous events such as hurricanes. The techniques used in weather forecasting are different from those in economic forecasting, and the time scale much shorter. Nonetheless, the goal is essentially the same, namely to peer into the future with a view to guiding those with decisions to make. Both types of forecasting are notoriously inaccurate. Hurricanes, the subject of this chapter, are liable to change direction, strength and speed at any moment.

The origins of the US National Weather Service have been traced back to 1870 when an army weather service was established in the Signal Corps. An important function of the service was the provision of storm warnings for shipping on the Great Lakes. In 1890–91 the Department of Agriculture took over responsibility for weather forecasting (Pietruska 2011), and in 1940 there was a further move to the Department of Commerce. Forecasting techniques were slow to develop until the introduction of radar and computers. As in business and economic forecasting, much depends on gathering accurate information and then projecting it into the future.

Not all weather-related disasters are difficult to predict. The Mississippi floods of 1927 followed months of exceptionally heavy rainfall, although the precise location and timing of breaches in the levees could not have been anticipated. As early as November 1926, the *National Weather Review* reported that 'neither prophetic vision nor vivid imagination was required to picture a great flood in the following spring', provided the heavy rains continued (Henry 1927, 437). Anticipating a hurricane is another matter altogether. Hurricane researchers in the 1960s were able to offer no more than a three-day forecast. Following considerable investment in the weather service in the 1990s, a five-day hurricane forecast was introduced in 2003 (Rappaport et al. 2009, 415), although knowing that a hurricane is out there is not the same as knowing where it will roam.

The National Hurricane Center (NHC) in Miami was responsible for making hurricane forecasts and issuing warnings to the authorities in threatened locations. Even with the relatively advanced technology available in 2005, it was difficult to predict what a hurricane would do until it was too late. Hurricanes are very strong tropical storms. Once a tropical storm is identified, the NHC issues regular forecasts of its probable track, intensity and wind speed. The NHC is explicit about the probabilistic nature of its forecasts. In practice, most hurricanes stray a long way from their projected trajectory. New Orleans was threatened by hurricanes on a regular basis, but very few actually arrived. In the case of Hurricane Katrina, however, the NHC's track forecasts were unusually accurate, but that could not have been known in advance. Sixty hours before Katrina reached the vicinity of New Orleans, the 'strike probability' was a mere 17 per cent. The strike probability for New Orleans did not rise above 50 per cent until less than 24 hours before impact (Regnier 2008, 19).

In addition to specific, if unreliable warnings from the NHC, there were several other grounds for concern about the exposure of New Orleans to a hurricane strike. Hurricane activity was subdued between 1971 and 1994, but thereafter their frequency in the Atlantic basin, especially in the Caribbean, started to rise. Hurricanes were also becoming more intense. Whether the trend towards more frequent and stronger hurricanes was part of a natural cycle or the product of climate change was a matter for debate, but the threat to New Orleans and other Gulf Coast communities was clearly rising (Goldenberg et al. 2001; Mann and Emanuel 2006).

New Orleans experienced several near misses, including Hurricane Georges in 1998 and Hurricane Ivan in September 2004. Following Hurricane Georges, application was made to the federal government for funds to develop a comprehensive plan to respond to a major hurricane disaster in New Orleans. After an interval of five years, funds were released in 2004 to pay for an exercise called Hurricane Pam, which was designed to test the preparedness of the authorities in New Orleans and facilitate improved planning. Pam was visualized as a slow-moving hurricane of Category 3 to 4 in strength, characteristics that it would have in common with Katrina (United States House of Representatives 2006, 83). It was estimated that Pam would cause widespread flooding and more than 60 000 fatalities because there would not be enough time to get everyone out of New Orleans. Between 200 000 and 300 000 people would require evacuation after Pam made landfall. Hundreds of thousands of residents would be displaced; state and local governments would be overwhelmed by the challenges of evacuating and sheltering so many people; hospitals would struggle to cope with special needs patients; and many first responders would be put out of action. A loss of situational awareness would be experienced by some agencies: in other words there would be confusion and possibly a failure of sensemaking (United States Senate, Committee on Homeland Security and Governmental Affairs

2006, 109–16). Other than in relation to the number of fatalities, Hurricane Pam was a good predictor of what would actually happen during Hurricane Katrina. Efforts were made to incorporate the lessons of Hurricane Pam in disaster planning, but time and resources were limited and New Orleans was poorly prepared when Katrina arrived.

On the other hand, there were also grounds for thinking that the threat to New Orleans was exaggerated. The involvement of the USACE in the design and construction of the district's flood defences was a source of reassurance to many. Officially, the position of the USACE was that New Orleans was safe against all but a 1 in 200- or 300-year storm. The Lake Pontchartrain Project had been designed to cope with a Category 3 hurricane. But the measurement and categorization of hurricanes had evolved since the 1960s when the USACE's implicit guarantees were first issued, and in retrospect they seem optimistic. Partly because of poor coordination between the USACE and local agencies, the defences of New Orleans were incomplete and inadequately maintained. Some local USACE officers were less sanguine than their superiors about the safety margin. Faith in the USACE provided local politicians and residents with a false sense of security before Katrina, but then provoked a backlash against the Corps after 2005 (Parker et al. 2009, 209; United States Senate, Committee on Homeland Security and Governmental Affairs 2006, 133; Irons 2005).

Before 2005, then, New Orleans and its citizens had been given various warnings about the city's exposure to hurricanes. Hurricanes Georges and Ivan had veered away from the city at the last moment. The Hurricane Pam exercise reinforced the message that New Orleans was inadequately prepared, but came too late to have a decisive effect. Even so, it would be difficult to distinguish a false alarm from the real thing. Central bankers may face similar dilemmas when deciding whether or not to intervene as lender of last resort to stem turmoil in the banking sector. Similarly, political and military leaders must decide which threats to meet with diplomacy and which with force. The scene was set for the advent of Katrina.

THE TRIGGERING EVENT

On Tuesday, 23 August, at 4 p.m. Central (Daylight) Time, a tropical depression formed near the Bahamas.[1] At 2.30 p.m. on Thursday 25, the status of the storm was raised to hurricane, and the hurricane was named Katrina. As Katrina approached the Florida coast from the east at 4 p.m. on Thursday, some NHC models predicted that, after passing over Florida and entering the Gulf of Mexico, it would turn and come ashore a second time somewhere between Louisiana and Alabama. Katrina crossed Florida, inflicting some but not a great deal of damage, and then travelled south west into the Gulf of Mexico. At 11 a.m. on Friday 26th the NHC predicted that the hurricane would change course and move in the general direction of New Orleans. The forecast track for Katrina was amended several times that day. At 10 p.m., however, the NHC predicted that landfall would take place east of New Orleans on the border between Louisiana and Mississippi on Monday. Katrina was also gaining in strength. At 4 a.m. on the morning of Saturday, 27 August, the NHC forecast a direct hit on New Orleans by a Category 3 hurricane on the coming Monday (United States Senate, Committee on Homeland Security and Governmental Affairs 2006, 67; Knabb et al. 2011). It should be remembered, however, that all hurricane forecasts have a very large margin of error. The triggering event, then, occurred between Thursday afternoon, when a vague threat to New Orleans emerged, and early Saturday morning, when the NHC forecast a direct hit within 48 hours. In the absence of computers, satellites and aircraft, the threat to New Orleans would have taken longer to identify. The triggering event was generated by the forecasting process, and its timing was influenced by the technology and human capital available to the NHC.

SENSEMAKING AND DECISION MAKING

Katrina arrived with only three or so days' warning, as did most hurricanes. Making sense of what was happening (or likely to happen) was conceptually quite straightforward. The challenge for policy makers was to make the right decisions with little time for reflection. To some extent the task of sensemaking had been delegated to the NHC which gathered and processed meteorological data from a wide range of sources: 'satellites, aircraft, airborne and ground-based radars, conventional land-based surface and upper-air observing sites, Coastal-Marine Automated Network (C-MAN) stations, National Ocean Service (NOS) stations, ocean data buoys, and ships' (Knabb et al. 2011, 4). The data were then packaged by the NHC and presented in a digestible format to those responsible for the safety of the residents of New Orleans and Louisiana, including the Mayor and the Governor. A second round of sensemaking took place as those leaders and their advisors considered the implications of the forecasts, and pondered the possible responses.

Different layers of government reacted on the accumulating evidence about Katrina at varying speeds. The decision to evacuate a city is ultimately the responsibility of the Mayor, although he or she is expected to take expert advice. The state government was first off the mark. Governor Kathleen Blanco of Louisiana declared a state of emergency at 1 p.m. on Friday, 26 August, and began to implement the state's evacuation plan at 9 a.m. on Saturday. FEMA's emergency headquarters started work at 6 a.m. on Saturday. Mayor Ray Nagin of New Orleans issued a *voluntary* evacuation order for the city at about 1 p.m. on Saturday. Early on Saturday evening Max Mayfield, the head of the National Weather Service, spoke by telephone to local leaders, including Blanco and Nagin, and stressed the seriousness of the threat from Katrina. The hurricane had the potential to wreak devastation. But Mayfield would later deny pressing Nagin to order the *compulsory* evacuation of the city (United States House of Representatives 2006, 70). Nagin finally issued the mandatory evacuation order on the morning of Sunday 28th.[2] He would be heavily criticized for delaying that decision for so long.

The decision to evacuate a major city is not one to be taken lightly. Most hurricane threats to New Orleans proved to be false alarms. The cost of each evacuation ran into millions of dollars. If the mayor 'cried wolf' too often, the city authorities risked losing credibility, and might even be sued for the costs and lost revenue incurred by private businesses and citizens (Parker et al. 2009, 211). When Hurricane Ivan was expected in September 2004, Nagin had announced the voluntary evacuation of New Orleans. More than half of the city's residents left town on that occasion, but Ivan veered east at the last moment and missed the city (United States Senate, Committee on Homeland Security and Governmental Affairs 2006, 24). Nagin did not want to repeat such an embarrassing episode.

Fear of a false alarm had to be balanced against the risk to the city and its inhabitants. A thorough evacuation would take several days to organize. For a small city, it was recommended that evacuation start about 30 hours before the expected arrival of the eye of the hurricane. For a big city, such as New Orleans, evacuation needed to start sooner, perhaps 50 to 72 hours in advance of the eye (Regnier 2008, 17). Hurrevac, the NHC's decision-support software, set precise deadlines for the evacuation decision to be made by each area threatened by hurricane. At 10 p.m.[3] on Friday, 26 August, Hurrevac set a deadline of 4 a.m. on Saturday for the New Orleans authorities to decide whether or not to evacuate. Had a firm decision been taken at 4 a.m., there would have been around 50 hours left in which to implement it prior to Katrina's landfall, and several more until the hurricane approached the vicinity of New Orleans (Kirlik 2007), but even that would have been cutting it very fine. Nagin dithered, however, and did not proclaim a voluntary evacuation until Saturday lunchtime, and a mandatory evacuation until Sunday morning, less than 24 hours before landfall. Although Nagin could not have known that the NHC's forecasts would be accurate, his procrastination increased the likelihood that the evacuation would be incomplete, and that many of the least mobile members of the community would be stranded.

Whether Nagin panicked or went into denial, like the operators of the Three Mile Island nuclear plant in 1979, is difficult to ascertain, but his behaviour invited such an interpretation (Shughart 2006, 36). We do know that when faced with incomplete information and a tough decision, the mayor played for time. Nagin would attract a significant part of the blame for the extent of the disaster experienced by New Orleans. But he was also desperately unlucky because Katrina, like Ivan and Georges, could have changed course and spared the city.

The challenge facing policy makers once Katrina became a threat was conceptually quite simple. Either Katrina would hit or come close to New Orleans or it would miss, and if it hit or came close there would be enormous damage. A decision on evacuation would have to be taken whilst the probability of a hit was still quite low. The situation facing policy makers in Europe in the summer of 1914, or officials at the Federal Reserve and US Treasury in 1929–30 or 2007–09, was more complicated because there were more imponderables and permutations. Nonetheless, the decision on whether or not to evacuate was still a tough one.

THE DISASTER UNFOLDS

The eye of Katrina made landfall around 6 a.m. on Monday. Although Katrina had been downgraded to a Category 3 hurricane by the time it reached the vicinity of New Orleans, it was still immensely powerful. Wind speeds reached between 100 and 140 miles per hour. The eye passed a few miles to the east of downtown New Orleans. Nevertheless, the city was subjected to a triple attack of high winds, torrential rain and a storm surge of up to 29 feet high along canals and other waterways. Water began to spill over the top of some levees and flood defences, inundating low-lying districts. Other levees, especially the poorly maintained ones, began to crumble and collapse. The worst breaches in the network occurred on canals that in normal times drained water out of New Orleans. When canal walls were breached, storm water from Lake Pontchartrain poured into the city centre (Nicholson 2005).

Eighty per cent of New Orleans was flooded. Approximately 1800 lives were lost; at least 1100 of the fatalities occurred in New Orleans and other parts of Louisiana (United States House of Representatives 2006, 7). Economic activity in New Orleans ceased when the bulk of the population fled. Thousands of residential and commercial buildings were destroyed or damaged. The Port of New Orleans was closed for seven months, and the oil and gas industries experienced protracted disruption. It was several months before the flooding subsided and the city, or parts of it, became inhabitable. Residents without access to transport out of the city, and those unwilling to leave, were encouraged to take refuge in the Superdome sports stadium or the Convention Center. Uncomfortable, insanitary and dangerous conditions were their lot until they could be evacuated on the following weekend (United States House of Representatives 2006, 65, 117). About 20 per cent of the population was stranded in New Orleans during the worst of the disaster. As anticipated, following the Hurricane Pam exercise, those left behind were the least mobile groups: the poor, the elderly, the disabled and the sick (United States Senate, Committee on Homeland Security and Governmental Affairs 2006, 35). African-American residents and those with lower educational attainment were also represented disproportionately amongst the non-evacuees (Thiede and Brown 2013).

Whereas the floods of 1927 occurred at various points along the Mississippi over a period of months, the damage caused by Katrina was relatively concentrated both in space and time. Katrina did not linger. Within a few hours the hurricane had passed New Orleans and gone further inland, diminishing in force all the time. But the flood waters remained. There was a degree of looting and disorder in the city, which was only to be expected after any disaster, but it was not as bad as was portrayed in the media (United States House of Representatives 2006, 241–60). More importantly, hundreds of thousands of people lost their homes, whether temporarily or permanently, and/or their livelihoods and security. Some lost friends and family. The cost of Hurricane Katrina was far more than a matter of adding up the damage to property. Mental health levels deteriorated in the wake of the hurricane, not least amongst those living in temporary accommodation and those unable to access compensation. One study of mental health on the Mississippi Gulf Coast showed that African-American and female survivors of Katrina were particularly liable to depression and stress (Picou and Hudson 2010).

One very significant difference between Katrina and the epic Mississippi floods of the 1920s and 1930s concerns the manner in which they were reported. The floods of 1927, the suffering of the victims, and the inadequacy of the official response could not be seen on television because television did not then exist. By 2005, however, rolling coverage of disasters was available on competing news channels everywhere in the USA and across the globe. Katrina was the most prominent media story in the world in 2005 (Malhotra and Kuo 2008, 122). Desperate families could be observed sitting on rooftops in New Orleans and signalling for help. The appalling conditions in the Superdome and Convention Center could be witnessed from sofas in New York, Los Angeles or London. Chaos appeared to reign in the days following the hurricane. Live coverage introduced new distortions. News crews focused on the carnage in New Orleans and the inefficiency of the authorities, even though fatalities were only a fraction of those expected on the basis of Hurricane Pam.

The Centre for Research on the Epidemiology of Disasters (CRED) describes Katrina as the fourth most serious natural disaster to strike the USA between 1900 and 2014 when measured in terms of fatalities. A total of 1833 people, including a few in Cuba, are reported to have been killed by Katrina. The natural disaster with the highest number of fatalities between 1900 and 2014 was the Galveston hurricane of 1900 which killed 6000.[4] Although the death toll from the Mississippi floods of 1927 is uncertain, it was probably much more than the 246 recorded by the Red Cross and accepted by CRED (Barry 1997, 286). When a natural disaster affects a country that is less economically developed than the USA, the casualties tend to be very much higher. The Haiti earthquake in 2010 may have caused more than 222 000 fatalities (Gros 2011), whilst the Indian Ocean tsunami of December 2004 is estimated to have killed 350 000 people in several countries including Indonesia and Sri Lanka (Athukorola and Resosudarmo 2006). However insufficient the flood defences and emergency services were in Louisiana, they were far in advance of those available in developing countries.

Although Hurricane Katrina was not a disaster on the scale of the First World War or the depression of the 1930s, any attempt to count the cost is bound to be impressionistic. Willliam Nordhaus (2010, 5–6) suggests that 'Katrina was so costly not because of its intensity but because it hit the most vulnerable high-value spot in the United States', namely New Orleans. The city was vulnerable because of its location and its poverty by the standards of large US cities. According to CRED, Katrina resulted in $125 billion of damage. While enormous in absolute terms, $125 billion was actually just under 1 per cent of gross domestic product (GDP) in the USA in 2005.[5] By way of comparison, the 2010 earthquake cost Haiti more than an entire year's GDP. Despite its prominence in the news and public debate, then, Hurricane Katrina was not a major drain on the US economy. Katrina was world news because of where it happened – the United States – and the presence there of a well-equipped and relentless media. Having said that, Katrina's impact was felt most intensely by marginal households which were least able to protect themselves from disaster or start again.

RESCUE AND RELIEF

Rescue and relief work started at the weekend, several days before Katrina made landfall. The goals were firstly to expedite the evacuation of New Orleans, and secondly to gather the human and material resources needed for rescue work, making emergency repairs to flood defences, restoring essential services, and feeding and caring for the displaced, should the worst come to the worst. The bulk of the population of New Orleans did manage to escape the city before the hurricane arrived. Displaced residents from the city were provided with temporary accommodation and welfare payments.

Numerous governmental agencies were involved in rescue and relief. Each agency had its own emergency plan, but those plans were soon revealed to be fantasy documents. The City of New Orleans, the State of Louisiana and the Department of Homeland Security (which controlled both FEMA and the US Coast Guard), the army and the National Guard were major players in recue and relief operations. One of the biggest challenges was to coordinate the rescue and relief activities of so many agencies, each with its own distinctive procedures and specialized information and communications systems. Hurricane Pam drew attention to the challenge of coordination, but Hurricane Katrina arrived before any solution had been found. Competing jurisdictions added to the confusion. Nagin was in charge, or so it was supposed, in New Orleans; Blanco presided in Baton Rouge, the state capital; Michael Brown, the head of FEMA, and his boss Michael Chertoff, the Secretary of Homeland Security, were based in Washington, DC. FEMA intended to support local agencies through the provision of additional resources. President George W. Bush also kept in touch with the rescue effort, albeit to little effect. William Shughart (2006, 37) concludes that, from the outset, the 'public [sector] response to Katrina was hampered by a confused chain of command'.

The hurricane and floods damaged communication networks, making it harder for official agencies to maintain contact with their own personnel in the field, let alone with each other. Nagin's emergency headquarters at the Hyatt Regency Hotel lost all communications. Incompatibilities between the information and communications technologies used by different agencies exacerbated the chaos, as did individual and organizational failure (Garnett and Kouzmin 2007). Sometimes the only reliable method of finding out what was happening or conveying instructions was to send a human messenger. Haley Barbour, the Governor of Mississippi, quipped:

> My head of the National Guard might as well have been a Civil War general for the first two or three days because he could only find out what is going on by sending somebody. He did have helicopters instead of horses, so it was a little faster, but [it was] the same sort of thing. (quoted in United States Senate, Committee on Homeland Security and Governmental Affairs 2006, 287)

Effective disaster relief often requires risk taking and a willingness to bend or break the rules. Many public sector employees, however, baulked at improvisation because they feared punishment for not following correct procedure. Some embarrassing misunderstandings prevented the timely deployment of personnel and resources. Medical personnel arriving from other parts of the USA were kept waiting for authorization to proceed instead of being sent immediately into action. Despatching the right number of buses and trucks to their intended destination also proved a daunting task. Food, water and medical supplies were stranded at depots or in laybys because of misunderstandings or bureaucracy (Perrow 2007, 111–13). It took until Saturday 3 September, five days after the hurricane, for the authorities to complete the evacuation of those stranded at the Superdome and Convention Center.

Family members, neighbours and church congregations played important parts in the rescue and relief phase of the disaster. They helped to rescue some of the trapped and to convey those without cars out of the city. Some large businesses, including Walmart and Home Depot, appeared to be better prepared and organized than public sector agencies, and rushed emergency supplies into New Orleans faster than FEMA was able to do. Firms such as Walmart had a strong incentive to ensure that their customers continued to be served. Local managers at Walmart were given more discretion during the emergency than their counterparts in the public sector (Horwitz 2009).[6] That family, the community and the private sector would react more rapidly and flexibly than the authorities had been foreseen by George Horwich (2000, 529–30) in a study of the Kobe earthquake of 1995. To be fair, though, a degree of chaos is inevitable during any disaster, whether natural, industrial, financial, political or medical. Disasters are by definition overwhelmingly disruptive events. Perhaps one reason why the official rescue and relief operations in New Orleans in 2005 are viewed so negatively is that expectations of the emergency services in the USA are very high, perhaps unrealistically so (Neal 2013, 251). Walmart was good at delivering emergency supplies, but it had limitations and was not in a position to rescue people trapped on roofs.

In many ways the rescue and relief operation during Hurricane Katrina was more successful than that during the 1927 floods. Whereas President George W. Bush released funds almost immediately to assist the rescue and relief campaign in 2005, President Calvin Coolidge had declined to make any contribution to meeting the cost of flood relief in 1927 (Pearcy 2002). Coolidge was worried about the impact of such spending on the federal budget. Coolidge and Hoover were firm advocates of self-help. Floods were regular occurrences in the Mississippi Valley, and they believed that residents should be prepared to fend for themselves and not expect federal aid. Any outside relief was best left to the American Red Cross. Hoover was assigned to coordinate the relief work carried out by local communities and charities. He was not shy about giving orders to local agencies, but did not accompany those orders with dollars (Lohof 1970). In the early twenty-first century, Coolidge's non-interventionist position would not have been politically tenable.

Although Hoover claimed great credit for the restoration of flooded districts to normality, the relief programme in 1927 had a sinister side. African-Americans were used as forced labour. Some were detained and mistreated in relief camps until they agreed to return to agricultural work, when they might have preferred to migrate to industrial cities in the north. Several were shot for disobeying orders or committing other perceived offences. Some were even forced to lie on top of levees as human sandbags. Hoover left routine matters, including the operation of relief camps, to the discretion of local aid workers, many of whom were white farmers and businessmen anxious to prevent an outflow of black labour (Spencer 1994). Relying on local worthies to lead rescue and relief operations may have improved flexibility, but it imposed additional costs on those whose freedom was compromised. The grandees of New Orleans ordered the levees that protected St Bernard and Plaquemines parishes to be dynamited, believing that by flooding outlying areas they could relieve pressure on levees around New Orleans. In the event, St Bernard and Plaquemines were sacrificed unnecessarily in 1927, and their residents were paid a pittance in compensation (Barry 1997, 238–58). Hoover likened himself to a battlefield commander, waging a relentless campaign against the elements (Barry 1997, 280).

Hoover enjoyed a favourable press in 1927, regardless of the more questionable aspects of that year's rescue and relief effort. Nagin and Bush could not hope to match Hoover's popularity, and were the subjects of far more intense media scrutiny. Rescue and relief methods had evolved considerably since the 1920s. Much more was achieved in 2005 than in 1927, albeit at a higher cost to the taxpayer, but that achievement was obscured by rising expectations.

ALLOCATING BLAME

Several parties, including the media, the general public, politicians and academic experts, were involved, effectively from day one, in the debate over who was to blame for the severity of the damage caused by Hurricane Katrina, as well as for the imperfections of the rescue and relief operations.

Ever since the days of antiquity, the legitimacy of political leaders has depended in part on their subjects' perceptions of their behaviour during disasters, and in particular on their willingness to help the victims. Hoover passed that test in 1927, making up for Coolidge's coldness. In 2005, however, President George W. Bush was depicted by the media as either bewildered by Hurricane Katrina or indifferent to the fate of New Orleans and its inhabitants. Although Bush allocated federal money to rescue, relief and emergency levee repairs – to the tune of $75 billion (Comfort et al. 2010, 672) – he could not assuage his critics. Mischa Meier (2012, 23) notes that at the time of the Great Fire of Rome in 64 AD the Emperor 'Nero, at least in the perception of his contemporaries, had not fulfilled their expectations of him as a provider of disaster relief'.[7] Bush was portrayed as Nero in one contemporary illustration, playing his fiddle while New Orleans sank.[8]

One survey of US public opinion in the aftermath of Hurricane Katrina asked participants to rank seven key individuals in terms of their responsibility for the lives lost and damage caused to property in New Orleans. Democratic and Republican respondents came to rather different conclusions. For 65.5 per cent of Democrats, the principal villain was President George W. Bush. Republicans, however, were not as confident about allocating blame: 35.1 per cent identified Mayor Ray Nagin as the main culprit, with 21.6 per cent choosing Bush (Malhotra and Kuo 2008, 127). African-American residents of New Orleans, who had been ill-disposed to Bush even before Katrina, believed him to be indifferent to the fate of a city that had a large black population. From the outset, then, the media and the public were determined to politicize Katrina; an even-handed assessment of the disaster was unlikely to be forthcoming. There were even some far-fetched allegations that the levees had been deliberately destroyed to eliminate areas inhabited by African-Americans (United States House of Representatives 2006, 19).

Public sector organizations also came under attack. FEMA was believed to have performed poorly during the disaster, and the levee boards were judged to have failed miserably. Criticism was also directed towards the USACE over the defective design and construction of the New Orleans levee system. In addition, the USACE was accused of complacency prior to Katrina. The Corps of Engineers attracted yet more blame when attention began to shift from the shortcomings of the levee system to the inadequacies of the Mississippi River–Gulf Outlet shipping channel. Complex and contestable engineering and legal issues were at stake (Shrum 2014). The reputations of the USACE and of other agencies responsible for flood defences and waterways around New Orleans were severely tarnished by Katrina.

The Senate and the House of Representatives embarked on detailed hearings into the Hurricane Katrina affair. Glossy 'bipartisan' reports on the disaster were published by committees of both Houses of Congress in 2006. The Senate report, subtitled *A Nation Still Unprepared*, blamed all levels of government for underestimating the threat to New Orleans over a period of years, and for a lack of leadership and poor organizational skills during the disaster itself. The solutions offered were essentially bureaucratic: to replace FEMA with a new and more powerful body, and to give increased emphasis to mitigation, disaster preparedness, planning and coordination (United States Senate, Committee on Homeland Security and Governmental Affairs 2006, 589, 606–15). Government had failed, and therefore it was time for government to regroup and try harder.

A Failure of Initiative, the House report, discoursed on similar themes, criticizing all levels of government for lack of preparedness, errors of judgement and poor organization. 'Government failed because it did not learn from past experiences, or because lessons thought to be learned were somehow not implemented. *If 9/11 was a failure of imagination, then Katrina was a failure of initiative. It was a failure of leadership*' (United States House of Representatives 2006, xi). The House report did not spare the media from criticism, pointing out that its reports were often inaccurate and sensational (United States House of Representatives 2006, 360–61). But the report came back to the shortcomings of government: 'We are left scratching our heads at the range of inefficiency and ineffectiveness that characterized government behavior right before and after this storm. But passivity did the most damage' (United States House of Representatives 2006, 359). Unlike the Senate committee, the House committee was not asked to make recommendations.

Neither report showed much interest in the question of flood insurance. Recommendation 55 of the Senate document recommended that an interagency review board investigate the vulnerability of communities built on the flood plain, the adequacy of existing defences and the role of programmes such as flood insurance (United States Senate, Committee on Homeland Security and Governmental Affairs 2006, 625), but that was all. The official reports on Katrina were in essence fantasy documents. They focused on one aspect of the disaster, namely the role of government in mitigation, preparedness and relief. They did not address the question of why so many people chose to live in a dangerous area, whether it was sensible for them to do so, and what if anything could or should be done about it. The Senate report concluded rather limply that all levels of government needed to do better in the future.

The individuals criticized in the official reports and in the media did their best to shift the blame by attacking others or claiming they were victims of circumstance (Martinko et al. 2009). Ray Nagin self-published a memoir, *Katrina's Secrets*, in which he depicted himself as the hero of the relief effort, while others including Governor Blanco were obstructive or incompetent (Krupa 2011). Academic commentators on Katrina explored the themes of government failure and disorganization at the heart of the congressional reports. One article dissected the crisis management styles and performances of four key actors: Nagin, Blanco, Brown and Chertoff. Too often, concluded the authors, Blanco and Nagin had 'reacted to exigencies in the situation without undertaking careful analysis or planning' (Olejarski and Garnett 2010, 29). Brown had been overly concerned with following correct procedure, an approach that had reduced the timeliness and effectiveness of FEMA's response. There had been moments of paralysis. Chertoff did not want to get too involved; Blanco left things to Nagin; but Nagin dithered. In short, the responsible authorities did not understand what was required of crisis managers. The Bush administration was attacked for undermining the effectiveness of FEMA as an agency for responding to natural disasters, and for staffing senior disaster management positions with political appointees (Perrow 2007). Parker et al. (2009, 217) identified three factors that contributed to 'a pattern of denial and distraction' in the government sector before and during the Katrina disaster. There was a culture of complacency; bureaucratic systems and procedures were defective and discouraged cooperation; and flood protection and disaster management were not political priorities. Taking a longer-term perspective than some other commentators, Erwann Michel-Kerjan (2010) suggested that one reason why Hurricane Katrina was so devastating was that more people had moved into the flood plain since the 1960s. Perhaps those newcomers lacked adequate information about the risk; perhaps they believed the risk had been removed by the Lake Pontchartrain Project; or perhaps they were just myopic.

William Shughart (2006, 32) regarded Katrina as emblematic of 'the inertia, corruption and waste regularly found at all levels of public authority. In short, fiasco was predictable because politicians and bureaucrats have relatively weak incentives to prepare for emergencies and to promptly mobilize the resources necessary to alleviate hardship when catastrophe strikes.' Government, then, was part of the problem and not the answer. Whilst not focusing specifically on Katrina, Andrew Healy and Neil Malhotra offered a compelling analysis of the politics of natural disasters. They estimated that $1 spent on preparedness could reduce the damage from disaster by as much as $15 spent on post-disaster relief. The problem, however, was that 'voters offer scant incentive to presidents to pursue cost-effective preparedness spending, but do encourage them to send in the cavalry after damage has been done and lives have been lost' (Healy and Malhotra 2009, 388). Political leaders pray that if a disaster happens it will be under their successors. Political considerations influence the way in which FEMA disaster aid is actually spent. The electoral game ensures that politicians are confronted by perverse incentives.

The media, the public and politicians were inclined to focus overwhelmingly on the shortcomings of certain individuals and groups. If only more capable or more conscientious people had been in charge, if only public sector agencies had been more efficient, then Katrina would not have been quite so bad. Similar sentiments were expressed by the media, the public and politicians in the wake of the GFC of 2008–09. Collective hand-wringing allows the public and their representatives to let off steam and shame those who have failed after a traumatic event, but it could easily distract attention from the underlying causes of disaster, which in the case of Katrina go beyond the inadequacies of George W. Bush, Ray Nagin or FEMA.

RECOVERY AND RECONSTRUCTION

Hurricane Katrina was the worst natural disaster to affect a major US city since the San Francisco earthquake and fire of 1906. A prosperous city in a growing region of the country, San Francisco recovered quickly after 1906 and resumed its expansion. German and Japanese cities levelled by allied bombing during the Second World War bounced back strongly in the late 1940s and 1950s (Davis and Weinstein 2002). There was a positive statistical relationship at the county level in the USA between damage from environmental disasters and population growth in the 1990s. Increased flows of government funds, combined with reconstruction work, pulled people into the affected zone, and often raised population above the pre-disaster level (Schultz and Elliott 2013). Would New Orleans too stage a full recovery?

One of the most distinctive features of the recovery stage of Hurricane Katrina was the vigour of the policy debate over whether reconstruction, at least reconstruction subsidized by taxpayers elsewhere, was actually warranted. New Orleans has been in relative decline ever since the railroads began to draw traffic away from the Mississippi River in the second half of the nineteenth century. On the eve of Katrina, New Orleans was by US standards a poor city with low household incomes, high unemployment, and no viable industries other than tourism, the port and facilities serving the oil and gas sectors. It was a city that would flood again without massive investment in defensive infrastructure (Vigdor 2008). Some of those evacuated in September 2005 could have produced and earned more in other parts of the country. If responsibility for financing reconstruction had been left entirely to the private sector, then only those parts of New Orleans with a commercially viable future would have been rebuilt, and US taxpayers would have been spared needless expense, or so went one line of argument (Rockwell and Block 2010). From the free market perspective, economic incentives in New Orleans before the disaster had been distorted by welfare transfers, subsidies, excessive regulation and corruption. Remove those handicaps and a new and more prosperous, albeit much smaller, city would emerge.

In practice, however, no US government would dare risk the political backlash accompanied by the abandonment of a major city. The New Orleans lobby was localized and vociferous, whereas the sceptics were spread thinly across the country. Between 2005 and 2010, the federal government spent $45.5 billion on New Orleans, including $14.45 billion on improvements to the flood defences, $16 billion on flood insurance payments and $8.65 billion on the Road Home Program, the aim of which was to encourage families to return to the city and restore their properties (Comfort et al. 2010, 672). With so much at stake, the reconstruction process was bound to be heavily politicized. At least 19 plans and versions of plans were drawn up for rebuilding the city and its flood defences (Comfort et al. 2010, 671). Plans were adjusted continually in order to accommodate powerful and vocal interest groups, a method that added to uncertainty and may have delayed or deterred the return home of some families and businesses (Boettke et al. 2007, 371). A construction boom after 2005 drew in many workers, including immigrants, who had not been familiar with New Orleans before (Sisk and Bankston 2014). Recovery was slow, but by 2012 the population of New Orleans had attained 81 per cent of the pre-disaster level (Eggler 2012).

The recovery and reconstruction programme was attacked from both the right and the left. It was suggested that the post-disaster funding 'windfall creates new opportunities for political corruption' (Boettke et al. 2007, 367). Within the first nine months after Hurricane Katrina, up to $2 billion of official funds are said to have been wasted or diverted into the pockets of fraudsters (Lipton 2006). The courts found that Ray Nagin had succumbed to temptation, and in 2014 he was sentenced to ten years in prison for accepting bribes as mayor of New Orleans between 2002 and 2010. Some of those bribes were from firms seeking rebuilding contracts following Hurricane Katrina (Zucchino 2014). New Orleans was already a relatively corrupt city before 2005; an unintended consequence of the recovery programme was to strengthen the culture of graft. On the other hand, it is difficult to avoid some waste and corruption during the reconstruction stage of the disaster cycle when government funds have to be spent quickly. During and after the GFC, governments and central banks injected trillions of dollars into the financial sector, sometimes propping up badly managed financial institutions or purchasing assets of dubious value.

Left-wing critics of the reconstruction programme accused the authorities of spending too little on the city, and of using Hurricane Katrina as a convenient excuse for a form of ethnic cleansing. White suburbs and businesses tended to be rebuilt first. African-American suburbs were left to rot. Implementation of the Road Home Program was said to have been rigged in favour of whites: 'public policy [was manipulated] to physically and socially exclude the black urban poor from the redevelopment visions' for New Orleans (Gotham 2014, 787). Naomi Klein (2007, 406, 416) argued that the interests of big business were given priority in the drawing up of reconstruction plans for New Orleans and the allocation of contracts. In order to pay those firms, deep cuts had to be made in welfare spending and public services. Klein's analysis of New Orleans after Katrina was consistent with her wider disaster capitalism thesis: US corporations and their political allies take advantage of natural disasters and other catastrophes such as civil wars, demanding major policy shifts and large contracts in return for aid.[9] Klein (2007, 465–6) compared the situation in New Orleans after 2005 to that in Thailand after the devastating 2004 tsunami. In truth, New Orleans got off very lightly in comparison with the parts of Asia affected by the tsunami.

The fate of New Orleans and its inhabitants aroused strong emotions. Despite criticism from both ends of the political spectrum, reconstruction went ahead, aided by substantial amounts of assistance from taxpayers in other parts of the USA. New Orleans was rebuilt as much for political as for economic reasons. But politics cannot be extracted from the reconstruction phase of the disaster cycle.

MITIGATION AND REGULATORY CHANGE

In the aftermath of Katrina, and the other hurricanes in the 2005 season including Rita, the US Congress passed a number of laws relating to disaster mitigation and management. This legislation ranged over a vast area from the Pets Evacuation and Transportation Standards Act to the Student Grant Hurricane and Disaster Relief Act, but the most important measure was the Post-Katrina Emergency Management Reform Act 2006, commonly known as the Post-Katrina Act. Responding to some of the concerns expressed in the Senate report on the mismanagement of hurricane preparedness and response, the Post-Katrina Act enhanced the status and autonomy of FEMA, albeit without liberating it altogether from the DHS. FEMA was given additional powers to coordinate national disaster planning, preparedness and response. Measures were taken to increase the attractiveness of FEMA to existing and potential staff members (Bea 2007; Government Accountability Office 2008).

Reforms were also implemented at lower levels of government. For example, Louisiana passed a new law on construction standards in 2007, partly with a view to enhancing protection against hurricane-force winds. Levee boards around New Orleans were merged into the Southeast Louisiana Flood Protection Authority–East and Southeast Louisiana Flood Protection Authority–West, which became responsible for operating and maintaining flood defences on the east and west banks of the Mississippi respectively. Wetland protection and the containment of coastal erosion were given a higher priority than before 2005. It was recognized that wetlands have the potential to absorb some of the force of an incoming hurricane, and that their gradual disappearance because of human activity had increased the vulnerability of New Orleans. The Louisiana Coastal Wetlands Conservation and Restoration Authority was converted into the Coastal Protection and Restoration Authority and given stronger powers (Cigler 2009, 329, 333).

Despite heavy criticism after Katrina, the USACE was given the task of rebuilding and enhancing the New Orleans levee system. Advice was taken from around the world including the Netherlands. The Greater New Orleans Hurricane and Storm Damage Reduction System, which cost $14.6 billion, overcame its first significant challenge, Hurricane Isaac, in

2012. While Isaac was only a Category 1 hurricane, it had features that led some experts to believe it could have overtopped the old defences (Zolkos 2012). Although designed to resist a one in 100-year flood, there can be no guarantee that the new flood defences will fulfil that promise. Complaints about the underfunding of the operation and maintenance of the levees persisted (Schleifstein 2013).

Payouts arising from Hurricane Katrina left the NFIP, which was already in a parlous state, with no option but to borrow $18.6 billion from the US Treasury (Michel-Kerjan 2010, 166). Private sector insurers also suffered huge losses, and responded by raising premiums or withdrawing from flood insurance altogether. The NFIP was a ramshackle mechanism, and policy premiums did not adequately reflect risk. Barring a major ideological shift, the federal government would always stand by the victims of major floods, reducing the incentive for property owners to seek cover. Making flood insurance compulsory for all households, as it was in some European countries, would have contained the liability of taxpayers, but compulsion would not be popular. The debate over flood insurance proceeded at a desultory pace after Katrina, despite other extreme weather events such as Hurricane Ike which devastated parts of the Texas coast in 2008. At length, the Biggert Waters Flood Insurance Reform and Modernization Act 2012 promised to raise premiums on some properties, and introduce new procedures for estimating risk and adjusting premiums. Authority was given for the NFIP to seek a measure of reinsurance in the private sector. Biggert Waters attempted to balance the interests of groups that sought higher premiums and private sector involvement with those of environmentalists who wished to discourage further building on the flood plains (Lehrer 2013; Knowles and Kunreuther 2014). Biggert Waters provoked howls of outrage in states bordering the Mississippi. After Hurricane Sandy wreaked havoc along the East Coast in 2011, the federal government began to waver on flood insurance reform. The Homeowner Flood Insurance Affordability Act 2014 slowed the rate at which NFIP premiums could be raised, thereby making reinsurance of NFIP a less attractive proposition to the private sector (Hofmann 2014).

As in other disaster arenas, including the financial industry and warfare, changes in the regulatory environment after Hurricane Katrina were the outcome of a process of bargaining and compromise. There was no objective analysis of how to prevent or ameliorate future calamities, but in a political world it could not have been otherwise. The perception of hurricane risk among a sample of Gulf Coast residents dropped between 2006 and 2008 (Trumbo et al. 2014). Evidently Katrina was already starting to recede in the people's memory. As memories of

Katrina fade, the public's willingness to contribute to the cost of elaborate mitigation measures is likely to fade too.

CONCLUSION

Hurricane Katrina is now history rather than current affairs, and it should be possible to start putting it into perspective. Katrina has often been depicted as a scandal perpetrated by incompetent leaders and bureau-cracies. Like the September 11, 2001 terrorist attacks, Katrina shook the confidence of the United States, and demonstrated the extent of its vulnerability.

Careful application of the disaster cycle, however, generates a less simplistic story. Hurricane Katrina was far from unique. Hurricanes and floods are commonplace along the Gulf Coast and the Mississippi Valley. Ever since the eighteenth century, there have been attempts to mitigate flooding in the region, primarily by the construction of levees and other defences. The effort put into levee construction and maintenance waxed and waned. The longer the interval since the last disaster, the greater was the sense of complacency. Levee building, moreover, attracted more people into the flood plain, offering them a false sense of security. Warnings about the vulnerability of New Orleans, much of which lay below sea level, were discounted, not least because the USACE appeared to guarantee protection against all but a one in 200- or 300-year weather event. Specific warnings from the NHC about the threat posed by Hurricane Katrina gave political leaders little time to respond. With only a day or two to decide whether to evacuate the city, and a high probability of a false alarm, the task of Mayor Ray Nagin was un-enviable. Nagin dithered before issuing the mandatory evacuation order. Katrina was immensely costly and disruptive for New Orleans, but casualties were a fraction of those that might have occurred in a developing country in the same situation. Rescue and relief efforts by the authorities were hampered by inadequate planning and poor coordination; nevertheless 80 per cent of New Orleans residents escaped the city before the hurricane struck.

That there were serious failures at all levels of government, both before and during the disaster, was the almost inevitable conclusion of the post-mortems conducted by both houses of Congress. Blame, much of it justified, was allocated through a ritualized process. Little attempt was made, other than by free market economists and political scientists, to point out that the severity of the disaster was a function of the number of people living in the danger zone. Nobody in the early twenty-first century would have chosen to build a city in that location. Yet New Orleans was important politically. The city had to be rebuilt and taxpayers in other parts of the USA would have to share the cost. The regulatory response to Katrina was hesitant. FEMA was given greater autonomy from the DHS, but the question of flood insurance was too difficult to tackle. In essence, the deckchairs were rearranged on the *Titanic*. The problem of New Orleans was not solved, but a compromise was reached that would hold until next time. Even natural disasters are social and political phenomena. Individuals and organizations prepare for and respond to natural disasters in predictable and suboptimal ways. Subsequent chapters demonstrate that broadly the same pattern of behaviour pertains in other fields where disaster threatens and strikes.

NOTES

1. All times are given in Central Daylight Time, as used in Louisiana.
2. Unfortunately the official reports on Katrina give different times for the mandatory evacuation order. According to the Senate Committee on Homeland Security, the decision was at 9.30 a.m., but the House Bipartisan Committee gives the time as 11 a.m. Both reports cite figures in Central Time. As it was summer, I take this to be Central Daylight Time (United States Senate, Committee on Homeland Security and Governmental Affairs 2006, 68; United States House of Representatives 2006, 109).
3. Hurrevac set deadlines in Eastern Daylight Time. I have subtracted one to convert them into Central Daylight Time.
4. Data from www.emdat.be/database.
5. GDP at current prices taken from OECD (2014, 21).
6. Bob Pickens, the desk editor of this book, recalls that, 'As my mother lives five miles east of where the eye of the hurricane made landfall, I was over there as soon as I could manage to help with the clear-up. Not only was the Walmart store in Waveland, Mississippi remarkable in its logistical ability to quickly bring in the right kind of supplies and food (as was the Sears store in Gulfport), but so was the Sonic drive-in restaurant in Waveland. Burgers and fries were being served by girls on roller skates within days of the disaster, a sight reassuring the population that normality would return, especially when viewed in context with the scene 100 yards away of a huge pile of boxes of donated clothing that victims were allowed to pick through.'
7. Meier sets aside questions of whether or not he started the fire, or fiddled or sang while it raged.
8. 'George W. Bush, American Nero', by Danny Hellman, September 2012. Available at www.dannyhellman.com/category_folders/politics/politics_nero.html (accessed 22 August 2014).
9. For a critical analysis of Klein's method see Norberg (2008).

3. The First World War

> [The First World War] was a cataclysm of a special kind, a man-made
> catastrophe produced by political acts ... Its victims died neither from an
> unseen virus nor from mechanical failure and individual fallibility.
> They owed their fate to deliberate state policy
> (David Stevenson 2004, xix)

The First World War was in many respects the key disaster of the
twentieth century. As well as being immensely destructive at the time, the
conflict between 1914 and 1918 generated economic and political
instabilities that helped to pave the way for the depression of the 1930s
and the Second World War. The years 1914 to 1918 brought an
unprecedented level of destruction to Europe. R.H. Mottram, a British
army officer on the Western Front, wrote that the world had become 'two
gigantic factories, equipped with an inconceivable plant of all sorts';
soldiers were 'the material on which the vast organisation worked, and
the finished article made out of them was Death' (Mottram 1929, 129).
The war was simply overwhelming. In *Dynamic of Destruction*, Alan
Kramer (2008, 240) states that many poor Italians 'regarded the war as a
natural catastrophe like an epidemic or an earthquake'. It must have
seemed that way to millions of people across Europe. Yet, as David
Stevenson points out, the war was not a natural catastrophe but a political
one.

The First World War of 1914–18 was an economic disaster of the
highest order. Millions of combatants and civilians died, either as the
direct result of military operations or indirectly from the disease and
starvation that accompanied war. An influenza pandemic in 1918–19
killed even more people than the war itself. Between 1914 and 1918
output fell in most belligerent countries. Men and horses were reallocated
from peaceful labour into the armed services. Factories switched from the
manufacture of civilian goods to the supply of munitions. Shortages of
food, fuel and raw materials soon emerged, and real incomes declined.
Millions of civilians were displaced from their homes, either temporarily
or permanently. War brought revolution and communism to Russia. The
old empires of Central and Eastern Europe were dismembered. It proved
difficult after 1918 to recreate the economic and financial stability that
had existed in Europe and the wider world before 1914. Angus Maddison

(1995, 65) concluded that the years between 1913 and 1950 formed a distinct phase in world economic development, one 'deeply disturbed by war [and] depression … It was a bleak age, whose potential for accelerated growth was frustrated by a series of disasters', starting with the First World War.

Each campaign or major battle would qualify as a separate disaster, but I focus here on the macro disaster of the war as a whole. The First World War was different from other disasters discussed in this book in one key respect: it was the deliberate intention of the belligerents to wreak destruction on their foes. At the start of the war, some economists of the German historical school did not share the conviction of their Anglo-American counterparts, such as A.C. Pigou, that the costs would far outweigh the benefits. On the contrary, they suggested that war might stimulate employment, technological change and economic development. A quick victory would be advantageous to Germany (Rotte 1997; Barber 1991). Such thinking became increasingly untenable as the conflict wore on, and the human and material costs accumulated.

MITIGATION AND REGULATORY CHANGE

Europe possessed various mechanisms for deterring war, settling international disputes peacefully and mitigating brutality should war break out. Some of those mechanisms were flimsy, and others were deeply ambiguous. In fact, deterrence and provocation often went hand in hand.

Substantial peace movements existed in several European countries and the USA in the early twentieth century, but they were weak compared with their successors in the 1920s and 1930s. The advent of a Liberal government in Britain in 1905 gave some encouragement to the peace movement. Henry Campbell Bannerman, the new Prime Minister, entered office advocating peace and disarmament. The government, however, could not ignore growing national security concerns or resist pressure from the naval lobby, and soon became embroiled in a naval arms race with Germany (Morris 1971).

Norman Angell (1913) argued that a general European war should be unthinkable in the twentieth century, for the devastating costs incurred by both sides would dominate any conceivable political gains. But the argument that war was either obsolete or unacceptable was not widely accepted in policy making circles. Carl von Clausewitz, the influential Prussian military theorist of the early nineteenth century, had taught that war was a rational instrument of policy. States went to war when their leaders calculated that force was required to achieve their foreign policy goals (Waldman 2010). War was not an exceptional state of affairs; although rarely the first option, it need not be the last. Such thinking was the norm in pre-war European capitals. A few extreme nationalists and imperialists even desired war. Military and naval professionals hungered for the glory and promotion that action could bring. Humans are aggressive creatures, and some who fought in 1914–18 enjoyed the adventure, the risk taking and even the killing (Ferguson 1999, 357–66). Hitler, who served on the Western Front, had some fond wartime memories. A short war, however, might have sufficed for all but psychopaths. A war that lasted too long was suggestive of some kind of miscalculation. Europe had been spared a lengthy continental war since Napoleon's downfall in 1815, but there had been localized conflicts, including the Crimean War of 1853–56, and several short wars between a pair of great powers, such as the Franco-Prussian War of 1870–71, not to mention various colonial escapades.

Military alliances simultaneously deterred and provoked potential enemies. Similarly, the maintenance of high military and naval spending was both a defensive and an aggressive strategy. In the early twentieth century Europe was split into two blocs: on one side were Germany, Austria-Hungary and Italy; and on the other were France, Russia and Britain. But these blocs were far from monolithic. The sincerity of Britain's commitment to France and Russia was opaque until August 1914. When Italy entered the war in 1915, it was not as a supporter of Germany but as a member of the other side. As discussed below, political scientists employ deterrence theory, a form of game theory, to explore strategic rivalry in Europe before 1914, and the behaviour that led to the outbreak of war.

The decade before 1914 witnessed two arms races: one between Britain and Germany at sea, and one on land involving all of the continental European powers. There was an element of disaster mitigation and preparedness in pre-war efforts to modernize armed forces. It would not do to be caught with a badly trained and poorly equipped army or navy in the event of war. For Admiral Mahan, the American naval theorist and historian, armaments were equivalent to an insurance policy (Mahan 1912, 322). But armies and navies were more than insurance policies, for they could be used aggressively as well as defensively, depending upon the intention of governments.

Technological change in the form of the dreadnought, a new class of capital ship, made the naval arms race particularly dramatic, but the underlying cause of Anglo-German rivalry was strategic. Imperial Germany felt hemmed in by Britain's traditional naval dominance. The British, however, regarded the Royal Navy as a deterrent, and responded to the rise of the German navy by introducing the dreadnought; Germany then began to build its own dreadnoughts but ultimately lacked the industrial capacity to match Britain (Maurer 1997). British war preparations also included planning for economic warfare, involving the disruption of German trade and the exclusion of Germany from world financial markets (Lambert 2012). Spending on land forces by each of the five largest continental powers was on a rising trajectory, accelerating as tensions grew in the immediate run-up to 1914. Total world defence expenditure increased from $19 billion in 1908 to $30 billion in 1913 (at 1980 prices). But rearmament was not on the scale of the 1930s, and the burden was eased by economic growth. Defence spending as a proportion of net national product did not reach 5 per cent in any of the big powers, including Britain, until 1913 (Stevenson 1996, 1–9). Even expenditure that appeared purely defensive, such as the strengthening of border fortifications, could also have offensive uses. Fortifications offered secure bases from which to launch an attack (Stevenson 2012). Interpreting the arms race is an art form. Would lower expenditure or higher expenditure have reduced the prospects of war? Jari Eloranta (2007, 272) speculates that: 'Higher military spending by the United States and Great Britain might have made the spending and capability gap between Germany and its rivals too large to overcome, thereby discouraging the expansion of the arms race and, ultimately, the First World War.' On the other hand, it might have spurred on the Germans to greater efforts.

If deterrence should fail, the accumulated arsenals of modern weapons, and the vast size of modern armies, were guaranteed to make battles larger and bloodier than ever before. Artillery would be the main killer between 1914 and 1918. The machine gun would also take a heavy toll, especially of troops advancing in the open. Mitigating the suffering caused by war was the objective of humanitarian organizations. The Red Cross was formed in Switzerland in response to the plight of the wounded at the Battle of Solferino in 1859. The principles governing the care of wounded enemy soldiers and the protection of medical staff were set out in the Geneva Conventions of 1864 and 1906. Red Cross societies were formed in many countries. By 1914, however, the national Red Cross societies had given up any semblance of neutrality, and Red Cross personnel were embedded in the armed forces, supporting the work of army medics and nurses (Hutchinson 1996).

International peace conferences at The Hague in 1899 and 1907 discussed a number of issues, including arms limitation, the rights of neutrals, the treatment of prisoners of war, the protection of civilians in occupied territory and the use of new and horrific weapons. Most of the nations represented at The Hague signed up to minimum standards of behaviour, which constituted an achievement of sorts, although there was little hope of sanctioning transgressors (Deperchin 2014). The Hague Conventions of 1899 and 1907 sought to discourage the adoption of poison gas as a weapon, but gas was used extensively by both sides between 1915 and 1918. War at sea was also discussed at the 1907 Hague Conference, and again at the London Naval Conference in 1908–09. There was extensive debate over the rights of neutral shipping and the definition of contraband. The British declined to commit themselves formally to any set of rules, wishing to retain their freedom of action to conduct a blockade (Offer 1988). Some of those involved in the peace conferences aspired to the abolition of war, but that was an unrealistic goal. It was made clear, primarily by Germany in relation to war on land and Britain with respect to war at sea, that military necessity would override any other concerns. A Permanent Court of Arbitration with a mandate to settle international disputes was established after the first Hague conference. Arbitration, however, could not be made compulsory, and disputes of significance were not submitted to the court. Geoffrey Best (1983, 140) concludes that the Hague negotiations were marred by 'theatricality'. Each party wished to appear noble without giving up its freedom of action. David Stevenson (1996, 417) dismisses the arms limitation talks at The Hague in 1907 as a 'charade'. For Avner Offer (1988, 111), the purpose of international law was to put the other side in the wrong and provide an excuse for retaliation. Belligerents in 1914 were constrained not by international law but by public and neutral (especially American) opinion and the fear of reprisals. They behaved humanely when it was convenient or expedient to do so.

It must be concluded that the means for preventing or mitigating a major European war in the early twentieth century were at best flimsy and at worst contradictory. In fact it was tricky, if not impossible, to separate deterrence from provocation. Rules of acceptable behaviour could be proclaimed but not enforced.

WARNINGS

Volker Berghahn (2014, 25) describes the cultural climate in Europe before 1914 as 'curiously schizophrenic': there was a tussle between optimists who foresaw the continuation of 'Victorian' economic, technological and social progress, and pessimists who believed that the old order was in decline and heading for disaster. Even liberals could be pessimistic about the outlook for peace. John Hobson (1902) argued that competition between the great powers for colonies as outlets for surplus savings would bring them into conflict, a theory greedily snapped up by Marxists. Novelists played on the fear of war. *The Riddle of the Sands* by Erskine Childers (1903) concerned the discovery of a German plot to attack England. *The War in the Air* by H.G. Wells (1908) also dealt with a German plot, this time a surprise attack on the USA using Zeppelins and aircraft. Wells was prescient about how technology would transform war in the twentieth century and place civilians in the front line. He anticipated that airpower would be deployed against cities as well as military and naval targets.

Although Germany had effectively lost the naval arms race by 1911 (Berghahn 2014, 32), the competition gripped the public all over the world, and provided confirmation of the tension between the great powers. The acceleration of military spending across Europe after 1910 was less obvious to the public than the launching of battleships, though no less significant. Troops and weapons do not have to be used, but their rapid accumulation signals a willingness to fight should the time come.

Germany's growing economic might and assertiveness posed a threat to its neighbours. The French had not given up hope of wresting back Alsace and Lorraine, the provinces occupied by Germany since the Franco-Prussian War. Britain wished to maintain a balance of power and to stop Germany from gaining ports within striking distance of the English Channel. The Balkans was an area of intense rivalry between the Ottoman, Austro-Hungarian and Russian empires, each of which was ailing and irritable. Fear of Germany brought France, Russia and Britain closer together in the decade before 1914. Germany was becoming surrounded politically and militarily, with only Austria-Hungary to count on, and it was debatable whether Austria-Hungary was an asset or a liability.

The arms races were warnings in themselves. In addition, a series of localized conflicts and diplomatic incidents generated anxiety in European capitals. A general war became increasingly likely. In 1904–05 Russia was defeated by Japan in a war for supremacy in north-east Asia. An attempted revolution in 1905 further dented Russian prestige. In 1905–06 Germany encouraged Morocco to resist French influence, a strategy that led to a Franco-German stand-off. At the Algericas conference in 1906 the other European powers, with the exception of Austria-Hungary, sided with France, and Germany chose to back down. In 1908 Austria-Hungary annexed Bosnia-Herzegovina. Technically an Ottoman territory, Bosnia-Herzogovina had been occupied on a de facto basis by Austria-Hungary for some time, but formal annexation soured relations between Vienna and Moscow, which claimed to have been double-crossed. Relations between Austria-Hungary and Serbia were invariably poisonous. Vienna feared Serbian collusion with Slav minorities in the Austro-Hungarian Empire. A second Moroccan crisis transpired in 1911, when Germany responded to French military activity in Morocco by sending a gunboat to Agadir. This was another exercise in brinkmanship. Germany pulled back again, accepting French supremacy in Morocco in return for the grant of land in tropical Africa. The great powers had come close to blows over Morocco, but in the end a diplomatic solution had been found. Even Italy was restless, conducting an imperial campaign in Libya. Apart from Morocco, however, the main flashpoint was the Balkans where the Austro-Hungarian and Ottoman empires were separated by a number of small and unstable nations. In the First Balkan War, 1912–13, Serbia, Greece, Bulgaria and Montenegro launched a successful attack on the Ottomans. Austria-Hungary was alarmed by the success of the Serbs and their allies, and considered intervening against them. After much soul-searching, the Germans opted to restrain their ally. A Second Balkan War broke out in 1913, as the victors of the previous conflict squabbled over the spoils, and the Turks took advantage of their disarray to fight back; this time Romania too was drawn into the fighting. The bigger powers watched closely. Austria-Hungary was particularly anxious to prevent Serbia from growing stronger. It remained uncertain, however, whether the Austro-Hungarians could rely on German support, or the Serbs on that of their Russian patrons in the event of a direct clash. Every incident was a warning, one that agitated the main players (Clark 2013; MacMillan 2013). But on each occasion disaster was avoided.

THE TRIGGERING EVENT

On 28 June 1914, a trigger was pulled several times by Gavrilo Princip, a Bosnian Serb radical. His target was Franz Ferdinand, an Austrian Archduke, on an official visit to Sarajevo, the capital of Bosnia-Herzegovina. Franz Ferdinand and his wife died in the attack. Princip was lucky to bump into the Archduke when he did. Earlier in the day Princip's colleague, Nedeljko Cabrinovic, had thrown a bomb which had bounced off the archduke's car and exploded without harming the royal visitors. No one expected the Archduke to drive through Sarajevo a second time after the first botched attack – he was reckless under the circumstances – and Princip must have been surprised to see him. The assassins had been granted two bites of the cherry. Political murders and attempted murders were commonplace in the Balkans, but Franz Ferdinand was an important figure, and there was already a high state of tension between Austria-Hungary and Serbia. Princip wished to create

Yugoslavia, a South Slav state that would include Serbia as well as certain Austro-Hungarian territories inhabited by South Slavs. The terrorists were armed by a Serbian Major who worked for Apis, the head of Serbian military intelligence (Strachan 2003, 64–6). Apis enjoyed considerable autonomy and may have had his own agenda. Although the Serbian government was eager to stir up trouble in Bosnia-Herzegovina, it was suspicious of the Yugoslavia project, and had little chance of winning a war against Austria-Hungary. But it was obvious to Vienna that Serbia was involved in the outrage, and it followed that Serbia must be punished.

SENSEMAKING AND DECISION MAKING

Between the end of June and the beginning of August 1914 the great powers of Europe were engaged in sensemaking and decision making. What should be done about the assassination in Sarajevo? Would there be a diplomatic solution, a Third Balkan War, this time between Austria-Hungary and Serbia, or a general European war? The game had many players and was extremely complicated. Within each state there were different opinions about what should be done and how other players would react, but some opinions counted much more than others. The decision to go to war was ultimately made by 'small coteries, most of them having fewer than ten persons', consisting of the head of state, senior ministers and the professional head of the armed forces, albeit with advice from outside (Hamilton and Herwig 2004, xv). What motivated Europe's leadership coteries? Each faced one or more external threats; some also saw opportunities. All wished to enhance, or at least preserve, the power of the states, whether empires, monarchies or republics, over which they ruled. The thinking and behaviour of individual coterie members was often convoluted. For example, Helmuth von Moltke, the Chief of the German General Staff, encouraged the Kaiser and civilian leaders to adopt a belligerent strategy, while in private doubting the chances of a German victory in a continental war (Mombauer 1999).

Leaders took huge risks with the lives and property of their subjects. Whether they realized it or not, they also took risks with their own lives and property and the lives of their families. The Tsar and his family were murdered by communists after war turned to revolution. The German Kaiser lost his throne and sought refuge in the Netherlands. The Hapsburgs' central European empire was broken up and their thrones abolished. The eldest son of Herbert Asquith, the British Prime Minister in 1914, was killed at the Battle of the Somme.

To what extent could the duration, nature and cost of a European conflagration have been anticipated, and taken into account when considering the use of violence as an instrument of foreign policy in 1914? During the most recent major European war in 1870–71, the Prussians had won swift and overwhelming victories over French armies, before encountering determined but irregular resistance from the French population. Weapons had become much more powerful and accurate since 1870, and the industrial capacity required to manufacture them had expanded rapidly. High casualties were accepted as inevitable in 1914, but the majority view was that even a continental war would be short-lived (Hamilton 2010, 20). Under the Schlieffen/Moltke Plan, Germany would attempt to defeat France in a lightning campaign, and then entrain troops for the east to deal with the Russians (Mombauer 2010). The French also expected a quick and decisive campaign against Germany. The French government and the Bank of France set aside emergency funds to finance a war on the assumption that it would be over within a few months (Horn and Imlay 2005).

That war might be more protracted was feared by some, albeit a minority. Pessimists could cite the work of the banker and military visionary Jean de Bloch. Like Norman Angell, de Bloch believed that war was an irrational enterprise. A European war might, he thought, last several years, although perhaps not four. Advances in weaponry favoured defenders over attackers. Both sides would be forced into trenches to escape from the devastating fire of artillery and machine guns. The result would be siege warfare on an unprecedented scale; which for more than three years is precisely what happened. Although de Bloch's analysis was relatively well known, most military thinkers and generals persisted in maintaining that a fearless and energetic attacker could overcome any obstacle (de Bloch 1899; Travers 1979; Dawson 2002). Perhaps there were shades of military euphoria in this outlook, similar to the euphoria that gripped financial markets before 1929 or 2007.

The Sarajevo assassination gave Austria-Hungary a pretext to smash troublesome Serbia. Vienna hoped that other countries would stand aside, permitting a quick and localized campaign. But if Russia elected to support Serbia, a wider conflict was possible. The Russians had shown weakness in the past, and perhaps could not afford another diplomatic humiliation. Germany encouraged Austria-Hungary to attack Serbia in 1914, and promised military support if Russia became involved; this was the famous blank cheque. The Fischer thesis, or the argument that Germany was already planning to attack France and Russia before their armies grew too strong, has been debated at length but inconclusively. More mundanely, Germany feared that Austria-Hungary would be weakened fatally if denied revenge for the assassination. In the event of war in Eastern Europe, France was unlikely to abandon Russia and then risk facing Germany alone after a Russian defeat. Britain attempted to mediate, and sent mixed signals about whether or not it would intervene in a general war. The diplomatic dance proved fruitless. On 28 July, Austria-Hungary began its assault on Serbia. Russia then started to mobilize, prompting Germany to declare war and launch the Schlieffen/ Moltke Plan against France. The German invasion of Belgium led to Britain's reluctant entry into the fray: the British could not accept German occupation of the channel ports. It was the worst possible chain reaction (Strachan 2003, Ch. 1; 2014; Hamilton and Herwig 2008; Vasquez 2014).

Frank Zagare uses game theory to recreate the sensemaking and decision making stage of the disaster that started in 1914. In the 'asymmetric escalation game', Germany/Austria-Hungary is the challenger and Russia/France the defender. The players decide in each round whether to compromise or escalate. In another variant, Germany is the challenger, Austria-Hungary the protégé, and Russia the defender. Germany encourages its protégé to be intransigent by offering it a 'blank cheque'. Without German support, Austria-Hungary might defect or crumble. The British choose a 'straddle' strategy, attempting unsuccessfully to restrain France whilst deterring Germany. At some point war becomes the best option from the perspective of the players (Zagare and Kilgour 2006; Zagare 2009a; 2009b). The game theory approach stresses the rationality of decision makers, while acknowledging that they were working with incomplete information about the reactions of their opponents. But the decision to fight may have involved more than calculation. For Europe's leadership coteries, national and personal honour or 'face' were at stake. Upper-class Europeans were trained in a code of honour. They might show restraint in some circumstances, but if they or their friends were insulted too openly it was essential to hit back irrespective of the consequences. Not to seek satisfaction would be dishonourable. British notions of duty had similar implications. Germany had let Austria-Hungary down on several occasions before 1914, behaviour that verged on the dishonourable. Instead of backing down again, Europe's leaders resolved to fight (Offer 1995).

As war became more likely, business leaders and economic policy makers struggled to make sense of the situation and prepare for a period of disruption. War would be bad for most businesses, depriving them of labour, markets and material inputs. Financial markets around Europe were thrown into panic towards the end of July. A flight to cash put pressure on the reserves of banking systems. The normal pattern of international payments was threatened. The ability and willingness of potential belligerents, especially probable enemies, to settle foreign debts was called into question. A further cause for concern was the adverse impact of war on government finances, taxation and inflation (Strachan 2003, 818–50). London, the hub of global finance and trade, was particularly vulnerable to uncertainty. Business sentiment was depressed. The British authorities restored order by closing banks and financial markets, injecting liquidity and placing a moratorium on debt (Roberts 2013). The threat of war, then, was enough to disturb the business world across Europe.

Ultimately, the 'popular image of war proved insufficiently awful for deterrence to operate' in the summer of 1914 (Strachan 2003, 99). Europe went to war for a variety of reasons. The failure to find another diplomatic solution reflected the growing frustration and intransigence of the main parties, especially Austria-Hungary, Germany and Russia. Once they were committed, the other major powers, France and Britain, were pulled into the conflict. Had the length and the human and material cost of the war been known in advance, a different set of decisions might have been made. Perhaps, then, there had been a failure of imagination in 1914.

THE DISASTER UNFOLDS

As the distinguished Austrian economist, Ludwig von Mises, noted in 1919, 'not too much economic insight is needed to recognize that a war means … destruction of goods and misery' (Mises 1983, 153). The First World War was fought in northern France and Belgium, Eastern Europe, the Balkans, Turkey, the Middle East and parts of Africa; it was also fought on and under the Atlantic Ocean and the Mediterranean. The conflict as a whole lasted from August 1914 to November 1918, although some belligerents joined late or quit early.

Cost is ultimately a subjective concept. Each person affected by the war experienced it in a different way. We cannot see into the heads of any of the people alive in 1914, and even if we could we have no independent yardstick with which to measure and aggregate the collective cost of the war to the inhabitants of any one country, let alone the world (Singleton 2007, 12–14). We could use diaries, letters or poems from 1914–18 as a proxy for the psychological impact of war, but they would generate far too impressionistic a picture. We are stuck, then, with measuring the measurable: those costs that can be expressed in pounds or dollars or marks. Even this is a process fraught with difficulty, and one unlikely to produce a definitive answer because the matter is so complex.

The war imposed many types of measurable costs. Aggregate output of goods and services declined in many, but not all, belligerent countries as well as in many neutral countries. Although a value is given to military services in measures of national output, men are assumed on average to have been less productive in the armed forces than they were in factory, mine, office or farm. Output fell when supplies of fuel, steel and other material inputs became scarce, perhaps because of disruptions to the import trade. Less well-fed workers were less productive. As well as a drop in output in most countries, there was a shift in the composition of output away from goods and services that civilians desired and towards the munitions of war. Consequently, there was a significant decline in living standards, especially for those segments of the population that lacked bargaining power in the labour market. Many economic assets were destroyed or degraded. Buildings, machinery, ships, railways, mines and farm animals, not to mention land in the war zone, were either destroyed or damaged. Soldiers, sailors, airmen and civilians became casualties: millions died, and millions were seriously wounded. The First World War made the world, and in particular Europe, a poorer place.

Attaching a money value to each type of loss is difficult because of data inadequacies and methodological problems. Uncertainty over the appropriate exchange rates to apply at a time of dislocation and high and variable inflation hampers the aggregation of national figures into a global total. Shortly after the end of the conflict, however, Ernest L. Bogart (1920), an economist at the University of Illinois, made a brave if flawed attempt to calculate the First World War's overall cost to the world. His figure of $338 billion at pre-1914 prices includes the 'direct costs' of military spending by governments, and the 'indirect costs' arising from the destruction of human and physical capital. In other words he attempted to combine flows (government spending) and changes in stocks (the capitalized value of assets, including lives, destroyed). Stephen Broadberry and Mark Harrison (2005) reject Bogart's method on several grounds, and regard it as difficult enough to measure the cost of the war to each belligerent without hazarding a combined global amount.

Figure 3.1 shows what happened to real GDP in selected countries between 1913 and 1918. Britain managed to achieve an increase in output during the war. War mobilization was more gradual in Britain than elsewhere in Europe; the British, moreover, with their large merchant fleet and navy, were in a better position than other European nations to

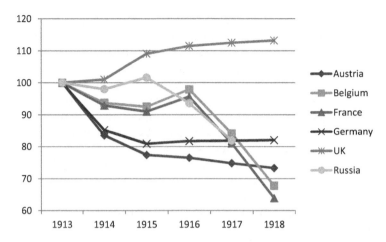

Note: Austria is modern Austria, not the whole Austro-Hungarian empire. Russia is the Russian empire minus Finland and Poland. GDP for Austria, Belgium, France, Germany and UK is measured in 1990 international Geary Khamis dollars (Maddison 2006, 426–7). The Russian series is net national income at 1913 market prices (Markevich and Harrison 2011, 680).

Figure 3.1   Change in real GDP of selected belligerents, 1913–18
*   (1913 = 100)*

maintain supplies of food, materials and other necessities from the rest of the world. Some economies, including France, Belgium and Serbia were affected by enemy occupation. Germany and Austria-Hungary may not have been invaded but they were cut off from major suppliers of key commodities in Western Europe and the wider world. Mobilization of farm labourers and horses, and shortages of fertilizer, led to a decline in food production. The figures for Russia are, perhaps, the least reliable because of the inadequacy of the statistical sources. Output in Russia dropped even more precipitously during the civil war that followed the 1917 revolution (Markevich and Harrison 2011).

Government spending figures are a good indicator of the extent to which the civilian economy was squeezed between 1913 and 1918. In France and Germany, for example, government spending as a share of gross domestic product (GDP) rose from approximately 10 per cent in 1913 to between 50 and 55 per cent in 1918. In the UK, government spending rose from 8 per cent to 49 per cent of GDP over the same period (Broadberry and Harrison 2005, 15). Since increased government spending was not fully covered by tax revenue or long-term borrowing, the money supply rose strongly, generating a rapid rise in prices.

Inflation further eroded the living standards of people whose labour was not required in munitions production and those dependent on fixed incomes.

Casualties were very high, especially amongst men of prime working age. Approximately 9.5 million members of the armed forces died during the war as a result of combat or disease: 5 million were on the Allied side (France, Russia, the British Empire and partners), and 4.5 million on the side of the Central Powers (Germany, Austria-Hungary and partners). Serbia suffered the highest rate of casualties. One-quarter of the Serbian male population aged between 15 and 49 died in military service (Winter 1985, 75). Military war deaths are estimated to have cost Britain 3.6 per cent of its pre-war human capital, France 7.2 per cent, Russia 2.3 per cent and Germany 6.3 per cent (Broadberry and Harrison 2005, 28). The seriously wounded, both physically and mentally, were even more numerous than the dead, and after the war their capacity for work was diminished. On average war took 11 years off the life expectancy of French men born in 1894 and 1895. The proportion of French women aged 25–44 who were widows rose from 5 per cent in 1913 to 10 per cent in 1920 (Héran 2014).

There may have been a further 5 million civilian deaths in Europe, excluding Russia, plus a large fall in the number of births because of the absence of men and, in some cases, worsening female nutrition. Food shortages were particularly acute in Central and Eastern Europe. An inadequate diet contributed to rising civilian mortality and declining stature in Germany. Whether hunger in Germany was caused primarily by the cessation of food imports, internal shortfalls in food production or weaknesses in distribution continues to be debated (Blum 2011; Kramer 2014, 471–6). The Germans blamed food shortages and the suffering that resulted, especially amongst children and the poor, on the British naval blockade. Regardless of the blockade, it had been reckless of Germany to go to war with some of its key food suppliers. The food problem in Russia was not a matter of the absolute shortage of grain, but rather of the failure of the authorities to ensure that grain reached the cities. Lack of food in urban centres helped to set the stage for revolution (Gatrell 2005). Millions of the Tsar's former subjects died in the Russian revolution, civil war and associated famine.

Population displacement was a feature of the war on all fronts. Although many refugees were in flight from the advancing enemy, others were forcibly removed from areas near the front by their own governments. Ethnic minorities were moved away from the fighting because of concerns about their loyalty (Gatrell 2008). Russia sent many minorities, including Jews, further into the interior. The Armenian population in

Turkey was subjected to a forced resettlement campaign that is often described as genocide (Kieser and Bloxham 2014). More than 50 million people died in the worldwide influenza pandemic of 1918–19. Although influenza was not caused directly by the war, it may have been spread from China to Canada and then Europe by members of the Chinese Labour Corps, who worked on the lines of communication in France, and then transmitted around the world by movements of military personnel (Humphries 2014).

The destruction of physical assets during the First World War was substantial, although very difficult to measure. The loss of non-human national wealth may have amounted to 14.9 per cent of the pre-war total in Britain, 54.7 per cent in France, 14.3 per cent in Russia and 3.1 per cent, before reparations are taken into account, in Germany (Broadberry and Harrison 2005, 28). British shipping losses were extremely high. Much of the fighting on the Western Front was conducted on French soil. Whole towns and villages were wrecked by shellfire and agricultural land was ruined. German forces sometimes engaged in the deliberate destruction of enemy property. The burning of the great university library at Louvain in Belgium created international uproar in 1914. When retreating to the Hindenburg Line in 1917, German forces adopted a scorched earth policy in the districts of France that were vacated (Kramer 2008). In general, however, the scale of destruction was less serious than it would be in 1939–45.

The cost of the war was felt immediately through death and destruction and the contraction and reallocation of output. But some costs continued to be incurred in the 1920s or even later. Productive capacity in some industries, including the Belgian and French coal mines, was seriously damaged. Normal patterns of economic intercourse within Europe and between Europe and the rest of the world were not restored immediately. There remained the question of how to manage the financial liabilities created by the conflict. War resulted in the rapid expansion of government debt; attempts to repay that debt after 1918 involved an imposition on taxpayers. War also fuelled inflation, which reduced the real burden of government and other debt but eroded the savings of the middle classes. The financial burden arising from the war should not be seen as an additional net cost at the national or global level. It was rather a distributional matter: who should ultimately pay for the costs incurred by the state during the war. In effect the burden was passed around like a hot potato. The impact of the war on households and nations was enormous, and it would take Europe some years to recover (Singleton 2007, 28–42; Aldcroft 1977).

RESCUE AND RELIEF

What measures were taken to alleviate the suffering of the many victims – the wounded, the imprisoned, the bereaved and the displaced – of the First World War? Military medicine and the overall care of the wounded were much more effective during the First World War than in previous conflicts. Advances in treatment were particularly noticeable on the Western Front where the armies were relatively well resourced and the war zone stationary for long periods. Elaborate procedures were devised for collecting and sorting the wounded, and transferring them from first aid posts to clearing stations, and if necessary to more distant military hospitals. Army medical services underwent rapid expansion, and their work was supplemented by voluntary agencies including national Red Cross societies. Volunteer groups raised money for the purchase of motor ambulances and other equipment; they also supplied nurses and other medical staff, and sometimes operated their own hospitals. Before becoming a crime writer, Agatha Christie worked as a volunteer nurse and dispenser at convalescent hospitals in England.[1] Improved methods for treating wounds and better surgical techniques were developed by the medical services. The First World War also witnessed a new emphasis on efforts to prevent the spread of infectious disease through improved hygiene at the front and in hospitals. This was not easy: trench systems were liable to become open sewers shared by the living and the dead. Keeping water as pure as possible was essential. Mobile laboratories made a large contribution to the campaign against disease. In many previous wars, such as the Crimean, soldiers were more likely to die of disease than wounds, but that was not the case in 1914–18. Treating troops quickly and efficiently, whether their wounds were physical or psychological, was economical from a military point of view, for those who recovered could be sent back to the front. Press coverage of the First World War was extensive, and morale at home, as well as amongst the fighting units, depended on confidence that the wounded and sick would be looked after properly (Harrison 2010; Delaporte 2010).

The Geneva Convention established principles for the treatment of wounded foes, whilst the Hague Conventions set minimum standards for the treatment of prisoners. For the most part, the belligerents sought to meet those benchmarks, though the welfare of prisoners was hardly a priority when food and medical supplies were particularly scarce. The International Committee of the Red Cross, national Red Cross societies, the Vatican and other humanitarian organizations supplemented the food rations of prisoners and provided other comforts. Heather Jones (2014,

273) notes that there was a 'mammoth charitable aid effort' to help prisoners of war between 1914 and 1918. Neutral countries also offered some assistance, not least with the inspection of prisoner of war camps (Jones 2009).

On the home front, the widows of soldiers and sailors were granted modest pensions, partly to help with the bringing up of fatherless children. Disability pensions were paid to seriously wounded combatants. Some private insurance policies covered the holder in case of death in military service, but arrangements varied from company to company and nation to nation (Huebner 1917). Governments responded to food short-ages by introducing rationing of some items. Even so, there were marked disparities in the access of different social strata to adequate supplies of calories and protein (Bonzon and Davis 1997; Davis 2000). Refugees and forced deportees looked to government officials and voluntary agencies for food and shelter. In Britain there was an outpouring of public sympathy and generosity towards Belgian refugees, but openness towards the newcomers cooled over time. Refugees were not always welcome, especially when they were different in race, language or religion from the host population, an issue that was particularly acute in Central and Eastern Europe (Gatrell 2008).

Many Belgians fled to the Netherlands, France or Britain to avoid German rule. Belgium normally imported three-quarters of its food requirements, but was isolated from international markets after the German invasion. The Germans were not in a position to feed the Belgians adequately, given their own desperate food situation. Herbert Hoover, at that time a business leader rather than a politician, led the Commission for Relief in Belgium (CRB) which shipped food for the inhabitants of occupied Belgium. Hoover's mission was complicated by the attitudes of both the British and the Germans. The British were anxious to prevent vital food supplies from falling into enemy hands, whilst the Germans suspected aid vessels of supplying the Allies. Some CRB ships were sunk by German naval forces. Nevertheless, supplies did reach Belgium. The Spanish ambassador to Belgium also played an important role in the humanitarian effort (den Hertog 2010).

Relief measures were not confined to the Western Front. An American Jewish Joint Distribution Committee (JDC) was established in 1915 to provide relief to Jews in Eastern Europe. Lithuania and swathes of Poland, and some of their Jewish inhabitants, passed into German control when the Russians were pushed back. Funds were collected by Jewish charities in the USA and transmitted to the Warburg bank in Hamburg. There was also some conflict between the JDC and German-based Jewish relief bodies, for the JDC was anxious for its work to be seen as an

American initiative. After the entry of the USA into the war in April 1917 it became even more difficult to send aid to Poland and Lithuania because of US and British government concerns about assisting the enemy. Nevertheless, the JDC made a worthy contribution to relief work in Eastern Europe (Tessaris 2010).

None of the noble work done to help the wounded, prisoners, the inhabitants of occupied territory and (in some cases) refugees would have been necessary if the great powers had not gone to war in the first place. Relief was always subsidiary to the war effort. Whilst funds were being raised to aid the civilian victims of conflict across Europe, much larger sums were being applied to the purposes of destruction. Human behaviour is frequently contradictory: between 1914 and 1918 destruction and the relief of suffering were pursued simultaneously.

ALLOCATING BLAME

The quest to attribute blame for the war began as soon as hostilities commenced in August 1914. Both sides issued reams of propaganda in order to vindicate themselves and demonize their opponents. Propagandists combined the written word with gruesome depictions on posters of the enemy and their shameful acts (Robertson 2014). The primary objective was to demonstrate culpability for starting the war and causing the ensuing costs. Considerable interest was also shown in individual war crimes or atrocities. Should the war be blamed on powerful individuals, such as the German Kaiser, or on entire nations? What, moreover, was the appropriate punishment? When the war ended, Germany and the other vanquished powers needed to find someone other than themselves to blame for defeat: the French and the British were the obvious candidates, but perhaps disloyal left-wing forces at home were equally or even more culpable. In the climate of 1919, a dispassionate approach to the allocation of blame for the war was simply not possible.

Victors in a war invariably blame their opponents for starting the conflict and demand that they be punished in some way. The motives of the victors in 1918 were mixed. They desired justice, a degree of revenge and some form of compensation for war damage and perhaps other costs. Most of all they craved a guarantee of long-term security, principally from Germany but also from one another. Leaders of the Allied nations also had one eye on domestic public opinion which demanded that Germany be punished severely. The USA, an 'associated' power and not formally one of the Allies, tended to adopt a more lenient stance than the Europeans or the Australians (MacMillan 2003; Boemeke et al. 1998).

At a preliminary meeting of the Paris Peace Conference in January 1919, a Commission on the Responsibility of the Authors of the War and on Enforcement of Penalties was established by the Allied and associated powers. The Commission concluded that the war was 'premeditated by the Central Powers' (Commission of Responsibilities 1919, 11). Responsibility for the war lay 'wholly' with the Central Powers, first and foremost with Germany and Austria-Hungary, but also to a lesser extent Turkey and Bulgaria (Commission of Responsibilities 1919, 4). The majority report of the Commission recommended a more detailed investigation of war crimes, and the creation of an international court to try alleged war criminals. Not even heads of state would be exempt from prosecution. Wilhelm II, the former Kaiser, now living in exile in the Netherlands, was in the sights of the Allies. The USA, however, was ambivalent about prosecuting Wilhelm. It was questionable whether there was any legal as opposed to moral case for Wilhelm to answer; could a head of state be held responsible for government policy? A fair trial was unlikely, and making a scapegoat of the ex-Kaiser would inflame rather than defuse political tension in Europe, possibly leading to further instability. A request was made for Wilhelm's extradition, but the Dutch would not cooperate, and the matter was dropped (Kampmark 2007). Germany also refused to hand over 850 suspected war criminals. Forty-five persons accused of mistreatment or atrocities were subsequently tried in German courts, and six found guilty. Turkey also resisted handing over alleged war criminals for trial by an international court, but did prosecute some internally. Nevertheless, the first steps had been taken towards establishing a mechanism for dealing with 'crimes against humanity' (Deperchin 2014, 636–8).

The Paris Peace Conference and the Treaty of Versailles redrew the map of Europe, granting independence to some nationalities, including the Poles, the Czechs and Slovaks, and the Yugoslavs, themselves a complex amalgam of national groups. Alsace Lorraine, seized by Prussia/Germany in 1870–71, was returned to France. The Rhineland was demilitarized, ensuring a wider buffer for France against future German attack. The Austro-Hungarian Empire was split up, and Germany cut down to size and deprived of some key industrial areas such as Silesia. These changes were less about punishing the losers than constraining German power and acknowledging the independence of some smaller European nations. Germany was stripped of its colonies; a symbolic act, for they were of little value. Article 231 of the Treaty of Versailles stated that Germany and the other Central Powers were responsible for 'causing' all of the losses suffered by the Allies after embarking upon a war of 'aggression'. Germany had little option but to sign the treaty or face further Allied blockade or military action, but objected strenuously to the 'war guilt' clause. Sally Marks (2013) argues that the German people could not accept defeat because the war had ended with an armistice rather than outright surrender. The German army, though battered, was still capable of resistance. Many Germans did not believe their country was at fault. The angry German reaction to article 231 surprised the Allies somewhat, but guilt had to be established in order to pave the way for reparation claims. It was normal procedure for a defeated power to pay reparations. After the First World War the principal Allied claims related to the damage done to property (including land) in France and Belgium, plus Belgium's war costs. The Allies inflated their demands in order to play to the gallery of public opinion. As Marks (1998, 338) explains, 'those who study reparations must cope with technical complexity and political considerations wrapped in great clouds of misdirection and propaganda'. Despite the histrionics of the British economist John Maynard Keynes (1919), about a 'Carthaginian peace', the Allies realized that Germany could and would pay only a proportion of the amount formally demanded.

Under the 1921 London Schedule of Payments, Germany was ordered to pay the Allies 132 billion gold marks, or about US$31 billion. Annual payments, including interest charges, were set at around 3 billion gold marks. In fact the London Schedule of Payments was an exercise in mystification to convince the public in Allied countries that Germany was being dealt with harshly. None of the Allies really expected Germany to pay more than the first 50 billion gold marks (Singleton 2007, 33). Germany did make significant contributions in the early 1920s, albeit partly in kind, but only 21.5 billion gold marks in total was forthcoming (Marks 1998, 367). Even that burden was offset to some degree by the financial benefits of a lower defence budget, for the Treaty of Versailles imposed severe restrictions on the size and equipment of the German armed forces (Hantke and Spoerer 2010).

For the Allies, the issue of reparations was primarily about obtaining some help with reconstruction costs for Belgium and France and mollifying domestic public opinion, but for Germany reparations were proof of Allied vindictiveness. The German interpretation enjoyed considerable rhetorical success in the Anglophone world, not least because of the efforts of Keynes and his unlikely bestseller *The Economic Consequences of the Peace* (1919). We might say that the post-mortem into the war generated several fantastic interpretations that continued to be debated in the following decades. Instead of enhancing European security, Versailles and reparations created new resentments and instabilities that would undermine security in the long run.

RECOVERY AND RECONSTRUCTION

Recovery was partly a matter of physical reconstruction, and partly one of restoring damaged institutions and normal patterns of life and commerce. In new countries it was often necessary to build institutions from scratch. Physical reconstruction was perhaps the easier of the two challenges, although in some war-ravaged localities it was not completed until the 1930s. France and Belgium regained their 1913 levels of GDP per capita in 1922. It took Britain until 1924, Poland and Germany until 1926, and Austria until 1927 to achieve comparable results (Roses and Wolf 2010, 187). The French and Belgian recoveries were impressive considering their wartime experiences. But Europe as a whole had lost a decade of intensive economic growth and rising living standards because of the First World War.

In the west, the fighting had devastated parts of Belgium and northeastern France, as Keynes observed at the time:

> During the winter of 1918–19, before Nature had cast her ameliorating mantle, the horror and desolation of war was made visible to sight on an extraordinary scale of blasted grandeur. The completeness of the destruction was evident. For mile after mile nothing was left. No building was habitable and no field fit for the plough. (quoted in Moggridge 1992, 286)

Villages, towns, cities and industries had to be rebuilt, coal mines repaired, farms restocked with animals, and land cleared as much as possible of trenches, shells, wire and other war debris. A 'cyclone' had passed over northern France between 1914 and 1918, according to Albert Demangeon, a contemporary geographer of Picardy (quoted in Clout 2005, 2). German war reparations, including deliveries in kind, were insufficient to cover the bill. Some aid was forthcoming from US private donors; John D. Rockefeller, for example, contributed funds for the restoration of Reims cathedral, which had been badly damaged by fire in 1914 (Clout 1989, 34). The Service des Travaux de Première Urgence, which used the labour of prisoners of war, was responsible for much of the initial clearing up in France, and the construction of temporary accommodation. Legislation in 1919 required each affected town or city to draw up a master plan for reconstruction. The procedures to be followed by property owners claiming compensation from the government were set out. The government would then meet the costs from German reparations. Once these mechanisms had been announced a growing number of citizens began to move back into the war-damaged communities. Villages and urban neighbourhoods often formed reconstruction cooperatives (Clout 1993). Since the government was unable to pay full compensation immediately, co-operatives raised loans to meet rebuilding costs. Some suburbs were rebuilt by mining or railway enterprises to house their workers. Reconstruction created work for architects, lawyers and builders. One of the most badly war-ravaged French cities, Reims, attracted construction workers from Paris, Italy and Spain (Clout 1989, 28). The process of rebuilding in France and Belgium was not complete until the 1930s. As in the case of Halifax after the 1917 explosion, reconstruction did bring some advantages. Sewerage systems and the quality of accommodation for working-class families were much improved (Clout 2005, 18), and services such as electricity were introduced where they had been absent before the war. Parts of France and Belgium also benefited to some extent from the popularity of war pilgrimages in 1920s, as the bereaved, often travelling from overseas, visited battlefields and war cemeteries (Winter 1998, 52).

Germany too required a degree of reconstruction. Valuable human capital had been lost between 1914 and 1918. Land, coalfields and certain industrial capacity had disappeared from German control under the Treaty of Versailles. The transport network, agriculture and industrial capacity, though not destroyed, were seriously run down and in need of urgent renewal. In much of Central and Eastern Europe, the situation was even more daunting. Dismemberment of the Austro-Hungarian, German and Russian empires led to the establishment of a clutch of new countries. Serbia (now the core of Yugoslavia) and Poland faced particularly difficult problems. Not only had those countries been devastated economically during the war, but they had to unite regions that until recently were under the control of other powers. They had to introduce new currencies, sort out transport systems built to serve the interests of their former imperial masters, and synthesize disparate financial systems. Yugoslavia inherited five practically unrelated railway systems and four gauges of track (Aldcroft and Morewood 1995, 7). Some financial assistance for reconstruction was available through international capital markets and the League of Nations, but it was fairly meagre. Foreign capital was scarce in the 1920s and Central and Eastern Europe lacked appeal for investors (Aldcroft and Morewood 1995, 26–7). John Komlos (1983) argues that splitting up the Austro-Hungarian customs union was a costly exercise. Only Czechoslovakia inherited a sizable industrial sector. Free trade within the empire gave way to protectionism and animosity. Trade between the former Habsburg states may have fallen by more than one-half after the First World War (Frankel 1997, 119–20). The gains from specialization were lost when each new country tried to develop a balanced economy. More recent research, however, argues that the impact on trade of the end of empire has been exaggerated (Wolf et al. 2011).

Financial as well as economic reconstruction was required. Governments had borrowed vast sums at home and, where possible, abroad to pay for war expenditure (Ferguson 1999, 325). All belligerents and most neutrals experienced high inflation between 1914 and 1918 because their governments were unable to raise enough revenue from taxation and borrowing to meet spending requirements (Balderston 1989). All resorted to the printing press and the inflation tax. Between 1914 and 1918, consumer prices rose by 69 per cent in the USA, 100 per cent in Britain, 113 per cent in France, 204 per cent in Germany, 1063 per cent in Austria and 1334 per cent in Belgium (Maddison 1991, 300, 302). Inflation gathered pace in a number of countries in 1919–20. An important side-effect of inflation was the redistribution of wealth and income, sometimes at the expense of the most vulnerable in society. Social tensions were stoked by rampant increases in the cost of living.

International financial and commercial relations were in disarray. Of the major economic powers, only the USA had sufficient gold reserves to remain on the Gold Standard by 1919. European currencies including sterling floated against gold and the dollar. Relative inflation rates and shifting perceptions about the imminence or otherwise of post-war recovery were amongst the factors that moved exchange rates. Restoring the Gold Standard was a key objective of European governments and central banks in the early 1920s, but it was a slow and painful process, not completed until France returned to gold in 1928 (Eichengreen 1998, 45–72). The onset of depression so soon after that achievement suggests that the emphasis on returning to the Gold Standard may have been misconceived.

The Allies were heavily in debt to the USA (and to each other) after 1918, whilst Germany was saddled with a substantial bill for reparations. There was little appetite in the USA for further intergovernmental lending to Europe. Washington wanted existing debts to be repaid as soon as possible, but belatedly agreed to a partial write-down. In the 1940s, the USA would preside over a very different post-war economic settlement, one designed to facilitate global recovery and stability. Material assistance and moral support were given generously to the war-torn nations of Europe after 1945. In the 1920s, however, the Americans were anxious to limit their commitments (Boltho 2001).

The orthodox route to financial stabilization and reconstruction, as practiced by the British, was harsh deflation to squeeze out inflationary pressure and set the economy on the path back to the Gold Standard.

Although the British achieved their objective and returned to gold at the old parity in 1925, deflation was costly in jobs and output foregone. By contrast Germany, Austria, Hungary and Poland all lost control of inflation and wrecked their currencies in the early 1920s. Internal debts were annihilated by hyperinflation, a process that was beneficial for debtors but crippling for creditors. Hyperinflation stemmed essentially from the inability of weak governments to control their budgets. In the case of Germany, the situation was aggravated by a policy of expanding the money supply in order to depreciate the mark, boost exports, and earn the foreign currency required to pay reparations (Ferguson 1998). Germany finally achieved a measure of stability in the mid-1920s, after currency and budgetary reform.

Taken as a whole, the post-war recovery was brittle. Europe was not in a position to withstand or even understand the economic shock waves of the early 1930s. Repairing and rebuilding physical structures that were damaged or destroyed in the fighting between 1914 and 1918 was the easiest part of the recovery phase. The hardest part was restoring normality to economic institutions both domestically and internationally. No blueprint was available to assist policy makers in 1918. Their successors in 1945 would be able to look back on the decisions and indecisions of the period following the First World War and avoid many of the same pitfalls.

MITIGATION AND REGULATORY CHANGE

The First World War was far more costly in lives and non-human wealth than almost anyone could have imagined in 1914. The post-war economic and political settlement, such as it was, had as its aim the prevention of further conflict. That objective was to be reached partly by weakening the defeated powers, and partly by creating institutions that could defuse international conflict and deter war.

It was anticipated that the League of Nations would be the institutional centrepiece of the new order. An international organization to preserve the peace was a concept that appealed to a variety of audiences, including the peace movement, advocates of international law and those countries, including France, that most feared renewed aggression. Such a body would supersede the more informal international governance arrangements of the pre-war era that had failed in August 1914. Some sceptics feared that the League would be dominated by the great powers. The key issue to be resolved, however, was whether the League would have the authority to make binding rules and judgements and enforce them, if necessary, by calling in the armed forces of member nations. Without such powers the League would be nothing more than a talking shop. President Woodrow Wilson was one of the most enthusiastic supporters of the proposed League, but the Congress declined to endorse US membership (Stevenson 2004, 531–2). From the outset, then, the League was fatally weakened by the absence of the USA. France and Britain were effectively left to manage the organization. When the League of Nations finally encountered serious challenges to world peace in the 1930s, in the form of Japanese aggression in China, the Italian invasion of Abyssinia and German expansionism, the response was hesitant. The League of Nations was revealed as a talking shop after all (Wertheim 2012; Dunbabin 1993).

The League proved unable to satisfy the advocates of disarmament. Peace movements grew rapidly in the aftermath of the First World War. Permanent reductions in armaments and the regulation of the arms trade were amongst the objectives of the League of Nations covenant. In the early 1920s a certain amount of progress was made in the direction of arms control. The Treaty of Versailles imposed draconian restrictions on the German armed forces. The major naval powers, including Britain, the USA and Japan, met in Washington in 1921–22, and accepted far-reaching restrictions on the absolute and relative size of their navies. Most governments in the early 1920s were struggling financially, and faced strong incentives to restrain military and naval expenditure. British budgets were based on the assumption that there would be no major war for at least ten years (Peden 1979). However, the great powers were reluctant, except in the naval arena, to commit themselves to any permanent reduction in their armed forces. They wished to retain sufficient flexibility to respond to new threats, and were not prepared to put all of their trust in the League to secure the peace. Consequently, the League's efforts to obtain substantive international agreement on arms reduction were thwarted. Although there was more support for the regulation of arms dealing, many European countries were large arms producers and were not prepared, especially at a time of high unemployment and balance-of-payments instability, to forego exports. Perceived national self-interest prevailed over internationalist ideals (Webster 2005; Eloranta 2002; 2011).

The efforts after 1918 to prevent future wars, genuine though they may have been, ended in failure. The desire for peace and the imperative of retrenchment were compatible in the early 1920s, but governments could not ignore other considerations. To what extent could responsibility for national security be delegated to an organization as flimsy as the League of Nations? The answer was, very little. Nevertheless the decisions of the early post-war era pointed to the future and the creation of a United Nations and other international institutions after the Second World War, if only because policy makers in the 1940s could reflect on what had gone wrong in the 1920s and 1930s.

CONCLUSION

Although the First World War was a complex and lengthy disaster, it still followed the broad contours of the disaster cycle. A loose diplomatic mechanism was in place before 1914 to resolve international conflicts short of war. Military and naval preparedness offered a measure of deterrence, but was double-edged because large defence budgets were also a provocation that encouraged competition. There was a wish to mitigate the effects of the war through international agreement on such matters as the treatment of civilians and the wounded. Red Cross societies were established to provide humanitarian assistance in wartime. The outbreak of the First World War was preceded by plenty of warnings in the form of confrontations that were defused by threats and diplomacy and localized campaigns. The trigger that initiated the period of crisis that led to war in the summer of 1914 was the assassination in Sarajevo of Archduke Franz Ferdinand. Diplomacy now failed. The small groups that led the European nations and empires were faced with a complex situation. How would other players in the game react to a range of possible actions from acquiescence to mobilization? How many moves ahead was it necessary to calculate? European leaders' sensemaking abilities were not up to the challenge. Moreover, they were under the impression that any war was likely to be brief, and therefore less costly than the one that transpired.

Once the fatal decision to fight had been made, the events of 1914 to 1918 unfolded in all their horror. Casualties, both military and civilian, were extremely high, as was the damage caused to physical capital and institutions. Improved military medicine and care of the wounded were notable features of the rescue and recovery phase. Humanitarian agencies also intervened to provide food and other support to the inhabitants of occupied territories on both the Western and Eastern Fronts. At the end of the war the Allies were determined to ensure that the Central Powers took all the blame for the conflict, and that they provided some measure of compensation for damage inflicted. Germany, however, managed to turn some of the blame back onto the Allies, citing the naval blockade and reparations demands as evidence of unreasonable behaviour. Reconstruction was more than a matter of rebuilding lost towns and villages. The institutions of the European and world economies, including the Gold Standard, were unhinged by the war, and were slow to recover in the 1920s. Europe was set back at least ten years economically by the war.

Although the leaders of the USA and the European Allies were determined that mechanisms be established to avert future wars, their aspirations could not be put into practice. The League of Nations proved hopelessly weak. It failed to achieve lasting disarmament in the 1920s, and in the 1930s offered little resistance to the rise of militarism. The World War of 1914–18 was not the war to end all wars. It was a disaster that would be repeated on an even more gigantic scale between 1939 and 1945.

NOTE

1. Christie was a member of the Volunteer Aid Detachment. Her service record is available online at www.redcross.org.uk/About-us/Who-we-are/History-and-origin/First-World-War/Agatha-Christie (accessed 27 April 2015).

4. The Great Depression

> The world has been slow to realise that we are living this year [1930] in the
> shadow of one of the greatest economic catastrophes of modern history.
>
> (John Maynard Keynes 1978, 126)

The Great Depression of the early 1930s was the worst pure economic disaster of the twentieth century. It was a pure economic disaster because it did not happen in wartime and was not caused by events in the natural world. For Ben Bernanke (1995, 1), the quest to 'understand the Great Depression is the Holy Grail of macroeconomics', and more than 80 years later there is still no consensus as to its ultimate causes or the policy responses that would have been most effective in dealing with it. Understanding the Great Depression was even more difficult for those, including policy makers, who lived through it (Parker 2002; 2007). They were unsure what to expect next, and they did not know how long the downturn would persist. Their efforts at sensemaking were confused and inconsistent, and at times they lapsed into panic or denial. It does not necessarily follow, however, that they were stupid. Individuals and organizations often struggle to find solutions to complex and pressing challenges, as was the case on a smaller scale at Mann Gulch (see Chapter 1). By using the disaster cycle framework we are able to see the Great Depression from a novel perspective, one that emphasizes parallels with other types of disaster. Although the Great Depression may lose some of its uniqueness, its historical significance is not diminished.

Figure 4.1 illustrates the severity of the Great Depression's impact on real gross domestic product (GDP) in seven leading industrial countries. The initial downturn occurred in the middle of 1929 in the USA, and somewhat earlier in Germany. Instead of bouncing back after a year or so, as would have been normal in a standard recession, the decline in output intensified in the early 1930s. Some economies, including the UK and Japan, began to experience recovery in 1932. Recovery in Germany and the USA was delayed somewhat longer, whilst France and other members of the European Gold Bloc slipped further into the mire of stagnation. Declining GDP meant hefty falls in the standard of living. By contrast with periods of inflation, however, those on fixed incomes fared relatively well in the Great Depression.

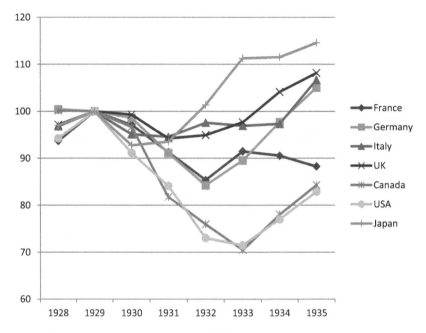

Note: GDP is measured in 1990 international GK$.

Source: Maddison (2006, 428, 429, 463, 550).

Figure 4.1   The G7 economies in the Great Depression: index of real GDP,
1928–35 (1929 = 100)

The scope of this chapter is confined to the leading economies of the capitalist world, and therefore excludes the Soviet Union. Although the Soviet Union was insulated by planning and semi-autarchy from the Great Depression, it underwent its own economic upheaval in the 1930s. Stalin squeezed the peasants in order to extract more food for urban centres at the heart of his crash industrialization programme. Combined with poor harvests, Stalin's brutal treatment of the rural population led to a disastrous famine (Wheatcroft 2004; 2009).

The word 'crisis' is largely avoided in this chapter, despite the fact that in the existing literature the Great Depression is portrayed as the classic macroeconomic crisis of the twentieth century. As explained in Chapter 1, a crisis is a period of challenge, a critical period extending from the triggering event through to the implementation of relief and rescue methods. The Great Depression was a disaster resulting from the failure of sensemaking and policy making during the critical or challenging period that began towards the end of 1929.

MITIGATION AND REGULATORY CHANGE

Policy makers and business leaders both before and after the First World War believed that good institutions were necessary for the mitigation of economic instability. Their ideal system consisted of the Gold Standard managed by independent central banks. The Gold Standard demanded fiscal discipline in the public sector and careful attention to costs in the private sector. Any country that allowed government spending and costs of production to run out of control would lose competitiveness. Gold reserves would tend to drain abroad, forcing the central bank to raise interest rates and the government to reassert fiscal discipline (Eichengreen and Flandreau 1997; Eichengreen and Temin 2000). In addition to guaranteeing the convertibility of domestic currency into gold at an irrevocably fixed exchange rate, the central bank was expected to avert financial disaster by standing ready to act as lender of last resort to the banking system. The lender of last resort function developed slowly, but was widely accepted by central bankers in 1914 (Singleton 2011, 34–46). Central bank independence was deemed important because of what could happen in its absence. In the early 1920s, the German Reichsbank, while autonomous in theory, was dominated by the government in practice. In order to accommodate large budget deficits, the Reichsbank engineered a rapid expansion in the money supply, and Germany descended into hyperinflation (Singleton 2011, 76–7).

The Federal Reserve System was set up in 1914 with the express purpose of mitigating financial instability and eliminating financial disasters. Unlike the major European countries and Japan, the USA had lacked a central bank in 1900, a state of affairs that exposed its financial system and the wider economy to considerable instability. The severity of the financial crash of 1907 was taken as evidence of the need for a central bank to manage the financial system and inject liquidity in an emergency. After considerable wrangling, the Federal Reserve Act was passed in 1913, creating a system of 12 regional reserve banks and a Federal Reserve Board in Washington. The system was established 'to furnish an elastic currency, to afford means of rediscounting [or purchasing] commercial paper, to establish a more effective supervision of banking in the United States, and for other purposes' (Board of Governors of the Federal Reserve System 1994, 2). Reserve banks were owned by 'member' commercial banks in the regions, whilst the Washington board included representatives of the government as well as of the reserve banks. These arrangements were an unwieldy compromise. Even so, the Federal Reserve was granted a large measure of independence from government control, and equipped with tools for mitigating financial and banking crashes (Meltzer 2003, 65–73; Singleton 2011, 50–56).

At the International Financial Conference convened by the League of Nations in Brussels in 1920, the institutional framework required for economic and financial stability in the post-war world was debated. The collapse of the Russian, German and Austro-Hungarian empires had led to the emergence of new nation states in Central and Eastern Europe. How should their economies be stabilized and linked into the international economy, and how should the world as a whole go about restoring a stable economic and financial regime? The conference recommended that all governments, including those beyond Europe, focus on balancing the budget, combating inflation and working towards the restoration of the Gold Standard. In countries without independent banks of issue (central banks) they should be established as soon as possible (Davis 1920; League of Nations 1920, 221–39).

The League of Nations and the three main central banks – the Bank of England, the Bank of France and the Federal Reserve – offered encouragement and assistance to other countries that were striving to achieve financial stability and set up independent central banks. Even Germany required external help to reorganize its monetary framework in 1924. A new currency was introduced and attached to gold with foreign assistance. The Reichsbank's autonomy was strengthened: a 14-person central bank General Council (seven Germans and seven foreigners) was created as a bulwark against domestic political interference in monetary policy. One foreign member of the General Council was empowered to veto further note issues if they considered gold convertibility to be endangered (James 1999, 24–5).

In 1919, the USA was the only developed economy still on the Gold Standard. During the 1920s the Europeans struggled back onto gold, in some cases to a watered-down variant called the Gold Exchange Standard (Eichengreen 1992, 188–90). Britain returned to gold at an overvalued exchange rate in 1925, whilst France did so at an undervalued rate in 1928. With the French back on board, the system appeared – in the event, misleadingly – to have returned to pre-1914 normality. The discipline exerted by the Gold Standard, supported by independent central banks, was supposed to mitigate economic and financial instability. When put to the test, however, these arrangements could not restrain the forces destabilizing the international economy in the late 1920s and early 1930s. In some respects the Great Depression was exacerbated by the institutions that were supposed to prevent or mitigate such a disaster.

WARNINGS

The economic outlook in the second half of the 1920s was different on opposite sides of the Atlantic. In the USA there was a mood of euphoria, as consumer goods production, property prices and the stock market boomed, fuelled in part by the rapid expansion of credit. Investors were encouraged to believe that this time was different, and that the boom was justified by a new economy. Only the agricultural sector was troubled. An advertisement for the Standard Statistics company of New York in September 1929 – just weeks before the Wall Street Crash – reassured investors that a bubble and crash were inconceivable because, unlike in the past, Americans now had access to full and timely information about investment opportunities (Reinhart and Rogoff 2009, 16).

In many European economies, however, there was unease. Unemployment was stubbornly high in Britain, while in Germany the economic recovery was fragile. By 1927–28, foreign observers, including S. Parker Gilbert, the Agent General for Reparations, were expressing doubts about the sustainability of German public finances at both national and local levels (Balderston 2002, 83). The German Foreign Minister, Gustav Stresemann, described the economic and financial situation in 1928 as akin to 'dancing on a volcano' that could erupt at any moment (Ritschl 2003, 105). Germany's balance of payments depended heavily on inflows of capital from US lenders. If American lenders decided to withdraw their funds (a 'sudden stop' in modern economic jargon), Germany's position would be dire. Nowadays an unusually high level of capital imports is interpreted as an early warning sign of financial instability (Reinhart and Rogoff 2009, 280). A German economic crash would reverberate throughout Europe, and any interruption in reparations payments would hinder recipient countries from servicing their own external war debts.

Not everyone in the USA shared the glib optimism of Standard Statistics. By 1928, the Federal Reserve was worried that stock market speculation might generate inflation, financial instability, or perhaps both. The US central bank tightened monetary policy in 1928–29, principally in order to deter borrowing for speculative purposes (Hamilton 1987, 148). The Federal Reserve believed that it had identified a bubble or potential bubble, and was determined to defuse it, albeit in a way that would have unintended consequences. Whether or not an increase in interest rates was justified by the economic situation is debatable. The USA still possessed vast gold reserves, and there was no inflationary pressure in the labour or commodity markets (Eichengreen 1992, 217).[1]

Reading the economic runes, and calibrating the policy response, posed a serious challenge. Once interest rates started to rise in New York, funds were sucked out of Europe, putting additional strain on the capacity of European central banks (except the Bank of France) to maintain gold convertibility.

During the 1920s the international financial community fretted over the adequacy of the supply of gold. Without sufficient gold in the system, the Gold Standard might not be viable. In retrospect, there appears to have been enough gold in aggregate. The destabilizing factor was the grotesquely uneven distribution of the precious metal. The lion's share had been held by the USA since the First World War. Restoration of the French franc to the Gold Standard at a heavily devalued rate in 1928 prompted large gold flows into France which continued during the early 1930s (Eichengreen 1996, 65; League of Nations 1944, 240). Those countries that were short of gold, however, were in constant difficulty in the late 1920s, a state of affairs that raised the spectre of a severe downturn.

There were strong grounds for thinking that economic policy makers were dancing on a volcano in the late 1920s. Equally, however, there were grounds for optimism, especially in the USA, where until the middle of 1929 the economy was in good health. It is worth examining whether or not professional economists, statisticians and business experts anticipated the slump that would strike in the early 1930s. In principle they were better equipped to do so than ever before. Economic and business forecasting blossomed in the USA and, to a lesser extent, Europe in the 1920s. Improved economic statistics enabled amateur and professional forecasters to offer prognostications. Businesses wanted to know how demand would hold up and whether the economy was approaching a cyclical turning point. Teams based at Harvard and Yale – the latter led by Irving Fisher, one of the most prominent economists in the USA – were at the forefront of these developments (Friedman 2013). But neither group predicted the Wall Street Crash of October 1929. Perhaps more significantly, after the crash they remained optimistic about the prospects for the US economy and did not foresee a depression. With the limited data and techniques at their disposal, their failure may not be surprising. Even with the advantage of more sophisticated techniques they might not have anticipated an economic disaster (Dominguez et al. 1988). Economic forecasting is better at predicting routine rather than dramatic changes in the direction of economic activity. As is often the case, then, the late 1920s was marked by conflicting interpretations of the economic outlook, and no sure means of choosing between them. If the tip of the iceberg was visible to those who looked closely, some of the others on deck were still intent on partying.

THE TRIGGERING EVENT

With some disasters it is difficult to identify a distinct triggering event. In the case of the Great Depression, however, the prime candidate is the Wall Street Crash of October 1929. The Dow Jones Industrial Average (DJIA) fell 11 per cent on Friday 24 October, and the panic continued after the weekend. The DJIA dropped 49 per cent between 3 September and 13 November 1929 (James 2010, 133–4). Industrial activity had already been falling for several months when the financial crash occurred. Stock market turmoil heightened uncertainty about the future, prompting consumers and businesses to reconsider or defer spending plans, with the result that demand for goods and services fell sharply (Romer 1993, 31). Individuals and firms that had borrowed in order to play the stock market found themselves in dire straits. Financial and real assets were sold at knock-down prices. Stock brokerages and banks faced possible insolvency if customer loans were not repaid. Banks responded by cutting back on new lending (Bernanke 1983).

The Wall Street Crash was one of the most dramatic news events of 1929, one that brought to a close a decade of euphoria in the USA. The crash was far more than another danger signal, and its ramifications were felt around the world. According to Harold James (2010, 131), the 1929 crash had 'really world-historical consequences (the Great Depression, even perhaps the Second World War)'. Reinhart and Rogoff (2009, 17) agree that a 'global stock market crash [of 1929] marked the onset of the Great Depression'. Charles Kindleberger (1987, 116), a leading scholar of an earlier generation, also regarded the Wall Street Crash as a turning point: 'One should not be dogmatic about it, but it is hard to avoid the conclusion that there is something to the conventional wisdom that characterized the crash as the start of a process' that led to depression.[2]

The other plausible but much more nebulous candidate for the triggering event was the tightening of US monetary policy in 1928. Higher interest rates in the USA put pressure on other countries that, to a greater or lesser extent, relied on continued inflows of capital from New York to prop up their balance of payments. Within the USA, the rising cost of borrowing increased the probability of an event such as the Wall Street Crash (Bernanke 2004). In the Minsky–Kindleberger framework, rising interest rates can spark a Minsky moment when borrowers and lenders realize that they have been imprudent and start to panic. But monetary tightening was a gradual process rather than a sudden break in the stream of events, and James (2010, 132) concludes that 'the specific trigger for the panic' on Wall Street – in other words the trigger of the trigger – remains unexplained.

Whether or not the October 1929 crash was the direct consequence of earlier changes in US monetary policy, it proved to be a decisive moment, especially when taken in the context of the mild weakening of the US economy over preceding months and the continued fragility of European financial systems. The crisis – in the sense in which that term is used in this book – had begun.

SENSEMAKING AND DECISION MAKING

Making sense of the emerging slump was a major challenge for policy makers and economists. It was not at all obvious in late 1929 that the collapse on Wall Street would be the prelude to a far more serious slump in the US and world economies (Crafts and Fearon 2010, 291). It seemed more likely that America was entering another routine recession from which it would soon recover.

Although the Federal Reserve loosened monetary policy in the immediate aftermath of the market crash (Meltzer 2003, 283–91), it adopted an essentially passive stance as the economy spiralled down during the early 1930s. The US central bank's efforts at sensemaking during a time of crisis were hampered by inexperience, tardy and incomplete data, and the application of misleading theory. Commercial banks that were members of the Federal Reserve System could borrow from reserve banks if they possessed acceptable collateral. Under the so-called Riefler–Burgess doctrine, it was assumed that member banks would not borrow from reserve banks until they were in difficulty, whereas in fact member bank borrowing was driven largely by the extent to which such funds could be put to profitable use. The Federal Reserve, then, interpreted the absence of a sustained surge in member bank borrowing in the early 1930s as evidence that monetary conditions were easy and appropriate to foster recovery. But low member bank borrowing was in fact a reflection of the desperate state of the economy and the lack of profitable outlets for funds (Wheelock 1990). The Federal Reserve also misunderstood interest rates, believing that low nominal interest rates were evidence of monetary ease. But negative inflation or deflation during the early 1930s meant that real interest rates were rising and becoming unaffordable. Allan Meltzer, the official historian of the Federal Reserve, argues that instead of panicking the central bank stuck stubbornly to ideas and methods that were no longer relevant: 'People see most clearly what they are trained or disposed to see' (Meltzer 2003, 400).

There may not have been panic but there was an element of denial in the US central bank's thinking. Dissenting voices were heard from time to time, but in general the Federal Reserve saw no need for a sustained programme of monetary stimulus. Meltzer (2003, 315–21) contends that in September 1930 the Federal Reserve missed its last chance to prevent calamity in the financial system. That the recession was one of the most serious for 50 years was not disputed. Some central bankers pressed for large open market purchases to inject liquidity into the banking system, but the majority view was that monetary conditions were already sufficiently easy: nominal interest rates were low and member bank borrowing was modest. The central bank's Open Market Policy Conference met on 25 September 1930 to consider strategy for the next period. George Harrison, the Chairman, informed the full Federal Reserve Board later in the day that bold measures of monetary stimulus had not been considered because 'the majority of the conference felt so strongly that there is no need for any further easing of the present easy money rate position at the present time' (Federal Reserve System 1930, 6).

In the latter months of 1930 the money supply began to spiral down, and in December the first of several waves of bank failures (described in the existing literature as crises) was encountered. The Federal Reserve would take the view that bank failures were often the consequence of imprudent management or corruption. That many banks had expanded recklessly in the 1920s was undeniable. Although there could have been no justification for rescuing individual banks, a central bank was expected to counter an epidemic of failures through the creation of more liquidity in the system as a whole. But the Federal Reserve proved unwilling to act as a lender of last resort and one-third of US banks collapsed in the early 1930s (Friedman and Schwartz 1963, 342–59).

Were professional economists in a better position than policy makers to engage in sensemaking during the slump? The 'business depression' of 1930 was the focus of a session at the American Economic Association (AEA) conference in 1931. Carl Snyder, the statistician of the Federal Reserve Bank of New York, noted in his paper that the depression was 'one of the most severe' cyclical downturns on record (Snyder 1931, 173). The slump illustrated 'the complete absence up to the present time of any kind of adequate procedure for the control, or even the mitigation of the severity of the business cycle in this country' (Snyder 1931, 173). An influx of gold from Europe during and after the Great War had fuelled a 'speculative mania' (Snyder 1931, 174) that gathered pace over the 1920s. Speculation had eventually bid up interest rates in the USA, which reduced the attraction of lending abroad, intensifying the pressure on European gold reserves. When the mania collapsed, demand for imported raw materials declined and foreign lending contracted again. The downturn spread rapidly from the USA to other countries. The slump in commodity prices had been catastrophic. For Snyder, then, the global collapse was the outcome of an orgy of speculation, of uncontrollable and perhaps irrational forces in the economy.

The distinguished Austrian economist Josef Schumpeter emphasized that economic activity is marked by waves of expansion and contraction, driven ultimately by changes in production methods. Three waves of varying duration could be identified: short, medium and long. During 1930, the trough of a short wave coincided with downswings in the medium and long waves. Although phenomena such as the collapse of a credit boom or stock market bubble 'may intensify a depression or even be the immediate cause of the location of a turning point ... it would be quite wrong to look upon them as a cause' (Schumpeter 1931, 181). The cyclical conjuncture had been aggravated by other factors, including weakness in the agrarian sector, wage and price rigidities, the deflationary climate created by Britain's return to the Gold Standard, reparations and inter-Allied debt repayments, and capital flight from some countries including Britain and Germany. Schumpeter added that he did not want to 'exaggerate the influence of monetary policy' (Schumpeter 1931, 180) in causing the slump or in providing a solution; he doubted whether low interest rates would prompt businesses to expand. Schumpeter ended cryptically: 'there is no difficulty in devising on the basis of this diagnosis remedies both for the situation in general and for any particular feature of it', although they might not be popular (Schumpeter 1931, 182). He did not, however, spell out those remedies.

In the ensuing discussion, Arthur Adam offered an alternative explanation of the depression: between 1922 and 1929, the value of consumer goods production had outstripped disposable incomes because wages had lagged behind profits. Growth had been unsustainable. Joseph Demmery described the situation in the Pacific north-west in great detail without saying much about the wider depression. Willard Thorp wondered how all three of Schumpeter's cycles could be managed at the same time without some movement towards a planned economy. He believed that the international dimensions of the depression were important, and felt that the business cycles in major economies were more in step than in the past. Alvin Hansen pointed out that the unequal distribution of world gold reserves, with France and the USA holding far more than their fair shares, made it hard for other countries to maintain convertibility without deflating. Hansen feared that the depression would be prolonged if, as seemed likely, the long (or Kondratieff) wave was in a downswing. Economic cycles led to imbalances in the development of different industries and between production and consumer demand (Adam et al. 1931).

The course of the debate at the 1931 AEA conference shows that participants found it difficult to agree on an interpretation of the depression let alone a solution. If the underlying issue was multiple economic waves driven in part by changes in production, including the introduction of new products and process technologies, there remained the conundrum of how, if at all, such waves could be managed. The Gold Standard appeared to be misfiring but what, if anything, could be done to make it work more smoothly? In short, no coherent policy recommendations emerged from the AEA discussion. Economists were no less at sea than policy makers.

Perceptions of the downturn varied considerably in European countries. During the early 1930s, France enjoyed a measure of insulation from the Great Depression, courtesy of lavish gold reserves and an undervalued currency, although both proved to be waning assets. The other large European economies, Britain and Germany, were far less well endowed with reserves. As world trade contracted and international credit markets tightened, the threats to the convertibility of the pound and the mark would intensify. Overall, the international dimensions of the slump were far more obvious to Europeans than they were to Americans. Most policy makers in Europe interpreted the downturn first and foremost as a threat to convertibility. The maintenance of convertibility was the primary aim of economic policy because without it there would be chaos, or so it was believed, and perhaps with some reason in post-hyperinflation Germany (Eichengreen 1992, 222–57; Eichengreen and Temin 2000).

The British Prime Minister, Ramsay MacDonald, resorted to meteorological metaphors in an effort to make sense of the depression. In 1930 he judged that Britain was suffering from an 'economic blizzard'. By 1931 that blizzard had become a 'typhoon' (Morgan 2006, 68). MacDonald's Labour government of 1929–31 was bemused by the unfolding disaster. The Labour leadership meekly assumed that there was no alternative to the Gold Standard, and that in order to remain on gold until the world economy improved, the government would have to pursue a policy of austerity to reassure financial markets and staunch the loss of gold. The Chancellor of the Exchequer, Philip Snowden, accepted the Treasury and Bank of England position on gold with some enthusiasm. Although one minister, Sir Oswald Mosley, advocated a more active policy he was unable to win over the Cabinet (Skidelsky 1970).

Outside the government, the prominent economist John Maynard Keynes did have radical ideas, but out of loyalty to the establishment refrained from criticizing the Gold Standard in public. Keynes persuaded MacDonald to commission a report on the depression from a Committee of Economists in 1930. Keynes chaired the committee, the other members being A.C. Pigou, Lionel Robbins, Hubert Henderson and Sir Josiah Stamp. The British case had distinctive features. Even before 1929 the economy was floundering, as old industries declined faster than new ones could expand to take their place. Rigidities in labour markets, stemming from the power of trade unions and the comparative generosity of unemployment benefits, were believed by many observers to have hindered the transfer of labour to new industries and growing regions. Consequently, it was difficult to know how much of the British slump to attribute to the global depression and how much to deeper-seated problems. Most members of the Committee of Economists were inclined to regard the global downturn as a serious, albeit temporary, aggravation. They believed that rigidities, including inflexible wages and prices, were the main source of Britain's woes, including high unemployment. Keynes disagreed: he contended that the key issue was high interest rates, not just in Britain, but globally. Interest rates were excessive because central banks were competing to attract and keep enough gold to maintain convertibility. The consequence of high interest rates was that savings exceeded investment, placing downward pressure on economic activity and prices (Howson 2011, 179–93). The economists struggled to reach a consensus, especially on policy recommendations,[3] and in any case the government was not really listening.

No agreement on the origins and nature of the slump emerged from the protracted deliberations of policy makers and economists on either side of the Atlantic. It is interesting, however, that they did not favour an interpretation that became popular in the late twentieth century, namely the theory of Milton Friedman and Anna Schwartz (1963) that the slump resulted from a series of policy errors by the US central bank. In the absence of any common understanding of the causes and dynamics of the downturn, it was impossible to develop a coherent strategy for dealing with the situation. Consequently the crash of 1929 mutated into disaster in the early 1930s.

THE DISASTER UNFOLDS

Instead of bouncing back in 1930, the US economy continued to contract. In December 1930 there occurred the first in a succession of regional banking collapses that continued until 1933. One in three American banks failed during the Great Depression. The annihilation of uninsured bank deposits, combined with the public's growing preference for holding currency, contributed to a massive fall in the US money supply. Surviving banks became ultra-cautious, cutting lending to households and businesses, and building up reserves. The failure of so many banks and survivors' reluctance to lend produced a credit crunch. Even sound businesses had difficulty borrowing funds in the 1930s (Bernanke 1983; 2000).

Millions of American workers lost their jobs, the price level and wages dropped sharply (though wages proved stickier than prices), businesses closed, and farmers and homeowners were thrown off their properties after failing to make mortgage repayments. Business confidence collapsed and was slow to recover. The incidence of poverty increased. There were suicides. Some people lost everything in the Wall Street Crash or the following depression. There was an increase in deaths from cancer and heart disease, possibly because the slump resulted in higher levels of stress (James 2010, 137–8).

The Great Depression was also a global phenomenon, albeit one that had a disproportionate impact on the most industrialized and urbanized societies. In *Golden Fetters*, the classic economic history of the interwar decades, Barry Eichengreen (1992, 222–316) argues that the Gold Standard served as the transmission mechanism for the diffusion of the slump from the USA to Europe and the rest of the world. The tightening of US monetary policy in 1928 caused a rise in interest rates and the curtailment of US capital exports. Recession, then depression, in the USA weakened demand for the commodities and manufactured goods supplied by Europe, Latin America, Africa, Asia and Australasia. International capital markets became extremely cautious. Gold began to drain from some European central banks and banking systems. Commodity prices fell steeply, reducing farm incomes around the world. Nations on the Gold Standard were unable to devalue their currencies in order to cushion the impact of falling export revenues on the domestic economy. They had few options, and had to take their medicine in the form of unemployment, bankruptcies and wage cuts. Net capital outflows exacerbated the strain on gold reserves, necessitating an increase in interest rates that further depressed demand. International trade contracted in a vicious circle. Falling exports led to declining real incomes and output, and lower demand for imported consumer and producer goods. Trade wars intensified the downward spiral. To be fair, however, not all of the turmoil in international finance markets could be attributed to the slump. Under the terms of the Young Plan on reparations in 1929 the protection afforded to private creditors of Germany was reduced, leading to a sudden stop in the flow of funds (Ritschl and Sarferaz 2014). Moreover, the Great Depression was not as serious in developing as in industrial countries. When demand for export crops plummeted, many families in developing countries could switch back to subsistence farming (Brown 1997, 222–5). But workers in Detroit could not eat automobiles.

Banking collapses afflicted many countries in the early 1930s. Some debtors were unable to meet their obligations, whilst their collateral proved to be worth less than expected, rendering their banks insolvent. Heavy withdrawals were made from some countries by foreign depositors who were keen to repatriate funds and shun risk. Illiquidity and insolvency stalked the banking systems of the USA and Europe. Systemic banking collapses in Austria and Germany in 1931 ushered in a new stage in the European depression, putting businesses and households under increased strain, and eroding political support for the Gold Standard (Grossman 1994; James 1984; Kopper 2011).

Trends in unemployment rates in six major industrial countries are shown in Figure 4.2. The rise in unemployment and the decline in output (see Figure 4.1) illustrate the cost of the Great Depression. Living standards were considerably lower in the 1930s than they would have been without the slump. The world economy was now in the middle of Angus Maddison's (1995, 65) 'bleak age' from 1913 to 1950. Despite international differences in the definition and measurement of unemployment the upward trend is unmistakable. The French experience, however, was somewhat different from that of other countries shown in the chart. Unemployment in France remained rather low during the early part of the Great Depression. Several factors explain this phenomenon: the franc was undervalued until Britain left gold in September 1931, France was not as heavily industrialized as either the UK or Germany, and French labour statistics are particularly unreliable (Salais 1988).

Unemployment rates do not provide the whole story of distress. Many workers were underemployed in the early 1930s, labouring fewer days in the week or shorter hours in the day. There were large regional differences in unemployment rates within nations. In Britain, the South-East (around London) and the Midlands (around Birmingham) were not affected as severely as the North, Scotland and Wales, where older and less competitive industries were clustered. Long-term unemployment was a growing phenomenon. A minority of workers lost hope and motivation and their skills (Crafts 1987). Whilst many of the unemployed became apathetic, others were radicalized by their experiences. Recent research confirms that the more protracted the national depression in the 1930s, the greater the rise in support for extreme political parties (de Bromhead

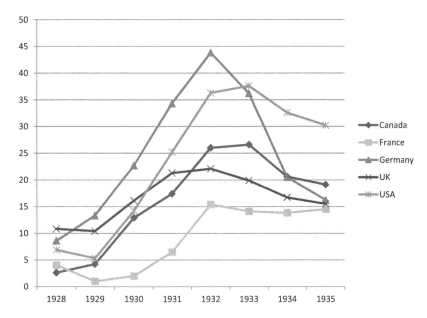

Notes: Methods of calculating industrial unemployment differed from country to country Eichengreen and Hatton (1988, 5–11). The French figures are particularly unsatisfactory and almost certainly underestimate industrial unemployment by a considerable margin (Salais 1988, 252–5, 270–76).

Source: The graph uses data from Eichengreen and Hatton (1988, 6–7).

Figure 4.2   Percentage unemployment rates among industrial workers in five countries, 1928–35

et al. 2013).[4] Social and political conflict and the failure of democracy in some countries, most notably Germany, may be included amongst the costs of the economic disaster of the early 1930s.

The disaster cycle during the Great Depression did not follow an identical path in the USA and Europe. In the USA the depression was primarily a domestic phenomenon, driven by internal deflation and the credit crunch, and exacerbated by policy errors. In Europe, however, the slump was imported and the Gold Standard played a major role in its propagation.

RESCUE AND RELIEF

The response of policy makers to depression was generally inadequate, and in some respects counterproductive. After a flood or an earthquake first responders know more or less what they must do to rescue survivors and contain the damage, whether or not their efforts prove successful. After the onset of a financial or economic disaster, however, it is less obvious what should be done. Economists and policy makers are as likely to disagree over the remedies for economic and financial disasters as they are over their causes.

Some argued that the disaster should be allowed to run its course in order to purge the economic system of the rottenness that had accumulated during the credit-fuelled boom of the 1920s. In memoirs published after the Second World War, President Herbert Hoover claimed that Andrew Mellon, his Secretary of the Treasury, viewed the slump as the reaction to the previous 'inflation brainstorm', and thought it necessary to 'Liquidate labor, liquidate stocks, liquidate the farmers, liquidate real estate' (Hoover 1952, 30). There remains some uncertainty over the accuracy of Hoover's representation of Mellon's stance (White 2008, 758–60), but he was expressing a common sentiment.

Hoover treated the slump as a problem to be solved by the business sector itself and not by the government. A firm believer in self-help and voluntary endeavour, Hoover felt that his own role was to encourage business leaders and bankers to pull together to revive the economy. His actions during the 1927 floods had been similar, focusing on the coordination of community initiatives. Business confidence in the early 1930s was at a low ebb, however, and Hoover's efforts fell flat (Barber 1985). There was never any prospect of the administration intervening to stimulate demand through fiscal policy. Not only were Keynesian ideas of demand management unformulated, but they were unlikely to appeal to Hoover and his Cabinet. The Federal Reserve's fixation on member bank borrowing inclined it to wait until business started to pick up before injecting liquidity. In other words the Federal Reserve was a follower of economic activity rather than a leader. Its procyclical approach was the opposite of that which was required (Wheelock 1990, 423). Although Hoover and the Federal Reserve may not have adopted the slogan of 'liquidate, liquidate, liquidate', their policy decisions led in the direction of liquidation.

In Europe, with the exception of France, policy makers were far more constrained by the demands of the Gold Standard than were their US counterparts. The threat to gold convertibility arising from the depression was treated as a more serious matter than the accompanying threats to employment and banking stability. Safeguarding the gold reserves was the priority of the economic emergency services in the early 1930s. Interest rates were raised and fiscal policy tightened in a hopeless attempt to reassure flighty investors. Austerity was also intended to depress wages and prices and boost export competitiveness. It was assumed that economic turmoil would intensify in the absence of convertibility. The period of floating exchange rates in the early 1920s was indelibly associated by Germans with hyperinflation and chaos. Germany's concerns were shared by governments and central banks across Europe (Straumann 2009). Gold reserves could be used either to support convertibility or to support the banking system. In the early years of the Great Depression, central bankers gave priority to the Gold Standard, even in the midst of banking distress.

Nowadays natural and financial disasters usually trigger international cooperation, but the will to cooperate was more muted in the 1930s. President Hoover granted the Europeans an official debt moratorium in 1931, but such magnanimity was rare. Governments and central banks were reluctant to offer financial assistance to their neighbours (Eichengreen 1992, 277–8), whilst private sector lenders were understandably cautious about increasing their exposure to unstable countries. In July 1931, the Reichsbank approached other central banks with a request for a loan of up to $1 billion to stave off imminent financial collapse. The French effectively killed the negotiations by demanding major political and military concessions that Germany could not accept (Singleton 2011, 105–6). Conflict was no less endemic in the commercial sphere. The world was already on the edge of a tariff war in 1929, as a result of the Hawley–Smoot tariff bill in the USA which became law in 1930 (Kindleberger 1987, 123–5). Tariffs rose in every continent in the early 1930s. Trade restrictions offered an easy way of saving jobs and boosting revenue in the short run, but provoked a cycle of retaliation.

The longer the slump continued, the more difficult it became for governments and central banks to justify the sacrifices required by the Gold Standard, and in the summer of 1931 the system began to unravel (Eichengreen and Temin 2000). For Germany, the final straw came in July 1931 when the Danat Bank collapsed and the Dresdner Bank stood on the brink. Acknowledging that the costs of playing by Gold Standard rules now exceeded the costs of restricting convertibility, the German authorities introduced exchange controls. Henceforth the use of gold and foreign currency for international transactions would be rationed. Although the mark did not float after 1931, it was no longer freely convertible. The German banking system was rescued and partially nationalized, rather like its British counterpart in 2008–09 (James 1986, 288–323).

Workers in some European nations were eligible for unemployment benefit under officially supported insurance schemes. A fully insured industrial worker in Britain could claim unemployment benefit for 26 weeks,[5] although the scheme did not extend to agriculture or some service industries. Unemployment insurance schemes required emergency injections of government funds during the Great Depression because of the sudden increase in demand for benefits. In a period of austerity, ministers were anxious to reduce such unwelcome commitments. Conflict over proposals to cut the rate of unemployment benefit hastened the collapse of the British Labour government in 1931. The following National government reduced the level of benefits and tightened access especially for women (Hatton 2004, 356–60). Unemployment and emergency benefits were also cut in Germany, and rates of contribution increased for essentially the same reasons (James 1986, 67).

Unemployment benefits nonetheless provided a measure of relief to millions of European workers, one unavailable to previous generations. In the USA, however, the unemployed were in an even more difficult situation. Responsibility for relief was left to state and local authorities and charities, resulting in uneven provision. The payment of relief was often linked to the performance of hard labour, such as in road building or forestry. There was a long tradition of federal grants to aid the victims of natural disasters, and Hoover was pressed by Senator Robert La Follette Jr to designate the slump a 'disaster'. Although Hoover acknowledged that trade depressions and natural catastrophes had some features in common, he declined to commit the federal government to providing relief. He regarded trade depressions and many natural disasters, including droughts, as recurring events for which families and communities should take precautions.[6] Hoover expected local and state authorities and charities, including the Red Cross, to help the unemployed and drought victims. But charities struggled to relieve millions of families on a long-term basis (Landis 1999). When impoverished war veterans set up camp in Washington, DC, and demanded that the government bring forward payments on military service certificates, police and troops were sent to disperse them. Not until 1935 did the USA introduce an unemployment insurance scheme (Plotnick et al. 2000, 274).

The unsatisfactory response of policy makers to the slump was in large measure a reflection of their defective sensemaking. The Federal Reserve was supine and the US government, though worried, was unsure how to proceed. In Europe in particular, policy makers were misled by the assumption that their primary duty was to protect the Gold Standard. The fact that most countries, with the notable exceptions of the USA and France, were desperately short of gold made international cooperation especially difficult. Central banks were competing for gold. A robust institutional framework that would facilitate international economic cooperation did not yet exist (Singleton 2011, 91–109).[7]

ALLOCATING BLAME

Social conflict intensified in many countries, as did political instability. Fascism and national socialism already existed in the 1920s. The Great Depression led to a rise in support for radical political parties and ideas of all hues. Even the USA witnessed something of a populist revival. In the wake of any disaster, the public, political leaders and the media are driven by the need to pin blame on someone. The most convenient scapegoats are usually collared first, a process that is not conducive to sober debate on the underlying causes of disaster.

In Germany, the list of possible scapegoats for the slump was a long one, extending to the Allies who were responsible for the Treaty of Versailles and reparations, the leaders of the Weimar republic, and the Jewish minority. Nazis were inclined to believe that most bankers – whether Jewish or non-Jewish – were corrupt and disloyal to the German nation. They regarded the financial sector as a parasitical force exploiting German agriculture and industry. To be a banker *and* a Jew was to be doubly culpable. Once in power, the Nazis continued to fulminate against the banks, favouring local savings and co-operative banks over the big commercial institutions, and purging the financial system of Jews (James 2001; 2004).

For the British, the economic emergency came to a head in August and September 1931.[8] The convertibility of sterling was under increasing threat after financial collapses in Austria and Germany earlier in the summer. When the Labour Cabinet split over new austerity proposals in August 1931, a rumour was spread to the effect that Wall Street bankers had attempted to impose spending cuts, including benefit cuts, on the government in return for a rescue loan (Williamson 1984). One prominent socialist, Beatrice Webb, confided to her diary that the alleged 'bankers' ramp' involved 'an open declaration, without any disguise, of Capitalist Dictatorship' (Webb 1956, 283). Paul Einzig (1931), a financial journalist, portrayed the French as the wreckers of the international economy, alleging that they had manipulated the Gold Standard in order to ruin their European rivals. Whilst sceptical of the bankers' ramp theory, Sir Oswald Mosley, the Labour politician turned fascist leader, attributed many of Britain's economic problems to the machinations of bankers, both Jewish and gentile, whom he claimed were more interested in profiting from speculative activity overseas than in revitalizing British industry (Reveley and Singleton 2013).

Suspicion of Wall Street was endemic in the American psyche, especially in small towns and farming areas. After the October 1929 crash, financial professionals – stockbrokers, bond salesman and bankers, and especially investment bankers – were singled out for opprobrium. Central bankers escaped comparatively lightly, except insofar as they could be portrayed as stooges of Wall Street. According to Vincent Carosso (1970a, 300), the 'crash and the depression transformed the image of the investment banker from one with a halo to one with horns and spiked tail'. The euphoric narrative of the 1920s was replaced by a new narrative of 'unfairness, corruption, and deception' (Akerlof and Shiller 2009, 67).

A Detroit priest, Charles Coughlin, who made weekly nationwide radio broadcasts, became a channel for the disaffected. This Canadian-born demagogue demanded that the 'gamblers of Wall St ... and their lieutenants in crime' be brought to account (quoted in Brinkley 1983, 117). He interpreted the depression as a conspiracy to enrich the financial elite by impoverishing the masses and seizing their assets, such as houses and farms. The Jews played an increasingly prominent role in his demonology, as did the British. The Gold Standard was depicted as a mechanism for achieving the pernicious goals of international bankers and their fellow travellers (Reveley and Singleton 2013).

President Franklin D. Roosevelt was not averse to using populist rhetoric in order to identify scapegoats for the Great Depression (Ryan 1988, 77–80). In his inaugural address on 4 March 1933 Roosevelt declaimed:

> Plenty is at our doorstep, but a generous use of it languishes in the very sight of the supply. Primarily this is because rulers of the exchange of mankind's goods have failed, through their own stubbornness and their own incompetence, have admitted their failure, and abdicated. Practices of the unscrupulous money changers stand indicted in the court of public opinion, rejected by the hearts and minds of men. (Roosevelt 1933)

An investigation into the activities of Wall Street was commissioned by the Senate Committee on Banking and Finance in 1932. After Ferdinand Pecora, a New York lawyer, took over the management of the inquiry, the leading figures on Wall Street were subjected to withering cross-examination. The Pecora hearings demonstrated that some prominent Wall Street firms had indulged in unethical behaviour, including selling risky securities to naive investors, offering special deals to influential clients, concealing information about the financial health of their institutions and engaging in short selling so as to make money from a falling market. The worst offender was said to be Charles E. Mitchell, the great 'Sunshine Charley' of National City Bank, one of the most successful bond salesmen in the 1920s. Pecora succeeded in painting Mitchell as devious, arrogant and unethical (United States Senate 1934; Perino 2010).[9]

The Pecora Report was perhaps the most significant fantasy document to emerge from the Great Depression. It was a fantasy document because it dealt with surface phenomena, especially the business ethics of a few senior members of the financial elite, rather than the more fundamental economic processes and policy errors that actually caused the slump. Since Pecora had no expertise in economics, a more sophisticated approach was out of the question. Pecora, however, was well equipped to ride a wave of anti-banker sentiment.

RECOVERY AND RECONSTRUCTION

The departure of Britain from the Gold Standard in September 1931, so soon after the German upheaval, appeared to be a further step towards financial and economic chaos. Convertibility had been the centrepiece of British economic policy, and now the British had broken their word to holders of sterling. Yet one well-informed observer, Keynes, saw matters differently. Speaking on a British Movietone newsreel, he rejoiced that 'a great weight is lifted from us'. British industry had been given a huge boost and must never allow itself to be put back into 'the gold cage' (Keynes 1931). Much of the British Empire, plus Sweden and Japan, followed Britain off the Gold Standard in the final months of 1931, but the USA and many continental European countries decided to persist with gold.

Leaving the Gold Standard, whilst humiliating for governments and central banks, was in fact a precondition for recovery. When a currency ceased to be convertible it usually depreciated sharply against those currencies still on gold. Depreciation boosted the competitiveness of firms supplying exports and import substitutes, although this initial tonic was short-lived. More importantly, depreciation permitted the gradual relaxation of austerity. Interest rates could be lowered; cheaper credit helped to stimulate recovery. Prices rose, partly because depreciation increased the cost of imports, but inflation did not run out of control because there was plenty of slack in labour markets and plenty of idle machinery. In the British case, low interest rates prompted a housing construction boom, which spilled over into increased demand for consumer goods. An early departure from gold was also associated with a healthier banking system because central banks could now give priority to domestic financial stability. The decision to default on foreign debt obligations also aided recovery in some countries (Eichengreen 1992, 287–316; Grossman 1994; Eichengreen and Portes 1990).[10]

Most countries did not have a credible recovery plan when they were forced off the Gold Standard. Abandoning convertibility, whether through floating the currency or imposing exchange controls, involved acknowledging that the policy elite had failed, not that they had come up with a better approach. In the USA, however, suspending convertibility was part of a deliberate recovery strategy implemented by a new government.

After the defection of Britain in September 1931, and of Japan in December 1931, the commitment of other countries to gold convertibility could no longer be taken for granted. London began to attract funds from other financial centres including New York. France, the Netherlands, Belgium, Switzerland, Luxemburg and Poland – the European 'Gold Bloc' countries – faced increasingly vigorous competition from manufacturers in Britain, Sweden and Japan. The response of governments and central banks in Gold Standard countries was to intensify austerity and tighten monetary policy, measures that promised more unemployment, business failures and banking crashes. The Bank of France's large gold reserves became a curse rather than a blessing during the 1930s: they sustained membership of the Gold Standard until 1936, but only at the expense of domestic recovery (Wolf 2008).

Global recovery would have been faster if leading nations could have agreed on a package of measures including the dismantlement of the Gold Standard, or at least the realignment of exchange rates, combined with the loosening of monetary policy and the relaxation of austerity. But such an agreement was unthinkable at the time. When a World Economic Conference was at last convened in London in 1933, the proceedings ended in deadlock. Most Europeans wanted to salvage the Gold Standard, but they were unclear over how to achieve their goal. President Roosevelt, however, made it clear that his government regarded the conference as pointless (Clavin 1992). It would take another world war to persuade the liberal capitalist nations, led by the USA and Britain, of the need to agree on the main features of a new international economic architecture.

Even the USA bled gold following sterling's depreciation. The Federal Reserve responded by tightening monetary policy. Further banking collapses ensued and the USA sank further into depression. Roosevelt defeated Hoover in the 1932 presidential election and was inaugurated in March 1933. His economic strategy was marketed as the New Deal, aspects of which remain controversial. Regulation and bureaucracy were increased in all sectors of the economy, an approach that hindered improvements in productivity. In the key areas of monetary and fiscal policy, though, Roosevelt acted decisively to promote expansion. Gautti Eggertsson (2008) argues that Roosevelt was successful because he instituted a 'regime change'; the 'dogmas' of convertibility and balanced budgets were swept away. Roosevelt promised to raise the price level and restore the economy to normality, and enough people and businesses believed him. By changing expectations for the better, Roosevelt persuaded households and businesses to start spending again. Roosevelt backed up his commitment to recovery with actions. Troubled banks were saved by the Reconstruction Finance Corporation (set up earlier by Hoover), and federal government spending was raised. The dollar was taken off gold in June 1933 and allowed to depreciate, but then returned to gold at a lower exchange rate in 1934. With the dollar at a more competitive level, gold flowed back into the USA, and this time it was allowed to boost the money supply. The US economy recovered strongly until another recession occurred in 1937–38. Christina Romer (1992) contends that the increase in the money supply was the main force pulling the USA out of depression in the mid-1930s. Eggertsson disagrees, stressing instead the change in expectations – Keynes might have said 'animal spirits' – prompted by regime change in 1933. Fiscal policy played an important role, as did monetary expansion, but in Eggertsson's narrative neither of these initiated the recovery. Debate over the sources of the US revival will continue. It is evident, however, that it was more thoroughly planned than Britain's.

The recovery process varied from country to country. It usually involved a large dose of trial and error. Although the abandonment of convertibility was often the first step towards reconstruction, it had to be supplemented by measures to encourage spending. In Germany and Japan, increased government spending on rearmament or military campaigns created millions of new jobs. Falling interest rates stimulated a housing boom in Britain. Roosevelt signalled his intention to preside over a change in policy regime several months before the dollar was freed. But the Gold Bloc remained in denial and refused to break with gold until it was effectively too late. The Gold Bloc's stubbornness would be repeated by Eurozone countries in the 2010s. With hindsight, recovery everywhere would have been hastened by the earlier adoption of expansionary fiscal and monetary settings (Almunia et al. 2010).

MITIGATION AND REGULATORY CHANGE

The Great Depression led to radical changes in economic policy and the regulatory environment around the world. Several countries, most notably

Germany and the USA, underwent regime change of one sort or another. In others, including Britain, the process of reform was more subtle. Throughout the capitalist world in the 1930s there was an upswing in government intervention in economic life, albeit not to the degree attained during and after the Second World War. Laissez-faire capitalism appeared to have failed in the early 1930s; the new goal was to establish policies and institutions that would prevent or at least mitigate a similar disaster in the future. Except in university common rooms, however, a disinterested search for optimal policies and regulations was not on the agenda.

The content of reforms was usually based on a compromise between different sectional interests and their political advocates. Banking regulation was tightened sharply around the world in the 1930s.[11] Even in Britain, one of the few countries to avoid a banking collapse in the Great Depression, the Bank of England began to exercise a closer, though still informal, oversight of the financial system. In the realm of monetary policy making, central bank independence tended to give way to a relationship of partnership with, and in some case subordination to, government (Singleton 2011, 85–9).

Germany experienced the most drastic regime change. The introduction of exchange controls and the partial nationalization of the banking system by the Weimar authorities in 1931 made it easier for the subsequent Nazi government to manipulate the economy.[12] Despite the prominence in Nazi rhetoric of the struggle against joblessness, full employment was not the primary goal of the regime. Many new jobs were created, but unemployment did not disappear in Germany. Rearmament was the government's economic priority. Success depended on the careful allocation of foreign exchange and the containment of wage pressure and consumer spending. The independence of the Reichsbank, and its capacity to oppose inflationary policies, were whittled away. Ultimately, Nazi economic policies did not secure genuine prosperity, for workers and their families could not consume machine guns or live in tanks. Nor did Nazi policies mitigate future economic disasters, for they increased the risk of inflation and resulted in a devastating world war (Tooze 2007; Weitz 1997).

During the New Deal era, there was a substantial increase in economic and financial regulation in the USA. In principle, the aim of regulation was to restrain the forces that might unleash renewed instability on banks, firms and households. In practice, the measures adopted were the product of political horse-trading. Whether or not they served their intended purpose remains debatable. Like all reforms, however, they had some unintended consequences. As well as generating benefits for some, they imposed costs on others. In the industrial and agricultural sectors the New Deal incorporated measures to fix prices and wages, and restrict competition and output, largely with a view to halting the deflationary spiral and eliminating perceived overproduction. This type of regulation may have hindered recovery by constraining flexibility and innovation (Cole and Ohanian 2004), and it provoked strong opposition. Insofar as the roots of the disaster of the early 1930s lay in the financial sector, it is hard to see how the regulation of other sectors could prevent further slumps.

New Deal financial reforms were longer-lived, although not necessarily any better designed. The desire to punish and control perceived rogues – speculators, company promoters and investment bankers – was strong during and after the slump. Regulation would stop them from wreaking further damage in the future. Banks and stockbrokers fought back with all the influence at their disposal in order to secure moderate rather than draconian regulation. The Banking Act 1933, commonly known as the (second) Glass–Steagall Act, was introduced into Congress while Hoover was still President, and became law under Roosevelt (Carosso 1970a, 368–75). Glass–Steagall separated commercial from investment banking, established a deposit insurance scheme, and introduced controls over deposit rates. The separation of commercial from investment banking was a long-standing aspiration of the critics of Wall Street. Glass–Steagall was in part a response to populist agitation, fuelled by perceptions of reckless and unethical behaviour during the slump. Whether or not there was any deeper justification for separation is questionable. Eugene White (1986) found no evidence that commercial banks' participation in investment banking before 1933 had put them at greater risk. Randall Kroszner and Raghuram Rajan (1994) cast doubt on the evidence that national banks with 'securities affiliates' had knowingly marketed dodgy securities. Glass–Steagall was the outcome of a highly political process, as were other reforms including the creation of the Securities and Exchange Commission and the regulation of securities markets (Hendrickson 2001; Carosso 1970b). Deposit interest rates were restricted in order to reduce the pressure on banks to make risky high-interest loans (Singleton 2011, 136). Although there had been state-level deposit insurance schemes before the Great Depression, they had been poorly funded. Roosevelt was suspicious of deposit insurance, for if depositors knew that their funds were insured they might not monitor their bankers properly. Nevertheless, he bowed to political pressure and endorsed a federal deposit insurance scheme (Flood 1992).

Glass–Steagall was not repealed until 1999, though even before that date the distinction between commercial and investment banking had started to erode. The intrusiveness of banking regulation, both in the USA and globally, intensified between the 1940s and 1960s because of the upheavals of the Second World War and its aftermath which increased the size and reach of the state. Between 1945 and the early 1970s the developed world was free of systemic banking crashes (Bordo et al. 2001). It is difficult, however, to be certain whether this prolonged respite was brought about by the reforms of the 1930s or by the even stricter controls introduced in the 1940s. In any case there was a price to be paid for the elimination of risk from banking. With fewer opportunities or incentives to compete, innovate or reduce costs, the banking and financial system became lethargic.

Central banking reforms were at least as important. The collapse of the Gold Standard was accompanied by growing acceptance that the exchange rate was a policy variable and not a price set in stone. Responsibility for exchange rate policy passed from central banks to finance ministries during the 1930s and 1940s (Bordo et al. 2007). Internal economic stability would no longer be sacrificed for the sake of maintaining a permanently fixed exchange rate. Although there were Keynesian elements to the recoveries of countries as disparate politically as the USA and Germany, it was not until the 1940s that governments acknowledged in principle that fiscal policy could be used in tandem with monetary policy to regulate economic activity and mitigate shocks. That recognition was the belated product of the Great Depression experience which had prompted Keynes (1936) to write his *General Theory*. In short, the mitigation and regulatory change stage of the depression is difficult to separate from the legacy of the Second World War, which tended to amplify processes initiated in the 1930s.

CONCLUSION

Although the Great Depression of the 1930s was not a tsunami or a hurricane, at the conceptual level it developed along similar lines, ones that are recognizable to anyone familiar with the disaster cycle. In the 1920s policy makers did not neglect their duty to look for ways of mitigating economic and financial disasters, yet the framework that they created (or re-established) was flawed, principally because it was centred on the 'barbarous relic' (Keynes 1924, 172) of the Gold Standard. Central banks placed adherence to the Gold Standard above their responsibilities to maintain internal financial stability. Both the institutions tasked with mitigation, and the intellectual constructs that guided them, were defective. In the late 1920s it was possible to observe that all was not well –

euphoria in the USA and economic fragility in Europe constituted a dangerous cocktail – but it was by no means clear that a depression was on the way. Stock markets are volatile, and in the immediate aftermath of the Wall Street Crash (the triggering event) few could have predicted what would happen next.

Even as late as 1931, leading economists and policy makers were frankly bemused by the depression. They attempted to make sense of the crisis, but arrived at no consensus. With the failure of sensemaking, there was nothing to stop the crisis turning into a disaster. Central bankers and politicians focused on the wrong indicators. The Federal Reserve ignored the decline in the money supply and the collapse of thousands of banks because their significance was not grasped. Central bankers and finance ministries in Europe focused on the defence of convertibility, and allowed economic activity to plummet, unemployment to rise, and banking instability to spread. Relief measures were directed at saving the gold reserves and managing the balance of payments. The unemployed were not forgotten completely, but helping them was an afterthought. The public searched for someone to blame, and with the assistance of populists of one sort or another reached for the usual suspects: greedy bankers and bond salesmen, foreigners and Jews, Wall Street and the City of London in general.

Recovery came after the collapse of the Gold Standard, and was a rather messy affair of trial and error, even to some degree in New Deal America. It was a process of trial and error partly because the Gold Standard had for so long been the intellectual anchor for economic policy and no one except Keynes knew what to do in its absence. Yet once the decision was taken to float or impose exchange controls, economic policy makers discovered that their room for manoeuvre was enhanced. Monetary and to an extent fiscal straitjackets could be loosened, at least somewhat. Achieving power 18 months after Britain's departure from gold, Roosevelt was in a better position to effect a more sweeping change in policy regime. Given that the depression was not really understood, and that populists were baying for blood, the regulatory reforms that ensued were less about effective mitigation than about satisfying public expectations and achieving closure. The regulation of banks was tightened. A movement towards greater government management of the economy was set in train. But the policy regime that secured economic and financial stability in the developed world between 1945 and the early 1970s owed at least as much to the next global economic disaster, the Second World War, as it did to the Great Depression.

NOTES

1. If the US had been playing by the Gold Standard rules it would not have resisted inflation. Countries with high gold reserves were expected to inflate so as to release gold for use by others.
2. Kindleberger (1987, 116) argued that the crash was part of the deflationary process and not a 'superficial phenomenon, a signal, or a triggering', but a trigger need not be an event of superficial importance.
3. The (UK) National Archives, CAB/24/216, CP (363) 30, Economic Advisory Council, Committee of Economists, Report, 24 October 1930.
4. This is a tendency that does not fit all countries. The obvious exception is the USA.
5. In practice the government continued to pay the benefit after the 26 weeks were up.
6. Parts of the USA were hit by prolonged drought in the 1930s.
7. The League of Nations was weak and did not include the USA. The Bank for International Settlements was new and still defining its role.
8. Strictly speaking Britain did not experience a financial crisis (using that term here in the conventional sense) in 1931 because the banking system remained intact. It did, however, experience a currency crisis that led to the suspension of the Gold Standard (Billings and Capie 2011).
9. Thomas Huertas and Joan Silverman (1986) argue that Pecora was grossly unfair to Sunshine Charley. They are not entirely convincing.
10. Even Britain defaulted on its First World War debts to the USA after the end of the Hoover debt moratorium in 1934 (Reinhart and Rogoff 2013, 14–15).
11. For details of these measures see the League of Nations publications, *Commercial Banks* (1934; 1935) and *Money and Banking* (annually, 1935–40).
12. Although the Nazis would reprivatize the banks, they kept them under strict control.

5. Mining disasters

> On an average ... the number of men killed [in British coal mines] each year is
> 1240, or about an infantry battalion at full strength.
> (R.H. Tawney 1920, 83)

In *Tommy*, an account of the lives of British soldiers in the First World War, Richard Holmes (2004, 95) quotes a contemporary report of an incident in which stretcher bearers, wading up to their knees in water, struggle to carry wounded men to safety. Holmes then reveals that his source does not describe a battle in Flanders or France but rather a mining disaster in Wales. As Tawney and Holmes both explain, there were similarities between the risks run by miners and soldiers, although the risks were greater for the latter, at least between 1914 and 1918.

Coal mining has always been a very dangerous occupation. Miners were exposed to numerous hazards, including flooding, rock falls, explosions and asphyxiation, not to mention the long-term health effects of breathing in dust. Most miners who died underground did so in ones or twos, but the death toll occasionally ran into hundreds when there was an explosion. Few large-scale mining accidents have occurred in developed economies in recent decades. The Pike River disaster, which claimed the lives of 29 miners in New Zealand in 2010, was an exception to the rule (Young 2012). Yet accidents with numerous fatalities still happen regularly in developing countries such as China (Wright 2012) and Turkey. People and property in the vicinity of coal mines are also at risk from negative externalities including pollution, subsidence and the collapse of tips of waste material extracted from underground.

Casualty rates in British, US and Western European mines were high in the early twentieth century. Coal mining was a labour-intensive industry; large numbers of miners were placed in harm's way every day. The causes of accidents, especially of explosions, were not as well understood as they are today. Although there was considerable public interest in the safety of miners, conditions that would be intolerable in the twenty-first century were accepted as the norm.

This chapter focuses on two mining disasters in South Wales, one of Britain's major coal producing districts during the nineteenth and twentieth centuries. The Senghenydd Colliery disaster of 1913 was the worst in British history, taking the lives of 439 miners. The Aberfan disaster in 1966 was in some respects even more shocking: a mine waste tip on a hillside collapsed onto the village of Aberfan, causing 144 fatalities including 116 children in school. The disaster cycle framework is used to structure the analysis of the Senghenydd and Aberfan episodes. While on a smaller scale than other disasters examined in this volume, these disasters were significant events that devastated particular localities.

SENGHENYDD 1913

The Senghenydd explosion of 1913 was the worst in a sequence of major explosions that struck the British coal industry in the years leading up to the First World War. Although the mining industry was at the height of its fortunes, having expanded rapidly during the nineteenth century, there remained serious problems, not least in the area of health and safety. Firedamp (methane gas) was believed to be the principal danger, but there was a growing recognition that the ignition of coal dust was also a factor in many of the most serious underground explosions. As yet, however, there was no agreed solution to the coal dust problem. Some mining experts argued that coal dust could be rendered inert by the addition of stone dust. Standard practice today (Man and Teacoach 2009), stone dusting reduces the risk of explosion but does not provide an absolute guarantee of safety. In 1913, though, the value of stone dusting was only just being established scientifically.

Mitigation and Regulatory Change

Safety was a matter of serious concern for all involved in the mining industry in the nineteenth and early twentieth centuries, whether miners and their families, government representatives, or managers and employers. Neither the miners nor their employers wished to incur the human and financial costs accompanying a disaster. Government responded to public alarm over underground explosions by ordering the inspection and regulation of the mining sector. But all were agreed that safety had to be balanced against the requirements to earn wages and generate profits. The outcome was a tacit agreement by all parties to accept risk and often to cut corners. Piece work also encouraged miners to take chances. It has been argued that from time to time some groups of miners, whether of coal or other materials, actually sought out danger and flouted safety rules in an effort to prove their masculinity (Mills 2005; Wicks 2001).

Setting aside the important but separate issue of industrial diseases, most violent deaths in mining were the result not of explosions but of rock falls, transport accidents and other events that killed one or two men at a time (Boyns 1985). Nevertheless, explosions attracted the most attention. They could be caused and propagated in several ways. Firedamp, a gas released from the strata during underground operations, was responsible for many uncontrolled explosions. A naked light, or a bungled attempt to blast rock and coal (shot-firing), could set off a firedamp explosion that might kill or trap some miners. Underground explosions also generated further asphyxiating gases such as carbon monoxide, carbon dioxide and nitrogen, known collectively as afterdamp. More miners were liable to die from the effects of afterdamp than in the initial explosion. The presence of coal dust multiplied the risks. Digging and hauling coal created large amounts of fine dust that covered all surfaces. Coal dust could be dislodged and set alight by a methane explosion, a defective safety lamp or a naked flame. A coal dust explosion was likely to surge through the underground workings, producing more afterdamp, and claiming numerous victims, primarily from asphyxiation (Boyns 1986). The introduction of electrically powered machinery and communications equipment in some mines in the late nineteenth century, although welcomed as a sign of modernization, resulted in a serious new safety hazard. Electrical sparks could set off a methane and/or coal dust explosion (Jones 2006). Finally, the spontaneous combustion of coal, which was possible under certain conditions, could ignite firedamp or coal dust. But pits did not explode every day. The gassiness (or fieriness) of mines, and their liability to blow up, varied according to the geological conditions. More care was required from employers, managers and men in gassy mines. Unfortunately the South Wales coalfield possessed some of the most hazardous geological conditions in Britain.

Coal mining was one of the first industries in Britain to be regulated by the state, largely in order to improve working conditions and prevent the disasters – such as the explosions at the Oaks Colliery near Barnsley in 1866 which killed 361 men – that so horrified the Victorian public (Duckham 1976). Parliament conducted frequent inquiries into coal mine safety and passed a series of remedial Acts, culminating in the Coal Mines Act 1911. An embryonic official inspection system was created in 1844. The number of inspectors, the scope of their duties and the extent of their powers expanded during the second half of the nineteenth century. In 1872 the miners and their representatives were given the right to conduct their own inspections, supplementing those of the government. Legislation was passed governing the use of safety lamps,[1] the ventilation of mines (especially with a view to dispersing gas), the use of explosives underground and the certification of mine officials, to mention but a few of the more important themes.

A Royal Commission on Mines in 1906–09 gave special attention to safety, and called for new research to be carried out into coal dust explosions and their prevention. An official committee on explosions in mines was established. Employers' groups and the government sponsored scientific work on the coal dust problem, but definitive results were not available before the First World War. The Coal Mines Act 1911 rational-ized previous safety legislation and permitted the government to proclaim new safety regulations without seeking additional legislation. In 1912, for example, new regulations were announced concerning the provision of ambulances and rescue apparatus, and the training of staff in their use. The 1911 Act also required the operators of mines to take action to guard against coal dust explosions, but did not specify a particular method. Some companies elected to spray the underground roadways with water, a method that although well intentioned turned out to be less effective than stone dusting (Gowers 1927; Bryan 1975).

The early twentieth century was marked by a surge of enthusiasm amongst employers, the government and miners' representatives for the creation of rescue brigades. First aid equipment in Victorian mines often consisted of a stretcher and some bandages. Breathing apparatus for use in poisonous atmospheres was developed in the late 1870s. The British-made Fleuss apparatus was deployed at Seaham Colliery in County Durham to assist those helping to reopen the mine after an explosion in 1880. Breathing apparatus may have been used by rescuers at Killing-worth Colliery in Northumberland after an explosion in 1882 (Foregger 1974). The dual function of breathing apparatus – rescue and repair work – was an attractive feature. However, the equipment was cumbersome and allowed the wearer only a short time in a noxious atmosphere. New types of apparatus were designed and marketed by German and British manufacturers after 1900, and the technology became more widely diffused (Department of Scientific and Industrial Research Advisory Council 1918). Under the statutory order issued in 1912, all mines employing at least 100 men underground were required to train and maintain one or more 'brigades' of rescue men. Breathing suits and apparatus could be held on-site or at a district Central Rescue Station equipped with a motor vehicle (Bryan 1975, 70).

The death rate per worker from underground explosions in Britain and continental Europe was trending downwards in the late nineteenth century, but major disasters were by no means eliminated. The extent to which the fall in the death rate was driven by better regulation is unclear, and it has been argued that technical improvements in lighting, ventilation and explosives were important factors (Murray and Silvestre 2015). Regulation and technical change may have been interrelated: changes in regulation gave employers an additional incentive to develop and adopt safer methods. Any system of regulation will be imperfect, however, not least because business and worker representatives may be able to exert influence over legislators and inspectors. By the same token, banks often seek to influence the scope and content of financial regulation. It was also common for underground regulations to be broken. Having said that, coal mining was a very competitive industry, and without some form of regulation, the pressure to cut corners in order to boost wages and profits would have been greater (Lewis-Beck and Alford 1980). The purpose of the current chapter is not to discuss the pros and cons of regulation as a principle. Mines in Britain were regulated in practice, and the objective is to investigate how disasters occurred in such an environment.

Miners could insure themselves against fatal and other accidents through friendly societies, trade unions and provident societies, the latter often being promoted by employers' groups in an attempt to avoid compensation litigation. Provident societies collected subscriptions from men and employers. Employers also insured themselves against the costs associated with accidents and compensation payouts. Mines were included in the scope of the Workmen's Compensation Acts of 1897 and 1906. These Acts were designed to make it easier for injured workers and widows to claim compensation from the employer. The employers had an economic incentive to reduce their potential liability by improving the conditions underground (Benson 1975; Jones 1980).

By the standards of the early twentieth century, safety was taken seriously in the British coal mining industry. A sophisticated regime of inspection and regulation, intended in large measure to reduce the incidence of catastrophic explosions, was in place. But the system had weaknesses, not the least of which was an inadequate understanding of how to prevent the ignition of coal dust.

Warnings

Sir Ernest Gowers, the Permanent Under-Secretary of Mines in the British government, lamented in 1920 that, 'By a curious perversity of fate Royal Commissions on Safety in Mines and Coal Mines Regulations have usually been followed by epidemics of explosions' (Gowers 1927, 113). The aftermath of the Royal Commission of 1906–09 was particularly gruesome. At the Wellington Pit in Cumberland, 137 men died in May 1910 in a firedamp and coal dust explosion. In December 1910 the death toll at Hulton Colliery in Lancashire was 344 when an explosion of firedamp was followed by one of coal dust. Amidst the devastation underground it was difficult to identify the precise cause of a disaster with any certainty, but the official investigations into the events at the Wellington and Hulton pits suggested that a faulty or broken safety lamp (perhaps the result of a roof fall) was the likely cause of ignition. At any rate, it was clear that the severity of both disasters reflected the presence of coal dust (Redmayne and Pope 1911a, 26; 1911b, 32). The spontaneous combustion of 'gob' or waste material was judged to have caused the explosions at Cadeby Main Colliery in Yorkshire which took 88 lives in July 1912, but coal dust was an exacerbating factor (Bryan 1975, 77). Massive explosions were by no means a distinctively British phenomenon. At Courrières Colliery in France in 1906, an explosion attributed to coal dust rather than firedamp accounted for 1100 lives (Neville 1978). All 367 men working underground at the Monongah Nos 6 and 8 mines in West Virginia died in an explosion in 1907. Dangerous working practices at Monongah, involving the use of naked lights together with careless shot-firing, had finally taken their toll, igniting gas and coal dust (Aldrich 1995, 484). As a result of these disasters, there were solid reasons for mine owners and staff to take extra care. On the other hand, the recurrence of explosions may have induced a spirit of fatalism, as it sometimes does today in developing and transitional economies (Saleh and Cummings 2011, 765).

At the Universal Colliery in Senghenydd, Glamorgan there were even stronger grounds for focusing on safety. In May 1901, coal dust was ignited during shot-firing, setting off a great explosion. The 'first' Senghenydd disaster killed 82 miners. Shot-firing took place between shifts when fewer miners were on site, otherwise the casualty list would have been higher. The coroner's jury recommended action to prevent the accumulation of coal dust in mines, and urged mining companies to water underground passages in order to reduce the chance of any remaining dust catching fire (Galloway et al. 1902).[2] Although relatively modern, Senghenydd was a gassy or 'fiery' mine, at greater risk of explosion than some others. The official report into the second explosion in 1913 would show that safety procedures were not followed systematically at Senghenydd, despite the lessons of 1901, the unfavourable underground conditions in South Wales, and the recent spate of disasters at home and overseas.

The Triggering Event

At 8.10 a.m. on Tuesday 14 October 1913 there was an explosion underground in the West Side of the Senghenydd Colliery (Redmayne et al. 1914, 20). Given the extent of the damage and the lack of survivors, it was hard for investigators to find the precise location and cause of the explosion. Nevertheless, it was obvious that something had happened to ignite a pocket of firedamp or an accumulation of coal dust. Several theories were aired during the inquest and the official inquiry. A fall of rock could have released gas and at the same time produced a spark. The explosion could have been caused by an open safety lamp in the lamp station or a damaged safety lamp found in the debris. Alternatively, friction between a rope and some timber could have generated sparks which ignited gas or coal dust. The inquest concluded that the probable source of ignition was a naked light (*Manchester Guardian* 1914a). However, Richard Redmayne (Bryan 2004), the Chief Inspector of Mines, who chaired the subsequent official inquiry, disagreed. He suggested that a large amount of gas had been released in a roof fall in the Mafeking District of the mine, and that the most likely source of ignition was a spark from the mine's electrical communication system. Sparks were produced every time an electrical signal bell was rung (Redmayne et al. 1914, 26–32). The initial explosion had disturbed and ignited the coal dust, propagating the blast through the West Side of the mine. From the perspective of those underground and above ground on the morning of 14 October, a terrible explosion had occurred and the immediate challenge was to save as many lives as possible.

Sensemaking and Decision Making

Once ignition had taken place, the chances of survival for miners in the West Side were poor. Many fatalities occurred before personnel on the surface had time to react. The mine manager, Edward Shaw, accompanied by D.R. Thomas, an overman, quickly descended the damaged Lancaster shaft, encountering some badly injured miners as well as intense smoke and an inferno (Redmayne et al. 1914, 20). Following the disaster, there was an acrimonious debate over whether more lives could have been saved by reversing the flow of air underground so as to avert the propagation of the explosion through the entire West Side. But that option was not available on 14 October. In contravention of the Coal Mines Act 1911, the main ventilation fan was of an older design that could not be thrown into reverse without modification. Robert Smillie, the President of the Miners' Federation of Great Britain (MFGB), and an 'assessor' at the official inquiry, argued that some deaths could have been avoided if a reversible fan had been present. But Redmayne was not convinced by Smillie's argument. Although some miners in the West York District might have been saved by reversing the airflow, more afterdamp would have been pushed towards the Bottanic District where other miners were awaiting rescue (Redmayne et al. 1914, 24, 40–41). Had the apparatus been of the authorized design, Shaw would have faced a dilemma: which setting of the fan would save most lives? Shaw would have had to make a guess because the full picture was unknown. Moreover, he would have had far less time – effectively none at all – for decision making than Ray Nagin had before Hurricane Katrina. As matters stood, however, there was little scope for the manager to take action that could have altered the course of events. The constraints of the situation on 14 October, especially the suddenness of the explosion and its propagation, and the inflexibility of the ventilation fan, meant that sensemaking was less important during the Senghenydd disaster than in the disasters considered in other chapters of this volume. Senghenydd, then, had something in common with an earthquake.

The Disaster Unfolds

The explosion was propagated most rapidly and destructively in those parts of the West Side that contained the thickest coal dust. At Senghenydd, coal dust was watered regularly and removed from the floor of underground roadways. Although official regulations stated that coal dust should also be removed from walls and roofs, those stipulations were neglected. Purely by luck, however, a relatively high proportion of incombustible stone dust was mixed into the coal dust. Had it not been, then in Redmayne's view the explosion would have been even more powerful, perhaps spreading to the East Side of the mine where another 500 men were at work (Redmayne et al. 1914, 33).

A total of 439 lives were lost as a result of the explosion, including one at the top of the Lancaster shaft where the blast reached the surface. Another man died the next day in a rock fall. All but five of those killed on 14 October succumbed to carbon monoxide poisoning. Some bodies also showed signs of burning and trauma, but afterdamp was the main killer. One of the first effects of afterdamp was to make miners sleepy. The 18 men rescued from the Bottanic District were found alongside another 18 who were already dead (Davies 1914). The *Manchester Guardian* (1913a) reported that after visiting the scene, the Home Secretary, Reginald McKenna, 'did not exaggerate when he said that hardly a cottage was not either a house of mourning or a house of anxiety'. Sons of several miners killed in the 1901 explosion died in 1913 (Lieven 1989, 24).

The official inquiry into the Senghenydd disaster focused on the causes of the explosion rather than the cost, but the cost was considerable. Lewis Merthyr Consolidated Collieries Ltd, the owner of the Universal Colliery, lost the revenue from the production of 1800 tons of coal per day (Redmayne et al. 1914, 6). Production on the East Side of the colliery resumed before the end of November, but the West Side was slower to recover. Under the terms of the Workmen's Compensation Act, it was determined that Lewis Merthyr should pay a total of £75 855 0s 4d in compensation, inclusive of funeral expenses, to the dependants of those killed (Jones 1980, 152). The company incurred additional costs associated with repair work. In short, Lewis Merthyr was inconvenienced but not ruined by the disaster.

It should be stressed, however, that cost is a subjective concept. The miners who died were worth more to their families than they were to the employer. It was much easier for Lewis Merthyr to replace a lost miner than it was for his family. More than 200 families were deprived of their main breadwinner, and others lost an unmarried son who contributed to household earnings. In some coal mining areas, including parts of Lancashire and Yorkshire, women could find paid work in the textile industries, but in South Wales there were few such opportunities, rendering the situation for widows even more desperate.

Rescue and Relief

The priority of rescuers was to find survivors and extinguish fires. Redmayne thought it could have been possible to reach and save some miners in the West York District if breathing apparatus had been kept on site. Although some miners at Senghenydd were trained in the use of breathing apparatus, the nearest kit was eight miles away at the Porth Central Rescue Station. Porth was not alerted until 10 a.m., and the equipment and the rescue team did not arrive until 11 a.m., almost three hours after the initial blast. Other rescue teams from Crumlin and Rhymney Valley assisted. In the meantime, Shaw and his staff did their best to control fires in the vicinity of the Lancaster shaft. Miners in the East Side workings were brought safely to the surface, along with some badly wounded men from the West Side. Attempts to fight underground fires were hampered by an inadequate water supply, and it was not until the day after the disaster that a second water pipe could be inserted down the mine from the surface. Firefighters wearing breathing apparatus had to contend with debris from the explosion and roof falls as well as gas and fire. Redmayne arrived at 5.30 p.m. on the afternoon of the explosion to observe the scene. Along with other mining engineers, he offered advice to the rescuers. At about 10 p.m. a rescue team was sent towards the Bottanic District where it was believed there might be survivors. Eighteen men were rescued alive from the Bottanic, but others there had already perished. The rescue operation was fraught with difficulty and risk. It is possible, however, that more men could have been saved if the water supply had been sufficient, and if breathing apparatus had been available for immediate deployment (Redmayne et al. 1914, 20–25). The rescuers eventually had to give up and turn their attention to retrieving corpses.

Compensation payments to bereaved families ranged from £50 to £80 for boys and young men under 24 years of age, to £300 for experienced miners (Jones 1980, 152). Compensation took the form of weekly instalments of between three shillings and ten shillings rather than a lump sum (Welsby 1995, 96). The company paid an advance of £10 per fatality in the immediate aftermath of the disaster (*Manchester Guardian* 1913a). What did these amounts mean in practice? In his study of the cost of the First World War, Ernest Bogart (1920, 275) used figures published by a French actuary in 1910–11 to calculate the social value of an individual. The amount for a British person (whether man, woman or child) was $4140 or £851. An adult male, being more productive, would have been worth more, even after making a deduction to account for lifetime consumption. A simpler approach might start with the fact that the average coal face worker in Britain earned £112 per year in 1906 (Routh 1980, 99). Adult Senghenydd miners appear to have been valued for compensation purposes at slightly less than three years' wages.

In addition to monies received under the Workmen's Compensation Act, bereaved families could submit claims to their insurers, and apply to the disaster relief fund for small weekly pensions of a few shillings. Public relief funds were established after every mining disaster. According to Barry Supple (1987, 429), the public rarely thought about miners until there was unrest in the coalfields or a disastrous explosion. The public was liable to be generous following major loss of life. The Lord Mayor of Cardiff set up a relief fund for Senghenydd, with King George V as figurehead. It raised £33 000 within two weeks of the explosion; a further £22 000 was collected through other channels including a fund established by the Lord Mayor of London (*Daily Mail* 1913a; *Manchester Guardian* 1913a). The sum of £2350 was donated by visitors to an exhibition of presents from the wedding of Prince and Princess Arthur of Connaught at St James's Palace (*Daily Mail* 1913b). Blackburn Rovers, the football league leaders, played a charity match at

Cardiff City which collected £361 for disaster funds (*Daily Mail* 1913d). A total of £100 000 was amassed within 32 days of the disaster, a very large sum for 1913 (*Daily Mail* 1913c).

Local worthies administered mining disaster funds. Widows and other dependants could not expect generous benefits, as Trevor Griffiths (2001, 206–8, 224–33) explains in a study of the Hulton explosion fund. Trustees would rather keep money in the bank than support high living amongst the bereaved. Widows were given just enough to sustain a modest existence. The extended family was expected to chip in with additional help. Beneficiaries were monitored closely. Payments could be stopped if they engaged in immoral or drunken behaviour or gambling, or indulged in extravagances such as the acquisition of a piano. Official returns indicated that the Hulton Colliery Explosion (1910) Relief Fund was worth £107 325 in 1923, and could expect to retain a surplus of £8498 once all claims were met. The 1913 Senghenydd Explosion Relief Trust Fund was worth £60 000 in 1925; when in 1924 it was estimated that there would be a surplus of £9351 after all claims were met, the trustees resolved to raise benefits (Lane Fox 1925, 11, 13).

The Senghenydd relief fund was administered in an identical way to the Hulton fund. At the outset there were 749 recipients of weekly allowances, consisting of 217 wives, 480 children and 52 other dependants. Widows appear to have received around nine shillings per week. It was difficult, albeit not impossible, for women who had lived out of wedlock with one of the disaster victims to demonstrate eligibility. Misconduct could lead to the withdrawal of benefits. Inflation eroded their value during the Great War, but rates were increased in 1919 to compensate (Welsby 1995). Although tight-fisted and harsh by twenty-first-century standards, the controllers of the relief fund did make a vital contribution to the lives of many bereaved families.

Allocating Blame

In the immediate aftermath of the Senghenydd explosion, the press departed from their usual depiction of the mining districts as hotbeds of socialist and trade union agitation. Instead, they portrayed the miners and their community in heroic terms, and stressed the importance of national solidarity (Lieven 1989). That approach would be difficult to sustain as evidence of organizational failure at the mine was brought to light by the inquest and the official inquiry.

There was a relatively high level of public accountability for safety in coal mining and on the railways. Mining and railway disasters were followed not only by coroner's inquests, but also by official inquiries conducted by the Mines Inspectorate and Railway Inspectorate, respectively. Some investigations took the form of a public inquiry with evidence presented in open session. Whether or not there was a formal public inquiry, the findings were published by the government as a command paper. The stated objective of official disaster inquiries was to determine the cause of the incident and suggest safety improvements. Apportioning blame was not an explicit goal, though it could not be avoided altogether. Bridget Hutter (1992, 191) notes that the rationale for railway accident inquiries was 'to anticipate, respond to and even appease public and political concerns'. The public and its representatives were dismayed by accidents involving many fatalities and demanded answers.

All parties, including the trade unions, understood that the British economy was fuelled by coal, that coal mining was dangerous, and that disasters would not be eradicated in the foreseeable future, even if the coal industry was taken out of private hands. The mood, then, was one of realism about what could be achieved under prevailing circumstances.

After the Hulton Colliery disaster in 1910, Redmayne had conducted an 'official investigation'. A detailed report was published, but not a full transcript of proceedings (Redmayne and Pope 1911b). Miners and their employers appeared as witnesses, but did not act as assessors. After the 1913 explosion at Senghenydd, however, the MFGB lobbied for the appointment of a special court of inquiry with assessors representing the miners and the colliery owners. Animosity between miners and employers was greater in South Wales than in any other coalfield. Home Secretary McKenna and the employers tried to argue that the inquiry should be non-partisan, but eventually backed down and agreed to the MFGB's demand (*Manchester Guardian* 1913b). Smillie, the MFGB leader, and Evan Williams, Chairman of the South Wales and Monmouthshire Coalowners' Association, were appointed as assessors. Thus the conduct of proceedings and the conclusions drawn would not be left to Redmayne alone (*Manchester Guardian* 1913c).

The inquiry reached no definitive conclusion as to the proximate cause of the explosion. It did, however, identify serious shortcomings in the equipment and operation of the mine that led to prosecutions. Whether or not lives could have been saved after the explosion by reversing the airflow was debatable, but the failure of the company to install the appropriate type of fan constituted a breach of the Coal Mines Act 1911. The company had been given until 30 September 1913 to comply but had done nothing. Redmayne also concluded that the company was in breach of Regulation 77 of the Act because of deficiencies in the measurement of underground air currents and associated record keeping (Redmayne et al. 1914, 7). The type of glass used in the safety lamps at the mine did not have official approval, and the men responsible for relighting lamps that had gone out, whilst competent, had not been appointed in writing as was required by the law. In Redmayne's opinion, management had not fulfilled the requirements of the 1911 Act specifying that the roadways, including the sides and ceiling, must be cleared of dust every 24 hours (Redmayne et al. 1914, 9). The mine was very gassy, and reports of gas, though not necessarily in explosive quantities, had been made in the weeks, days and hours preceding the explosion. Redmayne calculated that the firemen, whose job was to inspect the workings for gas and other hazards before each shift, did not have enough time to do so thoroughly, resulting in further breaches of legislation, and noted that there were errors in their reports (Redmayne et al. 1914, 11–12). He also thought that the method used to test for the presence of gas – elevating a safety lamp on a pole – was unsuitable. One fireman, Richard Davies, admitted that his reports did not clearly indicate whether or not a potentially explosive amount of gas was present. In general, Redmayne was not satisfied with the internal procedures for inspecting the mine or for recording the results of inspections (Redmayne et al. 1914, 13–14). Electrical apparatus was another area for concern. Regulations prohibited electrical systems that permitted 'open sparking'. Counsel for the firm and management contended that sparks generated by the equipment used at Senghenydd were too small to ignite firedamp, and that in conse-quence there was no open sparking. Although Redmayne did not chal-lenge this assertion, he felt that more care should have been taken in such a gassy mine (Redmayne et al. 1914, 31–2).

Redmayne acknowledged that several of the regulatory breaches at the mine seemed relatively minor, but 'taken in the aggregate they point to a disquieting laxity in the management of the mine' (Redmayne et al. 1914, 35). He did not, however, go so far as to conclude that lax compliance with regulation was responsible for the disaster. Redmayne called for the tightening of regulations, especially with respect to underground elec-trical apparatus. He suggested that stone dusting might be the best solution to the coal dust problem, and called for more research into this theory. The manager, Shaw, and others were commended for their bravery on the day of the explosion.

Smillie stated that he was in 'general agreement' with Redmayne's findings (Redmayne et al. 1914, 40). As we have seen, Redmayne was far more critical of management than of the miners. Williams, however, wrote a substantial statement of dissent. He asserted that sudden falls of roof and outbursts of gas were inevitable under the geological conditions prevailing in South Wales, and contended that the mine was well ventilated. He accepted that there had been errors in the recording of air currents, but felt that this was understandable in view of the 'bewildering number of new regulations' imposed by the authorities on management (Redmayne et al. 1914, 43). Senghenydd was an efficiently managed mine, as the Inspectors of Mines had acknowledged on previous visits. Williams said that various methods of dealing with the accumulation of coal dust had been tried and found wanting, but agreed with Redmayne that stone dusting was worth closer investigation. He dismissed the theory that the explosion was caused by an electrical spark, and thought it probable that gas released in a fall was ignited by an open light in the lamp cabin. He did not criticize the miners – after all, 439 of them had died – or the union. In other words, in Williams's eyes the explosion was an unlucky and largely unavoidable occurrence in a gassy mine.

To summarize, Redmayne was critical of management for not ensuring that mining operations at Senghenydd were in all respects compliant with the law. Insofar as firemen and other miners had failed in their duties of inspection and record keeping, it was because of poor routines which were ultimately the responsibility of management. He believed that the most likely cause of the explosion was a spark from electrical apparatus. Smillie was convinced that more lives could have been saved by reversing the airflow, and that the absence of an authorized ventilation fan was a fatal error. Redmayne and Williams doubted whether reversing the airflow would have made much difference. Williams complained about excessive regulation, and argued that occasional escapes of gas and explosions were inevitable in South Wales, even in well-managed mines such as Senghenydd. All three, however, agreed that the accumulation of coal dust underground posed a serious hazard.

The official inquiry was hardly a cover up. Smillie had had his say and his views were recorded in the command paper. In fact the Senghenydd report provided much ammunition for critics of the employers and of the principle of private ownership of the coal industry. An editorial in the left-leaning *Manchester Guardian* was particularly unimpressed by the attempts of Williams, on behalf of the owners, to avoid responsibility:

> But is it not time that the use of every proved device and contrivance for ensuring the safety of mineworkers should be enforced, and every loophole for evasion closed? The ruin of all, or of many, minowners [*sic*], we may be told, would follow. If there were much evidence of the likelihood of that, it would look like a rather stronger argument for the nationalisation of mines than for the omission of precautions. But predictions of the kind have been as numerous as large improvements in the conditions of mining labour have been, and yet coal-owning has remained reasonably remunerative through them all. (*Manchester Guardian* 1914a)

Feelings against the Lewis Merthyr company ran high in Wales. The South Wales coalfield was the most turbulent in Britain and its union, the 'Fed', inclined towards radical socialism. The abrasive Lord Merthyr, founder of Lewis Merthyr, was widely detested in the mining villages. On the other hand, Edward Shaw, the manager of Universal Colliery, was a more popular figure. He represented Senghenydd on Caerphilly Council and played a leading role in a local Baptist congregation (Lieven 1999, 11). The Home Office decided to prosecute Edward Shaw and Lewis Merthyr for regulatory breaches, the most important of which was the failure to install a reversible ventilating fan. In July 1914, Caerphilly magistrates fined Shaw £25 for various breaches of safety legislation, including £10 'for not providing a contrivance for the immediate reversal of the air'. Shaw was also required to pay £5 5s in costs. Lewis Merthyr was found not guilty of any crime on the grounds that the company had published the Coal Mines Act and all regulations at the mine, and had appointed a properly certificated manager upon whom all responsibility rested (*Manchester Guardian* 1914b). The union expressed anger at the verdict, which exonerated the company and appeared to value the lives of each dead miner at about one shilling. The Home Office resolved to launch an appeal against several of the verdicts (*Manchester Guardian* 1914c; 1914d). But there was a lack of clarity in the 1911 Act over the extent to which coal dust must be removed from roadways, and the appeal was rejected.[3] Speaking at an army recruitment rally in Wales in October 1914, Tom Richards, an MP endorsed by the miners' union, was cheered enthusiastically when asserting that German shells were not as dangerous as 'the bombs of Senghenydd' (*The Times* 1914). He underestimated the capabilities of the German artillery.

Recovery and Reconstruction

Eight hundred miners were laid off work as a result of the explosion. There was little alternative employment in the locality. It took four weeks for the company to extinguish the underground blazes (Lieven 1989, 18). The undamaged East Side of the colliery resumed work on 26 November 1914. Some bodies had still to be retrieved form the West Side (Redmayne et al. 1914, 8; *The Times* 1913). Miners had voted to return to work on 26 November because they could not afford to endure further unemployment. Moving away from Senghenydd was an option, but an expensive one, and mining was risky everywhere. Changing to a different occupation was also risky and imposed further costs. Senghenydd and many other mines in South Wales proved vital to the war effort between 1914 and 1918, producing steam coal for the Royal Navy. During the

1920s, however, demand for coal fell sharply, and in 1928 the colliery at Senghenydd closed, resulting in many redundancies. The village of Senghenydd no longer served any commercial function. The Universal Colliery had had a brief but stormy life. South Wales as a whole was one of the most depressed industrial regions in Britain during the interwar period because of its dependence on declining industries such as coal.

Mitigation and Regulatory Change

Senghenydd was the last of the great pre-1914 coal mining explosions in Britain. Between 1903 and 1912 an average of 133 miners per year died in explosions, interrupting and temporarily reversing the downward trend of the late nineteenth century. The figure for fatalities from explosions in 1913 was 462, most of whom died at Senghenydd. Between 1914 and 1917 the average number of fatalities per annum was 27. There was a spike to 160 in 1918 – 155 died in an explosion at the Podmore Hall Colliery, North Staffordshire – but then a fall to 27 in 1919 (Chief Inspector of Mines 1920, 21). No significant changes to official safety regulations were enacted between 1913 and 1920. Explaining the reduction in deaths from explosions during the First World War is beyond the scope of this chapter. It could have reflected sheer good luck or increased vigilance after Hulton and Senghenydd. Younger and fitter miners, moreover, were the first to volunteer to serve in the war (Supple 1987, 48); it is conceivable that they were also the ones prepared to take the biggest risks underground, but this is conjecture. On the other hand, the fact that coal mines were under great pressure to meet the demands of the war economy with a less efficient workforce was hardly a recipe for increased safety.

An official Explosions in Mines Committee (EMC) had been established at the recommendation of the Royal Commission on Mines of 1906–09. Seven reports were published by the EMC between 1912 and 1915, focusing principally on the use of stone dusting to prevent or mitigate underground explosions (Bryan 1975, 72). The subject was complex, for much depended on local conditions. The proportion of stone to coal dust required to prevent ignition was hard to determine. But the EMC became convinced, and correctly so, that stone dusting was very important. R.V. Wheeler, who led the scientific team working for the EMC, was brought in during the Senghenydd inquiry to test the type of electrical bells used at the mine (Redmayne et al. 1914, 36–40).

The war delayed action on the findings of the EMC. In 1920, new regulations specified in greater detail the requirements for removing coal dust from underground roadways. The 1920 regulations also required the use of stone dust or water, the latter being less effective, to guard against coal dust explosions (Rockley 1938, 20–21). Research into the coal dust problem continued during the 1920s and 1930s, for the danger was by no means eliminated by the 1920 regulations. Stone dusting could not prevent firedamp explosions, and its capacity to render coal dust inert varied according to the peculiarities of each location. Some mines needed a higher percentage of stone dust than others. The electrical issue also festered. Researchers and manufacturers strove to develop flameproof equipment. During the 1920s, the University of Sheffield, a leader in the field of mine safety research, offered a service that involved the testing and certification of flameproof equipment for underground use, a function taken over by the government's Mines Department in 1930 (Jones 2006, 123).

The 1920s did not see the end of fatal explosions in British coal mines. Between 1925 and 1934, a total of 753 British miners died in firedamp and coal dust explosions, a figure boosted by the death of 265 at Gresford Colliery in North Wales in 1934. The Gresford disaster – probably a firedamp explosion that was propagated by coal dust – was the worst since Senghenydd (Williamson 1999). The Mines Department conducted an investigation into why the rate of death from explosions per 1000 miners was higher in Britain than in France. Several factors were identified, including the almost universal use of safety lamps and the less widespread use of electricity in French collieries. French ventilation regulations also appeared to be more stringent (Hudspeth 1937). Gresford provoked even more bitterness than Senghenydd, and the government decided to establish a Royal Commission to review all aspects of mine safety. Incremental changes to safety regulations and practice were advocated by the Royal Commission, which reported in 1938. It also observed that the mechanization of underground operations was generating more coal dust than ever before, meriting further investigation (Rockley 1938). The Second World War delayed new legislation until the 1950s. After the mid-1940s mining disasters became rare in Britain. There was no magic bullet. Change was gradual, driven by better science, amendments to the law, increased organizational emphasis on safety by managers and miners (Feickert 2007), and the slow replacement of men by machines.

Senghenydd 1913 was a major disaster in an industry that was moving, albeit slowly and with setbacks, towards greater safety. Regulation played a substantial (but not the only) role in the mitigation of disasters in the coal mining industry in Britain during the twentieth century, but the cycle would recur with a vengeance as nations such as China, India and Turkey industrialized.

ABERFAN 1966

The most serious coal-related disasters in Britain after 1945 were idiosyncratic ones above rather than below ground. About 4000 deaths have been attributed to unusually thick smog in London in December 1952. The lethal smog, produced by the burning of coal, settled over the city in a period of still weather. The death rate remained higher than normal for the rest of the winter, reflecting the after-effects of the smog combined with an outbreak of influenza (Stone 2002).

At 9.15 a.m. on 21 October 1966, a spoil or waste heap attached to Merthyr Vale Colliery collapsed and slid into the village of Aberfan in South Wales, killing 144 people, including 109 primary school children in their classrooms and five teachers. Aberfan, like Senghenydd, was a village, and the death of so many children ensured that the disaster attained national prominence. The most authoritative account of Aberfan and the ensuing inquiry is provided by Iain McLean and Martin Johnes (2000).

As Richard Couto (1989, 310) indicates, the Aberfan catastrophe, like the great smog of 1952, may be thought of as a negative externality of the coal industry:

> The elements of the disaster [at Aberfan] were the byproducts of the industry that sustained the economy of the village. These elements literally spilt over to kill children who never had the opportunity to calculate and accept or reject the odds of injury and death as miners had done every day for more than a century.

Following the disaster, some attempt was made to compensate the families of the victims for their loss and to punish the perpetrators, but the deceased themselves could be given no compensation.

Mitigation and Regulatory Change

At the time of Aberfan, there were 1753 coal spoil tips in Britain, of which 477 were in use (Ashworth 1986, 286). It was common for several tips to be located in close proximity. Often many metres high, spoil heaps consisted of discarded material produced underground and waste generated by the sorting and washing of coal at the pit head. Coal washing produced a slime called slurry which was dumped on the tips. Many tip complexes were accompanied by substantial 'lagoons' into which the slurry drained (Thomson and Rodin 1972, 4). The quantity of waste material that required dumping expanded rapidly in the mid-twentieth century as a result of the introduction of new, highly mechanized mining equipment.

Although there were strict safety rules governing work underground, relatively little thought had been given either by the coal industry or by the government to the issue of safety above ground, possibly because of the absence of disasters on the surface before Aberfan. Key legislation on safety, including the Mines and Quarries Act 1954, dealt exclusively with the industry's employees, and did not address the safety of its neighbours. Colliery waste was tipped at the most convenient location, regardless of the proximity of dwellings and schools. Tips and lagoons were not designed in any way. If a tip grew too high, another one was started next to it. Many mines and mining villages in South Wales were in steeply sloped valleys, and the only space available for tipping was on the valley side. According to two technical experts in the early 1970s, Aberfan 'brought to light a complete lack of knowledge of the physical properties of colliery spoil and of any rational basis for designing spoil heaps and lagoons' (Thomson and Rodin 1972, 24). Water was the main problem. Tips that were not drained properly were the most likely to become unstable. High Welsh rainfall added to the danger.

Warnings

Aberfan was not the first landslide involving a spoil tip, but none of the previous ones had caused death or injury. The official report into the disaster contained a history of spoil tips and landslides in the Aberfan district since the 1930s. A major slip occurred at Abercynon, five miles away, in 1939, blocking a main road and canal. Tip 4 at Merthyr Vale, Aberfan, slipped a considerable distance in 1944, but without doing any serious damage. Tip 5, built further up the mountain side after Tip 4 was abandoned, began to show evidence of instability in the early 1950s. Tips 6 and 7 were begun in the 1950s. The procedure appears to have been to wait until a tip became self-evidently unsafe, or until an influential neighbour made a fuss, and then start on a new one, but without bothering to check whether the ground was suitable or drainage was adequate. Tip 7 at Aberfan – the one that failed in 1966 – was built over a stream. Local residents complained about the tip complex, part of which had caught fire, to Merthyr Tydfil Borough Council in 1959. Sections of Aberfan village were flooded by water from the tip from time to time. In 1960 the Council approached the National Coal Board (NCB), which owned the coal industry after nationalization in 1947, and drew attention to residents' concerns about pollution and flooding, and their fears that in a heavy downpour a tip could collapse. The NCB replied that there was nothing to worry about. The dumping of tailings (a very fine discard material) at Tip 7 between 1962 and 1965 generated more local complaints, some of which focused on the threat to the ill-fated Pantglas Junior School. Finer discard was potentially more prone to slippage. Several partial slippages of Tip 7 occurred in 1963. No damage was done and, as usual, the NCB downplayed the incidents. At Tymawr Colliery in 1965 a lagoon wall failed, but once again no one was hurt. The Tymawr accident alarmed at least some NCB officials. Old records were searched and a memorandum written just after the Abercynon slip in 1939 was discovered. The Powell Duffryn memorandum, named after the company that had owned the mines at Abercynon and Aberfan, set out important safety advice relating to the building and maintenance of spoil tips (Davies 1967, 41–79). If the Powell Duffryn memorandum had been NCB policy in 1966, it is possible that Aberfan could have been avoided. In the event, however, the attitude of the NCB as a whole was not to take warnings of tip instability seriously.

The Triggering Event

During the months leading up to the Aberfan disaster, Tip 7 at Merthyr Vale exhibited further minor signs of instability, but as usual such warnings went unheeded. On the day of the landslide, workers arrived at Tip 7 at 7.30 a.m. to discover that a depression had appeared at the top of the spoil heap. Some rails had buckled and a crane was in danger of toppling over (Davies 1967, 28). This overnight slippage was the triggering event that led to the landslide at 9.15 a.m..

Sensemaking and Decision Making

Nothing could have been done that morning to stabilize Tip 7. If, however, the significance of the initial slip had been grasped and acted upon immediately by NCB officials, the authorities would have had about 90 minutes in which to evacuate Aberfan, or at least to have stopped children from going to school. The tip workers thought the depression was worth reporting to their boss, but there was no working telephone line available because of vandalism. A messenger had to be sent down the slope to the office, wasting valuable time. When alerted, officials at the valley bottom expressed concern for the safety of the crane (but not the village), and ordered a team to be sent up the tip with equipment to cut the rails. They also decided that someone should inspect the tip on Monday (it was then Friday), so there was no real alarm. When the cutting team reached the top of the tip at 9 a.m., they were told that it had sunk another ten feet (about three metres), making 20 feet in total. They decided to have a cup of tea before moving the crane to safety. A few minutes later a wave of muck and water started to surge out of the depression. It flowed down the mountainside towards the school and village (Davies 1967, 28–30). There had been no panic between 7.30 and 9.15. The efforts at sensemaking by workers and officials had led them in the wrong direction because they lacked even a basic understanding of what could go wrong (Turner 1976, 385).

The Disaster Unfolds

Once the fatal slide began, it would have been too late to warn the school even had there been a telephone to hand (McLean and Johnes 1997, 285). It is estimated that 140 000 cubic yards of waste were unleashed down the mountainside. The flow was so powerful that 50 000 cubic yards surmounted a railway embankment and entered the village. Total fatalities were 144. Of the 116 children who died, 109 were attending Pantglas Junior School. A further 29 children and six adults suffered injuries. Sixteen houses and the school were damaged. Other properties were damaged in the rescue operation (Davies 1967, 26). The disaster would have been worse if fog had not delayed a bus bringing children to school from other villages (McLean and Johnes 1997, 286). According to the Centre for Research on the Epidemiology of Disasters (CRED) International Disaster Database, Aberfan was responsible for more fatalities than any other natural or man-made disaster in Britain in the 1960s.[4]

Rescue and Relief

Emergency services and volunteers rushed to the scene to try and rescue those trapped by the landslide. Some were equipped only with shovels. Mine rescue teams and miners from several collieries converged on the village to offer assistance. None of those buried in the landslide could be retrieved alive (Davies 1967, 26). Aberfan occurred in the age of television, and the aftermath of the disaster was shown on news broadcasts. By 1966 there were 15.4 million television sets in British homes (Broadcasters' Audience Research Board 2014). TV reports from the disaster site shocked viewers, particularly because of the large number of deaths of small children.

Survivors and relatives of the victims often developed symptoms that would now be classified as post-traumatic stress disorder. Some treatment was available from locally based psychiatrists and general practitioners, but the stigma associated with mental illness in the 1960s deterred some individuals and families from seeking or accepting medical help. They would have been even less likely to trust outsiders. Church ministers also offered care to those affected by the disaster. Media interest in the disaster was felt to be intrusive, and intensified villagers' suspicion of outsiders (Johnes 2000). After previous disasters in the coalfields, including Senghenydd, there had been no specialist care available for the bereaved beyond that provided by churches.

An Aberfan Disaster Fund was set up by the Mayor of Merthyr Tydfil. The sum of £1.75 million was raised for the victims and their families, or so the Mayor, the management committee and subscribers believed. The fund soon ran into unexpected legal problems. To avoid taxation, the fund was registered as a charity, but that involved accepting tight controls over the use to which donations could be put. Under charity law, payments could only be made to those bereaved families determined to be 'in need'. After wrangling between the management committee of the fund and the Charity Commissioners, it was agreed that all families of children killed at Aberfan were 'in need' in an emotional sense if not necessarily financially, and each family was given £5000 from the fund. Given their reluctance to approve the disbursement of funds to the victims' families, it is perhaps surprising that the Charity Commissioners later expressed no objection to a proposal that the fund should contribute £150 000 to the cost of clearing away the Aberfan tips (McLean and Johnes 1999, 380–89).

Within a week of the disaster, the NCB had inspected all of its tips and taken remedial action at some sites. At Aberfan, emergency work was carried out to improve drainage and render the complex secure (Ashworth 1986, 286–8). The NCB did not question its liability to compensate the families of the deceased and those whose property was lost or damaged in the disaster. Working from precedent – a case involving the Yorkshire Electricity Board – the court tasked with determining compensation set the tariff at £500 plus costs for each dead child. The NCB had initially hoped to get away with £50 per child. All told, the NCB paid £159 944 in compensation to the people of Aberfan, but recouped £150 000 from the disaster fund to help pay for tip removal (McLean and Johnes 1997, 288–9). The NCB's stance was comparable to that of Lewis Merthyr collieries in 1913.

Allocating Blame

Whereas reporting of the Senghenydd disaster in 1913 concentrated on the heroism of the rescuers and the importance of unity in the midst of adversity, the media in its reporting of Aberfan was prepared, albeit somewhat condescendingly, to acknowledge the anger of local people towards the NCB. At the inquest on 24 October 1966, the *Daily Mail* reported that bereaved parents insisted that their children had been 'murdered' or 'Buried alive by the National Coal Board'. The coroner refused to entertain such accusations (Kennedy 1966). Letters highly critical of the coal industry and its management were also printed in correspondence columns, especially of Welsh newspapers (Pantti and Wahl-Jorgensen 2011, 114–15).

The Labour government had no option but to announce a major 'Tribunal of Inquiry' to investigate the disaster. Lord Justice Edmund Davies was appointed to chair the inquiry. In many respects the Davies report was damning of the NCB and its leadership. A lengthy section of the report addressed the issue of blame directly. There could be no doubt that 'at one level or another' (Davies 1967, 84) the NCB had been responsible for the disaster because it lacked a policy for ensuring the safety of tips. While accepting responsibility in general terms, the NCB and its chairman, Lord Robens, tried to convince the inquiry that the accident was caused by special geological circumstances and therefore completely unforeseeable. Only with the greatest reluctance did the NCB admit that its officials had been aware that Tip 7 was built over a stream (Davies 1967, 85–92). Davies savaged Robens in his report, and then went on to censure seven individual NCB officials at the local level (Davies 1967, 92–102). Those officials should have foreseen and responded to the danger of a tip collapse, regardless of the absence of any national policy. Davies accepted that the officials were innocent of the charges of 'callous indifference' and 'villainy':

> But the Aberfan disaster is a terrifying tale of bungling ineptitude by many men charged with tasks for which they were totally unfitted, of failure to heed clear warnings, and of total lack of direction from above. Not villains, but decent men, led astray by foolishness or by ignorance or by both in combination, are responsible for what happened at Aberfan (Davies 1967, 25).

The Tribunal recommended that a National Tip Safety Committee be established to advise the government. It should draw up a code of practice for tip safety, and the Mines Inspectorate should ensure the NCB's compliance. Better training of NCB staff and officials should be mandated, and the Mines and Quarries Act 1954 should be amended to cover tip safety (Davies 1967, 131–2).

The Davies report was clearly not a cover-up or a fantasy document (Birkland 2009). In fact, William Ashworth (1986, 285–9), the author of the standard history of the NCB, argues that Davies was swayed by the climate of emotion and indignation, and went too far in attacking the NCB and Robens, whose argument that Aberfan was an unprecedented event was factually correct. Yet the NCB could have done more to heed warnings of instability at Tip 7.

Davies's recommendations were implemented, and no further tip disasters occurred in the UK. When the draft report first reached Cabinet ministers, however, it had created alarm. Although Davies did not actually call for Robens's head, his position was threatened, and he offered to resign. After considerable debate, the Cabinet decided to stand by Robens, a former Labour MP. The Cabinet regarded him as indispensable to their plans for restructuring the coal industry, not least because he was acceptable to the National Union of Mineworkers. The errant local officials received no punishment other than loss of face (McLean and Johnes 1997, 287, 293–7; Tweedale 2004 [2008]). Davies did not agree with bereaved families that Aberfan constituted murder, and there were no criminal prosecutions. Iain McLean and Martin Johnes (1997, 300–303) point out that under British law it would have been almost impossible to obtain a conviction on a charge of corporate manslaughter. The NCB accepted its civil liability and, like Lewis Merthyr, provided compensation at what was then the going rate.

Recovery and Reconstruction

The Aberfan tips were removed by the NCB. The associated raid on the relief fund was a source of great animosity both at the time and in retrospect. According to Robens, the NCB had offered to render the tips safe by removing any material that still posed a risk, but the local community had insisted on total removal. Robens claimed that it was the government and not the NCB that had required the relief fund to make a contribution to the additional costs (Ashworth 1986, 288). Whether or not Robens's interpretation is the correct one, the village was convinced that its relief funds had been expropriated by the NCB.

Aberfan was part of a region struggling with industrial decline. It would be an exaggeration to suggest that the village ever made a complete recovery, though it did survive. Merthyr Vale Colliery, the largest employer, continued in production until 1989 when redundancy payments were offered to the remaining 526 miners. Since the mine was known to be loss-making, the closure came as no surprise (Hoyland 1989). Money from the 1966 disaster fund was used to pay for the construction of a community centre. Interviewed 25 years after the disaster, Arthur Jones, a long-serving doctor in the village, stated that the consequences were still being felt: 'By every statistic, patients seen, prescriptions written, deaths, I can prove that this is a village of excessive sickness' (quoted in James 1991). Many of those affected most closely by the disaster would never be able to put it behind them. In 1997, the government repaid the money taken controversially from the relief fund, but £150 000 was worth far less in 1997 than in 1967 (*The Times* 1997).

Mitigation and Regulatory Change

All of the substantive recommendations of the Aberfan inquiry were implemented. The NCB introduced a new code of practice for dealing with spoil tips in 1967, and then a more detailed technical manual in 1969. A government order in 1967 made it compulsory to report dangerous 'occurrences' on tips to HM Inspectorate of Mines and Quarries. A National Advisory Committee on Tip Safety was established. The NCB and the Mines Inspectorate took on a number of civil engineers. One hundred engineers were assigned by the NCB to the tasks of inspecting tips and ensuring their safety. New research was conducted into tip stability (Thomson et al. 1973, 677–80). The Mines and Quarries (Tips) Act 1969 focused on the issue of safety. That there was so little argument over the implementation of the inquiry's recommendations is evidence of the degree to which tip safety had been overlooked before Aberfan. While any additional expenditure was burdensome for an industry in secular decline, the action taken after Aberfan reduced the risk that further serious negative externalities would be imposed on the industry's neighbours.

Aberfan and its implications for tip safety were studied overseas. The US Geological Survey and the US Bureau of Mines conducted a survey of potentially dangerous spoil heaps. One of the complexes that aroused concern was at Buffalo Creek, West Virginia (Couto 1989, 310–11). In 1972, the lagoon at Buffalo Creek burst out of its protective barrier, creating a tidal wave that killed more than 125 people, flooded 16 small communities, and left 4000 people homeless. Pittston, the owners of the tip and lagoon complex, had failed to comply with regulations. Approximately 100 families affected by the disaster took the company to court, and won an aggregate $13.5 million in damages, of which $5.5 million was for damage to property and loss of life, and the remaining $8 million for mental suffering (Stern 1976). The families of Aberfan were disadvantaged by the comparative stinginess of British courts.

The threat to life and property posed by spoil tips and lagoons in the coal mining districts of Britain receded in the late twentieth century. The closure of most coal mines in the 1970s and 1980s reduced the supply of tailings and other coal waste (Glyn and Machin 1997). Some spoil was recycled for use in road building and landfill prior to construction (Winter and Henderson 2003; Davies et al. 1998). Many tips were landscaped, often with the help of government grants, a process that was not without risk. At Cwmaman in Glamorgan, in 1973, a botched reclamation scheme led to the inundation of a number of houses with water and slurry and the evacuation of residents, although no one was injured (Clwyd 1973).

Repetition of the events at Aberfan was avoided by a combination of factors: the realization by the NCB that tips could be dangerous and needed careful maintenance, regulatory reform and the decline of the coal industry. But similar disasters could happen in the future, especially in developing countries that still have large coal industries.

CONCLUSION

Senghenydd and Aberfan were much more localized than the other disasters considered in this book. Both had a major impact on their local communities, and both were to some extent the product of ignorance. By the time of the Senghenydd disaster in 1913, coal dust was known to play a role in many mine explosions, but there was no consensus as to the best remedy. Regardless of the many dangers to their health underground, hundreds of thousands of men chose to work in the pits because they needed to make a living. In the case of Aberfan, the NCB did not bother to assess the risk to the community of a tip collapse because there had never been any loss of life from such an event. Aberfan residents were worried, but their fears were dismissed as exaggerated.

Following both disasters, the government established comprehensive inquiries. Those inquiries were thorough and their recommendations for reform sensible – they were not fantasy documents. On the other hand, those held to be most culpable for the disasters faced only the mildest of punishments, whilst the families of the victims were shown little generosity by the authorities and the courts. The villagers of Senghenydd and Aberfan lacked power. In the interwar period the application of stone dust helped to reduce the incidence of major underground explosions, but they did not disappear altogether. Aberfan was the one and only spoil tip disaster in Britain. Perhaps there was an element of good luck in the avoidance of other tip slides in the late 1960s and early 1970s, but the dangers were ultimately removed by better safety procedures and the decline of the coal industry. With the decline of coal mining in Britain and many other developed countries the locus of the disaster cycle has shifted elsewhere, especially to countries in Asia.

NOTES

1. Safety lamps were not required to be used in all mines, only in those judged particularly at risk of explosion.
2. It was not yet understood that watering was inferior to stone dusting. Water could prevent coal dust becoming airborne but was unable to prevent it catching fire (Aldrich 1995, 501).
3. TNA, POWE 8/975, Transcript of *Atkinson v. Shaw* judgment, 6 May 1915.
4. Search using http://emdat.be/disaster_list/index.html.

6.   Tobacco

Even major tobacco companies now concede that smoking causes harm and death. According to British American Tobacco, 'Along with the pleasures of smoking there are real risks of serious diseases such as lung cancer, respiratory disease and heart disease' (British American Tobacco n.d.). In an interview with the *Independent* newspaper in 2012, John Seffrin, Chief Executive of the American Cancer Society, warned that on current trends tobacco smoking will cause the deaths of 1 billion people in the twenty-first century, and that would make it the 'biggest public health disaster in the history of the world' (quoted in Connor 2012).

Tobacco has been a disaster in slow motion. The adverse health effects of smoking took several hundred years to pin down scientifically. Damage to the individual smoker accumulates over a period of decades. Speed, however, is not an essential component of disasters. A far more pertinent benchmark is the extent of the disruption and loss incurred. In *Collapse*, Jared Diamond (2005) shows how a number of societies, from Easter Island to Viking Greenland, gradually destroyed themselves over long periods of time, most notably because of their failure to protect and manage the environment. Diamond's societal collapses unfolded even more slowly than the tobacco disaster in the mid-twentieth century. Nevertheless, the fact that smoking kills in slow motion does have implications for the disaster cycle. There may be less urgency at the sensemaking and decision making stage of a slow-motion disaster than when a hurricane or a banking collapse is anticipated.

One objection to examining smoking through the lens of the disaster cycle is that, unlike many other types of disaster, the tobacco disaster will not be repeated. That objection does not withstand examination. Firstly, the decline of smoking in the developed world in the late twentieth century was accompanied by an increase in smoking in the developing world. The disaster recurs, albeit not in the same location. In a similar fashion, coal mining explosions that result in major loss of life are now more likely to happen in China or Turkey than in Western Europe. Secondly, smoking could be regarded as an instance of a wider category of public health disaster. Tobacco is not the only addictive substance to be implicated in numerous deaths, nor is it the only supposedly harmless product subsequently discovered to be lethal. In the eighteenth century, for example, gin was the drug of choice for many, leading to the ruin and premature end of numerous lives (Dillon 2002). The parallels between the histories of absinthe and tobacco have also been noted (Huisman et al. 2007). There are similarities, moreover, between tobacco and asbestos. Manufacturers of both substances endeavoured to cover up any evidence that suggested they were serious health hazards (Tweedale 2000; McCulloch and Tweedale 2008).

MITIGATION AND REGULATORY CHANGE

When Europeans invaded the Americas in the sixteenth and seventeenth centuries, they traded diseases and commodities with the indigenous population. Tobacco was one of the most popular American commodities to reach Europe and the rest of the world. Tobacco could be chewed, snorted, or smoked in various ways, depending on the fashion. The crop was often grown on settler-managed slave plantations. As tobacco consumption expanded, European governments realized that tobacco could be a good source of revenue and imposed taxes accordingly (Goodman 1993).

Today most people understand that tobacco is very dangerous. As well as nicotine, itself a highly addictive drug (and a poison), tobacco contains an impressive array of carcinogens. Cigarette smoking is the most efficient transmission mechanism for those carcinogens: on average a higher proportion of smoke is inhaled from cigarettes than from pipes or cigars. But the threat to health and life posed by tobacco, and especially the cigarette, did not become evident until the 1950s. Previously there was no firm medical evidence with which to convict tobacco. From the early days, however, tobacco use was controversial. Many commentators felt that tobacco was health-giving as well as relaxing, but others condemned tobacco consumption unreservedly. King James I of England wrote in 1604 that tobacco's 'hatefull smell' was a warning of its vile properties (James I 1885 [1604], 17). Tobacco, the monarch contended, offered no health benefits. On the contrary, smoking was 'contrary to nature' and therefore 'hurtfull to the health of the whole body' (James I, 1885 [1604], 16). Tobacco was 'harmefull to the braine [and] dangerous to the Lungs' and its stinking fumes were like those of hell (James I 1885 [1604], 32). Although correct on many points, including the danger to lungs, the King's argument was essentially a combination of inspired guesswork and assertion. James, however, was unable to turn back the tide of tobacco arriving from the Americas. Royal disapproval was not an effective mitigation strategy, and tobacco continued to gain in popularity.

Smoking, taking snuff and chewing tobacco were overwhelmingly (but not exclusively) male vices in the nineteenth century. The cigarette reached Northern Europe and North America in the mid-Victorian era. Cigarette sales took off in the 1880s and 1890s, decades marked by widespread technological and organizational change in the tobacco industry on both sides of the Atlantic, and not only, as used to be thought, in the business empire of James Buchanan Duke (Hannah 2006).

The late nineteenth century saw the emergence of movements that campaigned to restrict or prohibit tobacco, and cigarettes most of all. Anti-cigarette activists were motivated by similar concerns to those of temperance reformers. They perceived smoking as wasteful, immoral, decadent and generally unhealthy, particularly for young people and the poor. Fathers who smoked were burning money that should have been spent on food and clothing for their families. But it was still not possible to make a scientifically conclusive connection between smoking and any major disease. In essence the anti-smoking movement was an amplified, Progressive Era version of King James's *Counter-Blaste to Tobacco*. The sale of cigarettes to minors was illegal in 26 US states by 1890, and in all but two by 1940. Three Canadian provinces banned the sale of cigarettes to youngsters in the 1890s. The Canadian parliament prohibited the use of tobacco by persons under 16 throughout the dominion in 1908. Fifteen US states, beginning with North Dakota in 1895, passed legislation to prevent the manufacture of cigarettes and/or cigarette use by adults. Whereas the laws against tobacco sales to children became permanent, those restricting the production of tobacco products and their sale to adults were strongly contested, and frequently evaded. Smoking became more acceptable during the First World War, when cigarettes were amongst the comforts appreciated by troops at the front. The struggle for and against tobacco continued after 1918, and the anti-smoking lobby began to lose ground. Tobacco supporters argued that anti-smoking legislation infringed the rights of the individual. None of the state laws affecting adults remained on the statute book by 1930. Conflict over smoking was a side show compared to the debate over the prohibition of alcohol (Alston et al. 2002; Dinan and Heckelman 2005; Tate 1999).

Doctors in Britain were divided over the merits of smoking, some even seeing it as beneficial for asthma sufferers. It was agreed, however, that smoking was bad for children. Insofar as smoking caused physical and moral weakness in the young, the empire would be weakened, or so it was often asserted. In 1908, the British parliament outlawed tobacco sales to children and smoking in public places by children, partly in an effort to improve the racial stock (Walker 1980). As was the case in the USA, the popularity of cigarettes was boosted by the First World War. The cigarette smoking habit started to extend to women between 1914 and 1918. The war gave many women more freedom, and the opportunity to earn more disposable income when they replaced men, albeit temporarily, in many occupations (Wrigley 2014).

Anti-smoking sentiment was strong in some quarters in interwar Germany. The Nazis took up the anti-smoking cause, and attempted to discourage tobacco use by women and teenagers in particular. Essentially, they regarded smoking as a filthy and degenerate habit. Under-18s were banned from smoking in 1940, and tobacco advertising was restricted (but not prohibited) in 1941. But no consistent line was pursued. Although Hitler detested smoking, some other leading Nazis and their wives – and even Hitler's girlfriend Eva Braun – were smokers. Tobacco consumption in Germany actually rose after 1933. Tobacco was scarcer during the Second World War, but not even the Nazis dared deprive the armed forces of the supplies that remained (Bachinger et al. 2008).

Despite some rather limited attempts at restriction, tobacco continued to be popular in the first half of the twentieth century. But the way in which tobacco was consumed changed, especially in the Anglophone world. Cigarettes displaced pipes, cigars and chewing tobacco, admittedly at rates that differed from country to country. Whilst sales of all tobacco products per head of the adult population in the USA declined slightly from 11.1 grams per day in 1920 to 10.4 grams in 1938, sales of manufactured cigarettes increased from 1.7 to 4.7 cigarettes per adult per day over that period (Forey et al. 2012b, 14). In Britain, tobacco consumption per adult per day rose from 4.0 grams in 1905 to 5.8 grams in 1920, and 6.7 grams in 1938. UK sales of manufactured cigarettes per adult per day increased from 1.1 cigarettes in 1905 to 3.0 in 1920 and 5.2 in 1938 (Forey et al. 2012a, 15). The manufactured cigarette was now a convenient and affordable luxury for all classes. The other key interwar development was the further rise of the female smoker. Cigarettes were advertised to women as tokens of emancipation and sophistication (Tinkler 2001). Smoking by women did not go unchallenged, and in 1929 Hugh S. Cumming, the US Surgeon General, issued a statement condemning the female tobacco craze. Cumming, himself a smoker, argued that women smokers were prone to increased nervousness and insomnia, and felt that they lowered the tone of society (Burnham 1989, 1). Regardless of the growth of female cigarette consumption, smoking continued to be more prevalent amongst males. Men accounted for 90 per cent of tobacco consumption in Britain in 1939 (Goodman 1993, 106).

Official efforts to discourage or regulate tobacco use, other than amongst children, were rather half-hearted in the first half of the twentieth century. Action was driven by a number of concerns, both moral and health-related, but no definite medical knowledge. The anti-smoking lobby was thwarted by countervailing forces, including nicotine addicts, advocates of personal freedom, the tobacco industry and the tax authorities. In short, mitigation was weak in the extreme.

During the Second World War, governments regarded tobacco supplies as important for military morale. US forces operating overseas during the Second World War and the Korean War were supplied with cigarettes free of charge, whilst those stationed at home could obtain tobacco at a subsidized price. The long-term results of this policy were very high rates of cancer amongst veterans. Such was the unfortunate consequence of a well-meaning intervention (Bedard and Deschênes 2006).

WARNINGS

The medical and moral critiques of smoking overlapped. In fact they could be hard to disentangle even for a senior medical bureaucrat such as Surgeon General Cumming. Although there was no 'smoking gun' to identify tobacco as a major killer before the Second World War, there was a gradual accumulation of health concerns that amounted to a series of warnings. It need not trouble us that early research into tobacco and health often involved mistakes: the point is that researchers were on to something even when they proceeded in a roundabout way.

An association between pipe smoking and cancer of the lip, tongue and mouth was observed in the eighteenth and nineteenth centuries. Tobacco, however, was thought to be incidental to such cancers, and the damage was attributed to the pressure of the pipe on the lips or the heat of the stem (Doll 1998, 90). Nicotine was found to be toxic in the late nineteenth century. If used in large enough quantities – more than a smoker would absorb – nicotine attacks the nervous system and the heart. Between 1917 and 1919, the British considered using nicotine as a chemical warfare agent, but decided other poisons would be more effective (Palazzo 2000, 163). The evidence as to whether nicotine itself is carcinogenic remains 'inconclusive' after more than a century of research according to the US medical authorities (Communicable Disease Centre 2014). The main objection to nicotine today is its addictiveness. Tobacco smoke contains a cocktail of carcinogens, and nicotine encourages their consumption.

Several studies in the late nineteenth and early twentieth centuries brought to light a statistical association between smoking and heart disease. Although vascular disease affected smokers and non-smokers, it appeared to be more common in smokers. The medical establishment was inclined to discount such findings. Doctors were uncomfortable with the idea that smoking (or any other factor) rendered people more susceptible to developing a particular disease. Given that some smokers remained healthy whilst some non-smokers became unhealthy, the link between smoking and poor health seemed tenuous to doctors unsympathetic to statistical methods. Many physicians demanded certainty when it came to causation, and expressed a strong preference for clinical evidence such as from post-mortems (Doll 1998, 93).

Lung cancer has been studied since the early nineteenth century. The disease was more prevalent in men than in women. Amongst the possible causes, researchers in the 1890s suggested pulmonary infections such as tuberculosis and influenza, and the inhalation of irritants (Rosenblatt 1964). Tobacco was not a major suspect, although one small study in Leipzig in 1898 found a high incidence of lung cancer amongst workers in the tobacco industry, implicating tobacco dust (Doll 1998, 90).

Lung cancer was comparatively rare in the nineteenth century. Malignant lung tumours were responsible for just 1 per cent of cancer cases observed in autopsies at the University of Dresden's Institute of Pathology in 1878. In the early twentieth century, however, the share of malignant lung tumours in autopsies of cancer patients rose strongly, reaching 10 per cent in 1918 and 14 per cent in 1927 (Witschi 2001, 4). Better diagnosis may have played a part in the rising lung cancer statistics, and not all physicians were convinced that there was a problem. Nevertheless, considerable scientific interest in discovering the source of lung cancer emerged in the interwar decades. As Peter Bartrip (2013, 145) explains, there were many candidates, including the use of tar in road surfacing, 'general atmospheric pollution, tobacco smoke, X-rays, motor exhaust fumes, poison gas employed during the war, the aftermath of the 1918 influenza epidemic, micro-organisms, heredity, diet and parasites'. In order to combat the nuisance of dusty road surfaces in an era of increasing traffic, many roads were coated with substances containing tar between 1900 and the 1930s. Tar was a known irritant and a carcinogen that had killed animals in laboratory tests. Intriguingly, tar was also produced during the burning of tobacco. There was a crude correlation between the incidence of lung cancer and the use of tar in road surfacing and in the consumption of tobacco, especially in the form of cigarettes. In the 1930s, the evidence in favour of smoking as the culprit was accumulating, but not yet conclusive (Bartrip 2013, 151).

Clinical tests showed that tobacco smoke could produce cancer in animals, but the results were treated cautiously by the medical profession (Doll 1998, 91). A number of non-clinical studies also pointed towards a connection between tobacco and cancer. In the late 1920s, for example, researchers in Massachusetts found a strong association between heavy smoking and cancer (Lombard and Doering 1928). German cancer researchers in the 1930s were interested in the possible link with tobacco (Proctor 1999). One German study, published in 1939, found an association between very heavy smoking – more than 25 cigarettes per day, or the equivalent in cigars or pipe tobacco – and death from lung cancer. The study was based on a questionnaire sent to relatives of men and women who had died from lung cancer in Cologne, and included a control group of healthy men. Further research was carried out along similar lines in Germany and the Netherlands during the 1940s (Doll 1998, 92–3), but made little impact in the USA or the UK. The Second World War obstructed the diffusion of medical research from continental Europe to the rest of the world, and may have slowed down the realization in the Anglophone world that tobacco was lethal to human beings as well as laboratory animals. American medical textbooks of the 1940s hardly mentioned tobacco (Doll 1998, 95–6).

The scientific debate over smoking and health was followed with interest by the public, and leading newspapers reported on the progress of researchers. For example, in 1935 the *New York Times* stated that Professor Alton Ochsner of Tulane University in New Orleans advised people against smoking before breakfast if they wished to avoid stomach ulcers (Associated Press 1935). The same newspaper reported in 1940 that Ochsner had told a meeting of the American College of Surgeons that cigarettes were responsible for the rise in lung cancer (Laurence 1940). But the flow of news and commentary was not one-sided, and smokers could take heart from more optimistic testimony. An article in the *Washington Post* in 1929 said that Nancy Fluth, the niece of the late Confederate President Jefferson Davis, was still alive and well at 101. Mrs Fluth attributed her long life to 'regular' habits. 'She still smokes her pipe and gives that some credit, for in smoking, she says, she finds beneficial relaxation' (*Washington Post* 1929). In 1941 Dr George C. Andrews of Presbyterian Hospital was said to have shown that cancer of the lower lip (known as 'smokers' cancer'), which was common amongst agricultural labourers, was in fact the result of sunburn and not smoking (*New York Times* 1941). That the Nazis objected to tobacco, as well as liquor, cosmetics and modern dances such as the 'animalistic' Lambeth Walk, was taken as further proof of their madness. Americans were not impressed by the moralism of Nazi 'zealots' (Peters 1939).

Warnings about tobacco had little impact, and smoking was the norm in the 1940s, especially amongst men. Britain devoted vital shipping space to tobacco imports during the Second World War, and spent dollars that it could barely afford on purchasing tobacco in the era of post-war austerity. The British war economy ran on tobacco (and alcohol), at least to some extent. Between 1938 and 1946 the share of tobacco in UK consumer expenditure rose from 4.0 per cent to 8.4 per cent, whilst the share of food and clothing fell (Cairncross 1985, 29). In February 1946 Hugh Dalton, the Chancellor of the Exchequer, said that it was important to maintain tobacco imports, which then made up 4.5 per cent of total imports, for as long as possible: 'In the maintenance of public morale both smoking and pictures [i.e., Hollywood movies] are important for many millions.' Slashing imports of tobacco and movies would 'crush the people', he concluded (quoted in Cater 1946).

In the USA, 76 per cent of men aged 20 or over were smokers in 1947, as were 29 per cent of women (Forey et al. 2012b, 18, 19). In Britain, 77 per cent of men and 38 per cent of women aged 16 or over smoked in 1950 (Forey et al. 2012a, 20, 21). In West Germany, 88 per cent of men aged 14 or above smoked in 1950, but only 21 per cent of women (Forey et al. 2011, 20, 21).[1] In such a climate, health warnings about tobacco were bound to face resistance. It did not help that so far those warnings had been intermittent and tentative.

THE TRIGGERING EVENT

The triggering event in the case of tobacco was a series of scientific reports published in the early 1950s that offered much stronger evidence of the link between smoking and cancer. Tobacco did not suddenly become dangerous in 1950; it had always been dangerous. The disaster cycle, however, is a tool for the analysis of human behaviour. The triggering event is a challenge to action that goes beyond a more routine or less specific warning. In the case of smoking, the disaster was already under way by 1950, but it could still have been checked somewhat by prompt action to reduce the level of smoking. The following sections show that the response to the triggering event was extremely tardy.

As Richard Doll (1998, 96), the doyen of British cancer researchers, explained in a historical review of the scientific debate on smoking and health: 'In 1950, the situation was radically changed by the publication of five papers – four in the USA and one in Britain.' All five were retrospective studies of lung cancer patients. The methods employed were more sophisticated than in previous papers. Results were checked against control groups. The conclusions of the five studies were consistent: smokers were much more likely than non-smokers to get lung cancer.

Two of the five papers are now regarded as classics. Ernest Wynder and Evarts Graham investigated 605 male lung cancer patients from hospitals across the USA. Wherever possible, interviews with the patients themselves were used to collect data for the study. They found that 96.5 per cent of male lung cancer patients, but only 73.7 per cent of male hospital patients without cancer, were moderately heavy to chain smokers. More than 96 per cent of male lung cancer sufferers had smoked for at least 20 years. Since few women had smoked for that length of time, the study did not reach firm results about them. The authors did not claim that smoking was the only factor involved in lung cancer in men, but that: 'Excessive and prolonged use of tobacco, especially cigarets [*sic*], seems to be an important factor in the induction' of the disease (Wynder and Graham 1950, 336). Richard Doll and Bradford Hill sought to explain the fifteenfold increase in deaths from lung cancer in England and Wales between 1922 and 1947. They investigated a group of 649 male cancer sufferers in London hospitals, gathering data from interviews with the subjects. The control group consisted of patients with diseases other than lung cancer. Doll and Hill found 'a real association between carcinoma of the lung and smoking'. The effect of smoking was stronger for heavy smokers. However, there was 'no association between smoking and other respiratory diseases or between smoking and cancer of the other sites (mainly stomach and large bowel)', a finding that would be contradicted by later research. Whilst conceding that association was not proof of causation, the lead researchers could think of no 'other common cause likely to lead both to the development of the [smoking] habit and to the development of the disease [of lung cancer] 20 to 50 years later' (Doll and Hill 1950, 746). Three smaller studies linking smoking to lung cancer came out in the same year (Schrek et al. 1950; Levin et al. 1950; Mills and Porter 1950).

The 1950 studies were noticed by a wider audience than just the medical profession. The *New York Times* summarized the Wynder and Graham and Levin et al. papers, albeit without comment (*New York Times* 1950). In Britain, the *Daily Mail* reported briefly on the findings of the Doll and Hill report, and spoke to Doll about the pipe versus cigarette debate and smoke inhalation (*Daily Mail* Reporter 1951). *The Times* also reported the Doll and Hill findings (Our Medical Correspondent 1950).

The 1950 smoking and cancer articles constitute the triggering event because they appeared as a cluster. Five groups of researchers produced results that cast strong doubt on the safety of tobacco use. What would be the reaction of policy makers and the public?

SENSEMAKING AND DECISION MAKING

The most intriguing part of the smoking saga is that it took so long – until the mid-1960s – for the conclusions of the 1950 studies to sink in. This was indeed a disaster in slow motion, with a 20-year or more time lag between a person beginning to smoke and (if unlucky) being diagnosed with cancer or another smoking-related disease, and then a 15-year hiatus after 1950 devoted to sensemaking and decision making. Several factors were involved in the delay: first, additional research was required to confirm the 1950 findings; second, tobacco firms leapt to the defence of their product; third, the tobacco issue raised a number of difficult questions for governments in the areas of revenue collection, public health policy and individual responsibility.

Further Research

The results of the 1950 studies drew a mixed response from the medical profession and establishment. Epidemiological (or statistical) methods were still suspect, or at least inferior to clinical methods, in the eyes of many experts. Moreover, it was perfectly justifiable to question novel results, especially ones with such devastating implications (Webster 1984; Talley et al. 2004). Doll and Hill decided that they might have more impact with a prospective study. Data would be collected on the smoking habits of a group of subjects. Their mortality would then be observed over time to determine how it was related to tobacco consumption. Doll and Hill chose to study doctors, the group they most wished to influence. More than 40 000 British doctors volunteered information about their health and habits, and 24 389 were included in the study. The first of several articles on smoking and doctors' mortality was published in 1954. Since the beginning of the experiment 789 doctors had died. The evidence showed that mortality from both lung cancer and coronary thrombosis (heart attack) was related to the amount of tobacco smoked by the subjects (Doll and Hill 1954). A follow-up study two years later reinforced the earlier results (Doll and Hill 1956). An even larger prospective study of almost 187 000 men commissioned by the American Cancer Society (ACS) found a statistical relationship between smoking and deaths from lung cancer and heart attack (Hammond and Horn 1954).[2] Epidemiological research into the dangers of tobacco was supplemented by animal experiments, cellular pathology and analysis of the chemical contents of cigarette smoke (Proctor 2012, 88–9). Medical opinion began to change, albeit slowly, in the face of the accumulating evidence against smoking. The board of the ACS gave unanimous approval in October 1954 to a resolution drawing attention to recent research showing an 'association' between smoking and cancer, as well as between smoking and heart disease. The ACS called for a debate amongst public health agencies (Plumb 1954). In the UK, the Medical Research Council, a medical quango, declared in 1957 that there were strong grounds for believing that smoking was the major cause of lung cancer (Medical Research Council 1957). But the debate within the medical community would not be resolved until the 1960s. Smoking was still considered to be normal. Some doctors even offered patients cigarettes to calm their nerves during consultations. Medical opinion had not reached the tipping point.

The Response of the Tobacco Industry

Cigarette sales in the USA, but not in the UK, dipped between 1952 and 1954, possibly as a result of adverse publicity for smoking. Tobacco was a major agricultural crop both in the USA and in parts of the British Empire and Commonwealth. The manufacture of cigarettes and other tobacco products was a large, oligopolistic industry. With jobs and profits at risk, the reaction of the industry was to do all in its power to reassure customers. According to David Courtwright (2005, 423), the US tobacco 'industry initially responded with denial and buck-passing'. Advertising material for particular brands promised smokers that those brands were perfectly safe. In December 1953, however, the major US manufacturers decided that a collective response would be more effective. They established the Tobacco Industry Research Council (TIRC) with a view to contesting the scientific evidence linking smoking and cancer. Hill & Knowlton, a prominent public relations company, was appointed to manage the industry's defensive strategy (Miller 1999). TIRC and Hill & Knowlton were well resourced by the industry to draw attention to flaws in the work of other tobacco researchers. Whenever there was a press report on the dangers of smoking, they were on hand to put the counterarguments, and to offer the old air pollution and road tar theories as alternatives (Courtwright 2005, 424). Some smokers appear to have been reassured by such methods, and cigarette consumption recovered in the mid-1950s. It has since been revealed that the big tobacco companies already knew that the weight of evidence pointed towards smoking being a major cause of lung cancer when they embarked upon their campaign (Proctor 2012, 89). They were not, then, in denial, but bent on deceiving their customers.

Questioning the accumulating evidence against tobacco was not the only response of the industry. New, superficially safer products were advertised more aggressively, including filter-tipped cigarettes. Between 1950 and 1959, sales of filter cigarettes in the USA rose from 0.6 per cent to 48.7 per cent of the manufactured cigarette market. Menthol cigarette sales boomed in the 1960s (Forey et al. 2012b, 17). The tobacco industry faced a somewhat different situation in Britain. As a result of tobacco's role in the war economy, the industry and its dominant firm Imperial Tobacco enjoyed a close relationship with the state. Imperial did not launch a public campaign in defence of smoking, preferring to work behind the scenes. Imperial even contributed funds to assist public sector research into the effects of tobacco. The British tobacco industry hoped to reach some sort of compromise should the evidence against smoking prove decisive. In the 1960s the industry sought to work alongside government to achieve a managed solution to the tobacco problem that was compatible with profitability (Berridge 2006, 1195–6).

Governmental Procrastination

Governments were reluctant to enter the tobacco debate, even as health concerns accumulated in the 1950s. Most political leaders were smokers: President Eisenhower was a chain smoker and Winston Churchill was famous for his cigars. Furthermore, many of the people who elected them also smoked. Would smokers tolerate government interference in their chosen form of relaxation? Was smoking a matter for individual choice and responsibility or was it a public health issue? Given that tobacco taxes were a useful source of revenue, and that the tobacco industry provided many jobs, could governments afford to take an anti-smoking position? Such were the quandaries that confronted politicians and their official advisors in the 1950s and 1960s.

The smoking debate in the early 1950s was particularly vigorous in West Germany. After the Second World War, the West German tobacco industry faced increasing competition from American-style cigarettes, many of which were sold on the black market. Not only were West German growers and manufacturers losing business, but the government was losing tax revenue. Despite the opposition of medical experts, the tax on tobacco products was cut in 1953 in order to weaken the black market and encourage consumption of home-grown tobacco. The lobbying of the domestic tobacco industry had proven decisive. The fiscal authorities also hoped that increased sales would compensate for the lower rate of tax, whilst consumers welcomed the reduction in the cost of living. The association between anti-smoking and the Nazis did not help the cause of health reformers. West German cigarette consumption rose from 700 per capita in 1953 to 1241 per capita in 1960, satisfying the domestic tobacco industry and the government. Health concerns, whilst noted, were over-ridden (Elliot 2012).

Prevarication and procrastination were in the ascendant in the USA and the UK. Tobacco taxes contributed $1.3 billion to federal and $0.4 billion to state coffers in 1950 (Tobacco Tax Council 1975, 5, 8). Tobacco was a major crop in parts of the South. The Secretary for Health, Education, and Welfare in the Eisenhower administration showed little interest in the smoking controversy. Leroy Burney, the Surgeon General, did make a statement in 1957, in which he acknowledged that most evidence now pointed towards a causal link between smoking and lung cancer. Burney was adamant, however, that his role was merely to inform the public, and that health policy was a matter for each state. Only in 1962 did President Kennedy determine that the Surgeon General should take a leading role in evaluating the case against smoking (Parascandola 2001, 201–2).

British governments also played for time. Ian Macleod, the Minister of Health, summed up the situation in a letter to a colleague in 1954: 'We all know that the Welfare State and much else is based on tobacco smoking' and the tax revenue it generated (quoted in Berridge 2003, 66). Nevertheless, the medical evidence was taken seriously enough for a Cabinet committee on lung cancer to be set up in 1957. Virginia Berridge (2003; 2006; 2007) argues that the smoking–cancer nexus forced the British state into a painful re-evaluation of its public health philosophy. The conventional view at the time was that the government should provide information about health threats, and then trust individuals to make their own choices. The alternative view, which was gradually accepted in the 1960s, was that the government should actively discour-age people from doing things that were bad for them and expensive for the National Health Service (NHS). But intervention could bring its own risks, including a possible electoral backlash against bossy politicians (Berridge 2003, 69), which in the case of tobacco did not materialize.

The Tipping Point

Two reports released in the early 1960s marked the turning point in the smoking debate in Britain and the USA. Both were given maximum publicity. In 1962 the Royal College of Physicians, a group previously known for its reticence, published a detailed study and set of recom-mendations about smoking. The report concluded that 'cigarette smoking is the most likely cause of the recent world-wide increase in deaths from lung cancer', as well as a factor in other diseases (Royal College of Physicians 1962, 43). Doctors were asked to warn patients against smoking, whilst the government was urged to discourage smoking by means of tax increases, advertising and regulation. The more detailed Surgeon General's report of 1964 was even more explicit: '*Cigarette smoking is causally related to lung cancer in men; the magnitude of the effect of cigarette smoking far outweighs all other factors*' (Surgeon General's Advisory Committee on Smoking and Health 1964, 37). The evidence about women was less clear-cut, but pointed in the same direction. Smoking was also implicated a range of other diseases. The situation was sufficiently urgent to merit '*appropriate remedial action*' (Surgeon General's Advisory Committee on Smoking and Health 1964, 33).[3]

THE DISASTER UNFOLDS

By the early 1960s the smoking disaster was already in motion, with millions of people suffering and dying from smoking-related illnesses around the world. Researchers at Oxford University have estimated the number of deaths from smoking in developed countries between 1950 and 2000. In the USA, 15 million deaths are attributed to smoking, including 6.6 million (or 30 per cent of) male deaths, and 1.9 million (or 15 per cent of) female deaths, in the 35–69 age range. In Britain, 6.3 million deaths are attributed to smoking, including 2.6 million (or 42 per cent of) male deaths, and 0.6 million (or 16 per cent of) female deaths, in the 35–69 age range. One in three deaths of 35–69-year-old males in the USA during the 1970s and 1980s are explained by smoking, according to the Oxford researchers. Almost half of all male deaths in Britain in the same age group between the mid-1960s and mid-1970s are attributed to smoking. The proportions for women peaked later. For both genders, the share of deaths explained by smoking was waning by the end of the twentieth century (Peto et al. 2006, 500, 512).

Smoking caused millions of premature deaths. Smoking also led to a net reduction in economic output when middle-aged workers died or became less efficient at their jobs because of worsening health. Many smokers required lengthy and expensive courses of medical treatment. One early study concluded that the net cost to the US economy from mortality and illness caused by smoking, including medical costs, was $5.3 billion in 1966 (Hedrick 1971), a figure that, like Bogart's estimate of the cost of the First World War, is almost certainly wrong, but nonetheless provides a useful early indicator of the severity of the issue. In the context of proposals for tighter restrictions on tobacco, the US Treasury calculated in 1998 that the annual cost to the economy of smoking was at least $130 billion, comprising medical spending, costs attributed to smoking during pregnancy, lost output from shortened working lives and unnecessary fires. The total would have doubled or more with the inclusion of other harder-to-measure costs, such as reduced productivity and the present value placed by victims on future years lost (US Treasury 1998; Viscusi and Hersch 2008). By any calculation, however, the amount was very large.

Depending on the healthcare system in each country, the financial burden of treating and caring for smokers falls primarily on the patient and their family and insurers, or the government and the taxpayer. Taking into account the large flows of revenue from tobacco products, the fiscal burden was sustainable, even for a country such as Britain in which the government was the dominant supplier of health services. The annual cost to the UK National Health Service of treating smokers was £5.2 billion (5.5 per cent of NHS spending) in 2005–06, a sum three times as high as previously estimated (Allender et al. 2009). However, the British government also collected £9.8 billion in excise duty and value added tax on tobacco, and in crude terms still profited from the smoking disaster (Tobacco Manufacturers' Association n.d.). It is sometimes argued that the average smoker, who may die early, is less of a drain on health resources than the average non-smoker (or ex-smoker) who may linger into their eighties or nineties, but the evidence is mixed, and research from Denmark suggests that smokers actually consume more health resources over a lifetime (Rasmussen et al. 2004). What matters most is the opportunity cost of treating smokers: other things being equal, the greater the medical resources devoted to treating smokers, the less are available for treating non-smokers. It should also be borne in mind that smoking generates negative externalities for non-smokers. The health risks of passive smoking became another issue for researchers and the public in the 1980s and 1990s. Measuring the social costs of passive smoking proved extremely difficult (Doll 1998, 110–11; Gruber 2001, 203).

Against the costs of smoking must be set the satisfaction or consumer surplus enjoyed by smokers from using tobacco. Some economists argue that the behaviour of people who appear to be 'addicts' is calculated or rational. Nicotine addiction, they claim, is a choice that can be reversed if smokers have a big enough incentive to give up. They will continue to smoke if perceived benefits exceed costs (Becker and Murphy 1988). But the extent to which people – young persons in particular – really understand the risks of tobacco use is debatable. If their understanding is inadequate then they may not be able to make a rational choice (Slovic 2001).

Tobacco growers and tobacco manufacturers, their employees and their shareholders, also derive certain benefits from smoking. On the other hand, the factors of production employed in the tobacco industry could be reallocated to other industries where they might be equally productive. Some developing countries, including Malawi, became dependent on tobacco growing for export earnings in the twentieth century. But tobacco cultivation degraded the quality of the land, and Malawi could have gained from switching to other crops (Tobin and Knausenberger 1998). The argument that the government depends on revenue from tobacco taxes overlooks the fact that there are alternative sources of tax revenue, at least in developed countries.

Although the rational addiction argument deserves to be taken seriously, it remains the case that millions of people around the world have died prematurely from the effects of tobacco smoking, and that is sufficient to make smoking a disaster from the perspective of this volume.

RESCUE AND RELIEF

Smoking is a cause of many types of cancer, as well as of heart disease, ulcers, diabetes and other serious health problems. The strongest link, however, is with lung cancer, where smoking is responsible for about four in five cases. Lung cancer survival rates have been low. The medical profession in the 1970s still had 'a tremendous nihilism about the treatment of lung cancer', and even in the early twenty-first century between 80 and 90 per cent of lung cancer patients died of the disease (Comis 2003, 230).

In the 1950s and 1960s, when the nexus between tobacco and cancer was becoming apparent, and the number of smoking-related cancer cases (not just lung cancer) was rising strongly, the outlook for sufferers was poor indeed. Surgery and radiotherapy, the main treatments available, were not very successful. David Monahan, a cancer specialist at Bridgeport Hospital in Connecticut, described as follows the treatment of lung cancer patients between 1947 and 1956:

> The [post-surgery] care of these patients, and of those clinically inoperable, in the six months to a year most of them had of remaining life, was directed to making them as comfortable as possible. Many were surprisingly free of disabling symptoms for a considerable period, while others suffered agonizing pain from metastasis and vertebral involvement, which frequently resulted in spinal cord paralysis. X-ray treatment occasionally relieved pain. (Monahan 1957, 584)

The painful nature, expense[4] and ineffectiveness of medically approved cancer treatment in the mid-twentieth century led many desperate patients to seek cures from alternative practitioners. Harry M. Hoxsey treated cancer patients with mysterious tablets. The US medical profession and government officials regarded Hoxsey as a quack and did their best to discredit him. Yet Hoxsey remained popular because he offered his patients hope, albeit false (Cantor 2006). Able surgeons like Dr Monahan of Bridgeport struggled to offer their patients even that much with the crude techniques available in the 1950s.

Methods of surgery and radiotherapy improved considerably between the 1960s and the early twenty-first century, as did techniques for the control of pain. Cancer research was accorded a higher priority by funders in the public and private sectors, and in 1971 the US government launched the 'war on cancer'. The 1970s saw the advent of chemotherapy, an approach that in its earliest days owed something to experience with mustard gas, a chemical warfare agent. Chemotherapy could be used to treat a range of cancers, including lung cancer. Some patients were given a combination of all three main approaches: surgery, radiotherapy and chemotherapy (Verellen et al. 2008; DeVita and Chu 2008).

The sooner cancer can be identified, the better are the prospects for effective treatment. More resources were devoted to early detection in the late twentieth century. Even so, less than 20 per cent of patients diagnosed with lung cancer in the early twenty-first century survived for five or more years. At the end of a review of improvements in cancer treatments between 1970 and 2003, Robert Comis (2003, 233) of the Coalition of National Cancer Cooperative Groups remarked that: 'And, obviously, we would not have this problem if cigarette smoking were to end.' Palliative care plays a crucial role in the relief of many patients. The modern hospice movement, which was pioneered by Dame Cicely Saunders in 1967, sought to provide pain relief and psychological support to terminally ill patients, including those suffering from cancer, as either inpatients or outpatients. By the start of the twenty-first century there were more than 7000 hospices and hospice-like units attached to hospitals around the world (Milićević 2002).

One form of relief that was unavailable for many years was compensation for loss of health from the tobacco companies. As the next section shows, the cigarette producers were adept at avoiding legal, if not moral, blame for their actions.

ALLOCATING BLAME

The purpose in this section is not to convict wrongdoers, but rather to explore how blame for the smoking catastrophe has been debated since the 1950s. The strategy of the tobacco industry from the mid-1950s onwards was for tobacco companies to deny that there was anything dangerous about their products. When that position became untenable, they argued that the decision to smoke was a matter of individual choice, to be made in the light of available information (Courtwright 2005). In some respects the presence or absence of blame is a legal matter, but in others it is decided by public opinion. In the case of tobacco, the courts were harder to convince than a large segment of public opinion.

Between the publication of the Surgeon General's report in 1964 and the end of the twentieth century public opinion turned against tobacco and the tobacco industry. The medical side of the argument against smoking was much stronger than it had been during the battles of the Progressive Era at the start of the twentieth century. Attempts by the tobacco industry to recruit teenage smokers attracted particularly sharp criticism. In 1984 the *New York Times* reported on the 'growing militancy of the nation's nonsmokers', and noted that in San Francisco anti-smoking lobbyists were 'Telling the Tobacco Industry to Butt Out' (Brody 1984). Wanda Siu (2009) shows how the tone of reporting on the tobacco industry in the *New York Times* became more critical in the interval between the Surgeon General's report in 1964 and the trial of tobacco manufacturers for consumer fraud and conspiracy in Minnesota in 1998. By contrast, the *Wall Street Journal*, a more specialist newspaper, continued to defend the tobacco industry, taking the viewpoint of investors rather than of the public.

The leak in 1994 of the so-called 'Cigarette Papers' was a major event in the process by which the big tobacco firms became wholly discredited in the eyes of the public. A box containing documents, dated from the 1950s onwards, belonging to the Brown & Williamson tobacco company, was sent to Stanton Glantz, a professor of medicine and anti-smoking campaigner at the University of California San Francisco. The documents showed that Brown & Williamson, a subsidiary of British American Tobacco, had known as soon as the 1950s and early 1960s that tobacco was dangerous, but continued to assure smokers that there was nothing to fear (Glantz et al. 1996). In the early twenty-first century, the tobacco industry's tactic of casting doubt on scientific evidence was portrayed as a template for the opponents of the global warming thesis. The tobacco companies and their scientific advisors were modern 'merchants of doubt', an allusion to the debate over 'merchants of death' in the arms trade in the interwar period (Oreskes and Conway 2011).

Legally, it was much harder to pin the blame for the health costs of smoking on the tobacco industry. US tobacco companies defended themselves vigorously, and successfully, against plaintiffs who, beginning in 1954, argued that they should be compensated for illness caused by smoking. It was very difficult to prove that a particular individual's lung cancer was the result of smoking cigarettes and not of something else. The Surgeon General's report, and the warnings placed on cigarette packets from 1966, permitted the tobacco manufacturers to contend that smokers knew exactly what they were doing and accepted the risks. Tobacco manufacturers could count on being able to outspend and therefore outgun their challengers in court. The legal tide started to turn after 1995. Plaintiffs began to pool their limited resources in order to compete with the tobacco industry's star lawyers in class actions. Release of the 'Cigarette Papers' equipped plaintiffs with an impressive new supply of ammunition. The industry began to incur significant defeats, but nearly always managed to secure the reversal of adverse judgments on appeal (Sirabionian 2005). For example, *Engle vs R.J. Reynolds* was a large class action in Florida that started in 1994. Howard Engle, the named plaintiff, was an elderly doctor who had smoked since his student days. The class was awarded punitive damages of $144.8 billion in 2000, although the decision was overturned on appeal. Engle did, however, receive a payment from the tobacco companies from a fund they had set up during the appeal process (Weber 2009). Juries were more sympathetic towards plaintiffs than the judges who ruled on appeals.

In 1998 the industry suffered a permanent reverse, when the four biggest US tobacco companies signed an out-of-court Master Settlement Agreement (MSA) with 46 states that had sued them to recover Medicaid expenditure. The MSA cost the tobacco industry $206 billion, which was to be paid in instalments over 26 years, and put another swathe of embarrassing historical documents into the public domain. Separate agreements were reached with other states (Woods 2006). The MSA was in effect a reparations agreement, comparable to that imposed on Germany after 1918. Unlike the Weimar Republic, however, the US tobacco industry had a reliable stream of revenue that facilitated payment. US manufacturers began to lose cases more frequently in the early twenty-first century (Alderman and Daynard 2006). In many other countries, however, the obstacles facing smokers who wished to use the courts to win compensation from manufacturers were even greater. In Britain, for example, there was no tradition of punitive judgments and class actions were considered unusual (Sirabionian 2005).

The tobacco industry did not meekly accept blame for the smoking disaster. Before the early 1950s tobacco companies were not to know that smoking was dangerous. After the early 1960s it could be argued that new adult smokers ought to have been aware of the risk. The murkiest period was the intervening few years. Public opinion was increasingly of the view that smoking was the fault of the big tobacco firms and not of the smoker, but it proved extremely difficult to make that charge stick in the courts.

RECOVERY AND RECONSTRUCTION

As discussed above, the probability that an individual will recover from lung cancer is low. Giving up tobacco, however, improves the odds of avoiding a serious smoking-related disease in the first place. Determination, support from others and in some cases nicotine replacement therapies (NRTs) are also required by those ceasing smoking. Various NRTs, including gum, patches and sprays, came on the market in the late twentieth century, starting with Nicorette in 1978. The e-cigarette was invented in China in 2003 and distributed commercially from 2006. Although NRTs contain nicotine, they are supposed to help smokers overcome their dependency or addiction. Most importantly, NRTs are free of the carcinogens produced when tobacco is burned (Bell and Keane 2012), but they remain controversial in some jurisdictions.

The extent of recovery from smoking is best measured at the national rather than the individual level. Smoking became less popular in the developed world in the late twentieth century. Tobacco consumption per adult in the USA peaked at 13.8 grams per day in 1963; thereafter consumption per capita declined slowly until 1980, and then dropped more rapidly, reaching 4.6 grams in 2010. The proportion of adult American men (18 years and above) who smoked cigarettes fell from 52 per cent in 1965 to 24 per cent in 2003, and of adult women from 34 per cent to 19 per cent over the same period (Forey et al. 2012b, 14–15, 18, 19, 26, 27). In Britain, the decline in tobacco consumption per adult started earlier, falling from 8.5 grams per day in 1960 to 3.1 grams in 2009. Cigarette consumption per adult peaked in 1973 and 1974. The proportion of adult British men (16 years and above) who smoked cigarettes fell from 61 per cent in 1960 to 25 per cent in 2005, and of adult women from 45 per cent in 1966 to 23 per cent in 2005 (Forey et al. 2012a, 16, 20, 21, 32, 33).

Why did smoking dwindle in popularity, thereby enabling the USA and Britain to recover, at least partially, from the tobacco disaster?

Policies that at first glance might appear to come under the heading of 'mitigation and regulatory change' were in fact 'recovery' measures. Once the tipping point was reached in the mid-1960s, government agencies in the USA at both state and federal levels, as well as agencies in many other countries, employed a combination of higher taxes, tighter regulation, and education and propaganda to combat tobacco use (Novotny and Mamudu 2008). In the USA and in Britain the official attitude towards smoking hardened in the final third of the twentieth century. The anti-tobacco lobby and the medical profession succeeded in portraying smoking as an addiction or illness rather than a personal choice. They stressed the dangers of passive smoking (not least to babies and children) and pointed out that smoking imposed a large cost on society. Encouraging young people to take up smoking was branded as immoral. As Christopher Bailey (2004, 54) explains, smoking was reframed 'as a social hygiene issue similar to campaigns to eradicate infectious diseases and not a matter of personal behaviour'.

Potentially the most effective tool in the war on tobacco is taxation. The price elasticity of demand for tobacco is low in developed nations, meaning that a relatively large price increase is necessary to persuade consumers to buy less of the product. Even so, the relationship between price and quantity demanded is robust. In the USA in the 1990s, a 10 per cent rise in the price of cigarettes was required to achieve a 4 per cent reduction in quantity demanded, giving a price elasticity of 0.4 (Jha and Chaloupka 1999, 41). In Europe, the price elasticity of demand for local brand cigarettes is estimated to have been 0.46 in 2000 (Gallus et al. 2006). Whether a change in tax results in an equivalent change in price depends on market conditions, but tax and price are almost certain to move in the same direction. The impact of higher cigarette taxes – set in cents per pack – in the USA was negated in the 1970s by high inflation. In the 1980s and 1990s, however, excise tax per pack rose more sharply and outpaced inflation; there was now a real and not just a nominal tax increase. US tobacco manufacturers used their market power, derived from inelastic demand and an oligopolistic industrial structure, to raise cigarette prices even faster than tax rates in the 1980s and 1990s, thus adding to their profits (Gruber 2001, 195–8). The 1980s and 1990s were decades in which smoking was falling out of fashion, except amongst the young and the poor. By magnifying the tax hikes, cigarette producers demonstrated that in the home market they were content to make larger profits from fewer customers. As a proportion of the price of cigarettes, tobacco taxes in Europe – and in Britain in particular – were higher than those in the USA in the early twenty-first century (Eriksen et al. 2012, 80).

Supplementary recovery measures included restrictions and educational programmes. The Cigarette Labeling and Advertising Act 1965 required cigarette packets in the USA to carry health warnings, albeit of a rather mild nature. Under the Public Health Cigarette Smoking Act 1969 cigarette advertising on television and radio became illegal in the USA. Tobacco companies took a great interest in the debate over smoking regulation, and lobbied, often successfully, to be given enough freedom to run a profitable business. Laws against smoking by young people were tightened in the 1990s. States also used their powers to deter smoking, by imposing additional state taxes and proclaiming smoking bans in public places. Restrictions on tobacco advertising and tobacco use on public transport and in the workplace were increased step by step until in some jurisdictions smokers were evicted from bars (Jacobson et al. 1997). Anti-smoking public education or propaganda campaigns were conducted in many states. California linked cigarette taxes and public education under Proposition 99 in 1988: tax per pack was raised from ten cents to 35 cents, and 20 per cent of the extra revenue collected was spent on anti-smoking education and media campaigns (Hu et al. 1995). A similar path of regulation was followed within the European Union (EU), albeit with considerable variation from country to country. Britain was one of the strictest EU members in the areas of tobacco taxation and control. Germany, by contrast, was one of the most tolerant towards smokers, a stance that may have reflected the lingering association between smoking restrictions and the authoritarianism of the 1930s and 1940s (Clancy 2009).

Taxation and regulation reinforced the message that smoking was dangerous and costly, not only to individual smokers but also to others. Although it is probable that tobacco consumption would have declined in the late twentieth century without any government intervention, particularly amongst the better educated, there can be little doubt that higher taxes, combined with tighter regulation and anti-smoking propaganda, accelerated the process.

MITIGATION AND REGULATORY CHANGE

Tobacco smoking is unlikely to regain popularity in developed countries such as the USA and the UK. What, then, is there to be said in relation to mitigation and regulatory change? There are two points to be made. Firstly, the focal point of the tobacco disaster has shifted to the developing world, where cigarettes are still treated as a cheap luxury good by people with low but rising living standards. Agencies such as the

World Health Organization (WHO) and medical professionals in the developing world are anxious to counter this trend. Secondly, experience with tobacco may provide regulators with a template when confronting other public health disasters, whether real or imagined.

As cigarette consumption per capita dropped in the developed world, the prevalence of smoking, especially amongst men, surged in developing nations. Rising prosperity was not the only factor at work in the spread of the smoking 'epidemic'. Trade liberalization exposed consumers in many developing countries to new imported tobacco products (Jha and Chaloupka 1999, 13–15). Tobacco multinationals, such as British American Tobacco in sub-Saharan Africa, devised marketing strategies to persuade young people to take up smoking, for example by sponsoring pop concerts (Patel et al. 2009). Promotional techniques used in Africa were influenced by experience in Western Europe and North America, even though they were no longer acceptable in those regions.

During the mid-1990s the WHO began to work towards an international agreement that would commit participants, including countries in the developing world, to controlling the tobacco epidemic through taxation, regulation, public education, and the conversion of land from tobacco cultivation to the growing of other crops. The World Bank had ceased providing loans to encourage tobacco farming in developing countries in 1992. Major international tobacco corporations did their best to resist and dilute the WHO proposals, just as global banks strove to influence the rules for international banking supervision and capital adequacy under the Basel process. Nevertheless, 168 countries (not including the USA) ratified the Framework Convention on Tobacco Control (FCTC). The Convention came into force in 2005. Many parties to the Convention were developing countries. The FCTC was designed to provide a global forum for governments and NGOs to debate tobacco control. Although the signatories could not be compelled to introduce tighter controls on tobacco, they were under strong moral pressure to follow up their commitments with actions. Governments without an efficient income tax system could achieve an immediate revenue boost by imposing higher taxes on cigarettes, although if taxes were raised too far they risked pushing sales underground. For the tobacco companies, the enactment of the FCTC was not the end of the story, and they continued to put pressure on governments in the developing world to look after their interests (WHO 2009; Ramin 2006; Novotny and Mamudu 2008). Developing countries progressed along the path of tobacco control at different speeds, and the regulations that were introduced were not always enforced (Sussman et al. 2007). Even so, the intention of the

FCTC and its supporters was to contain the epidemic at an earlier stage than it had been in the West; in other words, to mitigate disaster and save life.

Tobacco control could provide a template for policy makers concerned with mitigating other potential public health disasters, as the WHO (2009, 35) acknowledged:

> The Framework Convention provides a new approach to international health cooperation, with a legal framework to shape the future of health for all people. It provides a model for a powerful, effective global response to the negative effects of globalization on health with potentially other similar applications in public health.

It is conceivable that obesity will be the next global public health problem to be amenable to the sorts of measures used in tobacco control. Sugar-filled drinks and fat-filled convenience foods are contributing to the rise in obesity and associated health problems such as diabetes. Obesity is now being reframed as a threat to public health rather than a matter of individual choice. In the early years of the twenty-first century, the healthcare costs resulting from obesity in the USA may have amounted to $147 billion per year. According to Jonathan Klein and William Dietz (2010, 388), experts in paediatrics and nutrition, respectively: 'Overcoming the childhood obesity epidemic will require changes on the scale of a social movement similar to the shifts in attitudes and regulations toward smoking and tobacco.' Progress in the war against smoking was underpinned by the identification of a common enemy in the tobacco manufacturers. A new common enemy must be identified, Klein and Dietz argue, if the public is to be united behind the struggle to overcome obesity. Producers of obesity-inducing beverages and foodstuffs may face a rising tide of litigation and regulation similar to that faced by the tobacco industry (Alderman and Daynard 2006). Taxing sugary drinks and fast foods, banning them from public places such as schools, and prohibiting their advertisement are amongst the options. If the history of tobacco offers a reliable guide, those options will be exercised with increasing vigour.

CONCLUSION

Smoking is not so different from the other disasters considered in this book, except in the sense that it unfolded over a much longer period of time. In the case of smoking it took half a century for professionals to recognize that something was wrong, and that tobacco was killing thousands every year, especially from lung cancer. It took another decade and a half, until around the mid-1960s, for governments to react by introducing anti-smoking measures (higher taxes and more regulation) and for consumers to start thinking about changing their behaviour. For smokers, including many doctors, it was necessary to weigh the possible health risks of smoking against the immediate pleasure that it gave. Tobacco was a significant revenue source for governments, one that they were anxious not to undermine. Moreover, the pro-tobacco lobby was powerful, and for some time succeeded in casting doubt on the evidence that smoking was dangerous. Governments and consumers felt that they could afford to linger over the processes of sensemaking and decision making; most smokers were not going to drop dead immediately. In the late twentieth century, smoking was increasingly framed as an epidemic. Although that epidemic was on the wane in the developed world, it was spreading rapidly to the developing world. Efforts were made, not least through the WHO, to mitigate such contagion. It was also recognized that the lessons of smoking could be applied to the mitigation of other emerging public health concerns in developed countries.

NOTES

1. Figures for each country include all types of tobacco. Women, however, only smoked cigarettes.
2. Doll (1998, 99) claimed that Hammond told him that the Cancer Society had hoped to find no such relationship.
3. Emphasis in the original.
4. Note that patients of the British NHS did not have to pay for treatment.

7. The twin financial disasters of the early twenty-first century

Why did nobody notice it?
(Queen Elizabeth II,
November 2008)

On a visit to the London School of Economics in November 2008, Queen Elizabeth II expressed her perplexity over the failure of economists and market participants to predict the recent financial collapse. The Queen, it should be added, was not a disinterested observer. The crash is estimated to have reduced the value of her £100 million investment portfolio by 25 per cent (Pierce 2008). The period beginning in 2007 saw two inter-related financial disasters, both of which had large macroeconomic consequences. Whereas the first of these disasters, commonly known as the Global Financial Crisis (GFC), was largely an Anglo-American affair, the second was based in the Eurozone. The Anglo-American disaster of 2007–09 punished those European financial institutions that had dabbled in the US bubble, destabilized the Eurozone more generally, and sparked a global economic contraction and credit crunch. American and British policy makers were more successful than their Eurozone counterparts at making sense of the situation and finding remedies. Eurozone policy makers were hampered, both intellectually and practically, by their commitment to monetary union, just as their unfortunate predecessors had been by the Gold Standard in the early 1930s.

The twin financial disasters of the early twenty-first century prompted numerous comparisons with the early 1930s (Eichengreen 2012; 2015; Eichengreen and Temin 2010; O'Rourke and Taylor 2013; de Bromhead et al. 2013). Furthermore, Ben Bernanke, the Chairman of the Federal Reserve Board between 2006 and 2014, was steeped in the lessons of the 1930s. An academic economist for the bulk of his career, Bernanke was a leading authority on the financial aspects of the depression in the USA (Bernanke 2000). Once the extent of the danger became evident in 2008–09, he was determined not to repeat the Federal Reserve's policy errors of the early 1930s. This chapter begins by examining the Anglo-American disaster of 2007–09, and continues by investigating the

Eurozone disaster that began in 2010 and, at the time of writing in 2015, persists. We cannot escape the phrase 'Global Financial Crisis' altogether because it is in common use, but 'Global Financial Disaster' would be a more accurate description.

THE ANGLO-AMERICAN FINANCIAL DISASTER

The Anglo-American disaster is easier to explain than the Eurozone disaster. As the Minsky–Kindleberger cycle predicts, a period marked by growing euphoria and systematic underestimation of risk will eventually give way to panic when the truth dawns that paper wealth is built on insecure foundations (Kindleberger and Aliber 2011). In fact, policy makers exacerbated the upswing in the early years of the twenty-first century, by suppressing interest rates and encouraging financial institutions to lend freely to uncreditworthy persons in order to boost home ownership for political reasons.

Mitigation and Regulatory Change

At the start of the twenty-first century the conventional view was that financial instability should be mitigated by light-handed prudential supervision rather than heavy-handed banking regulation, within a macroeconomic policy framework in which central bank independence (CBI) and inflation targeting took pride of place.

The period between 1945 and 1970 was distinguished by the absence of systemic banking collapses or macroeconomic disasters in the developed world, although there was some instability in exchange rates (Bordo et al. 2001). By the late 1960s, many economists, bankers and policy makers were convinced that the banking and financial regulations imposed in the 1930s and 1940s were no longer necessary, and that their removal would encourage competition and innovation. Larger banks and financial sector firms, not least in the USA, the UK and West Germany, expected to benefit from liberalization and regain market share from smaller competitors. Financial liberalization began in the USA and West Germany and spread to Britain and other developed and developing countries. Controls over the interest rates advertised by banks were lifted. Restrictions on the volume and direction of bank lending were removed. The barriers between different financial activities, such as commercial and investment banking, were relaxed. International banking had been growing since the early 1960s, driven by the development of the eurodollar markets, especially in London where the authorities took a liberal view of activities that did not involve sterling. After the demise of the Bretton Woods system of pegged exchange rates in 1971–73, the need for tight restrictions over international capital flows diminished. Controls over the activities of multinational banks and financial institutions became much less onerous (Abiad and Mody 2005; Kaminsky and Schmukler 2008; Abiad et al. 2010). The retreat of the US financial authorities from the regulatory ethos of the mid-twentieth century culminated in the Gramm–Leach–Bliley Act 1999, which effectively repealed Glass–Steagall's separation of commercial from investment banking (Barth et al. 2000). But there was no relaxation in the sphere of depositor protection. Indeed the number of countries with explicit deposit insurance schemes grew during the final third of the twentieth century (Demirgüç-Kunt and Sobaci 2001).

But it would be inaccurate to describe the late twentieth century as an era of unalloyed financial deregulation. Governments and central banks accepted that some form of oversight of financial institutions was still required. Under a new approach, dubbed prudential supervision, banks and other financial institutions were expected to maintain various prudential ratios, the most important of which was the ratio of capital to risk-weighted assets. Compliance was checked by on-site inspection or the analysis of financial information submitted confidentially or published by banks. Prudential supervision was deemed necessary at both the national and international levels. In the mid-1970s, the lack of coordination between bank supervisors sometimes resulted in the failure of a bank in one country destabilizing financial markets in others. Closure of the Bankhaus Herstatt by West German regulators in 1974 caused a period of turmoil in New York money markets because of uncompleted payments. The threat posed to global financial stability by contagion was addressed by the 'Basel group' of central bankers and supervisors. Under the Basel Concordat of 1975 agencies in different countries agreed to cooperate in the supervision of internationally active banks. The first Basel Accord of 1986 (Basel I) specified a minimum level of capital to risk-adjusted assets for internationally active banks. Basel II, signed in 2004, was more sophisticated, and allowed the biggest banks to calculate their own capital requirements. The Concordat and Accords set benchmarks, and it was left to each country to decide how they should be implemented. Large banks were able to influence both the content of the Accords and their application. Prudential supervision did not extend to 'shadow banks', such as investment banks and hedge funds, that operated on the fringes of the main banking industry. Even so, the supporters of the Basel process, including the world's leading central banks, believed that the new regime was a force for stability (Singleton 2011, 227–40; Wood 2005; Lastra 1996). When put to the test in 2007–09 it proved to be of limited value.

Most experts in the 1990s and early 2000s insisted that CBI and sound monetary policy were the ultimate keys to financial and macroeconomic stability. High and variable levels of inflation in developed (as well as developing) countries, from the late 1960s through to the 1980s, were perceived by policy makers and academic economists to be the main threat to prosperity and economic security. Inflation was attributed to political manipulation of monetary policy for short-term advantage. West Germany, whose central bank, the Bundesbank, was designed in a way that limited the scope for political interference, enjoyed relatively low inflation rates, and was widely admired for that reason. Beginning with New Zealand in 1989, many other countries decided to grant their central banks greater independence. At the same time – and also starting in New Zealand – there was a movement towards the adoption of inflation targeting as a monetary policy framework. Under inflation targeting, price stability became the overriding objective of the central bank. Inflation had been a source of economic disruption and uncertainty, and if it could be squeezed out of the system the risks of a financial or macroeconomic crash would be reduced, or so it was believed. Even those countries, including the USA, that did not formally commit themselves to CBI and inflation targeting, permitted their central banks to operate as if they did (Singleton 2011, 204–21, 241–58; Siklos 2002; Singleton et al. 2006).

The classic 1990s recipe of CBI, inflation targeting and light-handed prudential supervision was assumed to underpin financial innovation and efficiency as well as stability. A false sense of security was generated, one that in the run up to the retirement of Alan Greenspan as Chairman of the Federal Reserve in 2006 sometimes descended into triumphalism (Kahn 2005; Calomiris 2006).

Warnings

Barry Eichengreen (2015, 3–4) remarks that although the lessons of the interwar era were influential between 2007 and 2009, they had been ignored by policy makers and other economic actors in the years of feverish activity before the crash. The global financial system had been on a bumpy ride over the previous two decades, and no country with open financial markets was immune. Yet the mood in the USA and other Western economies was increasingly euphoric, not least because of Greenspan's remarkable record of averting disaster when it threatened to engulf the American financial system.

Financial liberalization did not go smoothly in the late twentieth century. Scandinavia, Japan, Mexico, Argentina, Russia and East Asia all experienced financial disasters of one sort or another with attendant social and fiscal costs. For example, the 'Asian crisis' of 1997–98 began when the Thai baht plummeted in the foreign exchange market. Panic spread to neighbouring countries, causing bank failures, severe falls in equity and property prices, a credit crunch and a sharp recession (Noble and Ravenhill 2000). More generally, liberalization exposed banks and other financial institutions to competition for the first time in decades, and many were unable to adjust. There was often a period of credit expansion, lasting a few years, during which inadequately trained banking personnel made ill-considered lending decisions. After the inevitable crash, surviving banks at last achieved the efficiency improvements that liberalization was intended to deliver (Kaminsky and Schmukler 2008).

Not even the most sophisticated financial systems escaped undamaged. Britain experienced a 'secondary banking crisis' in the mid-1970s, whilst the USA suffered the savings and loan debacle in the 1980s (Capie 2010, 524–86; Mayer 1990). Several potential economic disasters were defused by Greenspan, including the stock market crash of 1987, the failure of the hedge fund Long Term Capital Management in 1998, and the dotcom crash in 2000–2001. Greenspan always saved the day by flooding the market with liquidity or organizing a last-minute rescue operation. Well-timed interventions – brilliant crisis management – earned Greenspan a reputation for financial wizardry (Singleton 2011, 24–5). In some respects, however, he was fuelling an even larger bubble. By offering an implicit guarantee that the central bank would always step in to defuse market turmoil, Greenspan encouraged rather than deterred excessive risk-taking. In other words he stoked moral hazard. Fearing a deep recession in the wake of the dotcom crash, moreover, Greenspan kept interest rates down for much longer than was justifiable on the basis of the Taylor rule, the standard approach to interest rate setting that takes into account inflationary pressure and spare capacity (Taylor 2009). Cheap credit after 2000 was fuelled not only by the Federal Reserve's accommodating monetary policy, but also by large inflows of savings from China and other Asian countries, loose financial regulation, the introduction of new financial products derived from the property market, and government encouragement of home ownership. US monetary policy was at length tightened in 2004, and the housing market began to cool, but few expected a cataclysmic crash (Rajan 2010).

Mathematical models developed in the 1990s and 2000s to assess risk in financial markets, including those derived from housing mortgages, proved to be seriously flawed. Modellers and model users assumed that they were operating in a world in which house prices would never fall. No allowance was made for a sudden, catastrophic change of fortune.

Financial products such as asset-backed securities, collateralized debt obligations and credit default swaps, which were designed and priced using those models, were not as safe as they appeared to be (Dowd and Hutchinson 2010, 65–135). Warnings of impending disaster simply could not be generated within such an intellectual framework.

Euphoria over Greenspan's achievements in the USA was accompanied by a degree of complacency in Western Europe. In April 2007, the Bank of England, which would soon witness the UK's worst ever banking collapse, assessed the risks to financial stability as follows:

> The UK financial system remains highly resilient. But strong and stable macroeconomic and financial conditions have encouraged financial institutions to expand further their business activities and to extend their risk-taking ... That has increased the vulnerability of the system as a whole to an abrupt change in conditions. ... [Nevertheless the] operating environment for UK banks and global financial institutions has remained stable over much of the period since the July 2006 [*Financial Stability*] *Report*. Conditions are likely to remain favourable. (Bank of England 2007, 5)

The most important note of caution, although by no means a prediction of doom, came from the Bank for International Settlements (BIS) in Basel in June 2007. Credit was expanding rapidly on both sides of the Atlantic. Although the consensus forecast for the world economy and financial system remained positive, there were uncertainties, not least in relation to asset markets (housing and financial securities), which appeared fully priced. Turning points, noted the BIS, are always hard to anticipate:

> [V]irtually no one foresaw the Great Depression of the 1930s, or the crises which affected Japan and Southeast Asia in the early and late 1990s, respectively. In fact, each downturn was preceded by a period of non-inflationary growth exuberant enough to lead many commentators to suggest that a 'new era' had arrived. (Bank for International Settlements 2007, 139)

It was difficult for anyone, whether a central banker, an academic economist or the chief executive of a major financial institution, to step off the escalator of euphoria and question whether the good times would last. And when the escalator reached the top everyone was thrown off into the abyss.

The Triggering Event

During the course of any disaster, decision makers will be confronted with a series of events that pose a challenge of one sort or another. The collapse of the US shadow bank Lehman Brothers, on 15 September 2008, generated panic and confusion both domestically and internationally, and was perhaps the single most dramatic moment of the Anglo-American financial disaster. Nonetheless, Lehman Brothers did not initiate the critical period, which had in fact started more than a year before. According to the BIS, the triggering event may be dated with precision:

> The simmering turmoil in financial markets came to the boil on 9 August 2007. On that day, a number of central banks felt compelled to take extraordinary measures in an attempt to restore order in the interbank market. The disorder was triggered by a freeze on redemptions from a small number of funds that had invested in structured finance products backed by US subprime mortgages of recent vintage. (Bank for International Settlements 2008, 3)

Financial market participants panicked in the summer of 2007, realising belatedly that the value of securities derived from subprime mortgages was unknowable in a period of declining property prices and rising mortgage defaults. This was the Minsky moment. It was obvious that some banks and other financial institutions must have sustained huge losses, but in view of the complexity of the derivatives involved, and their distribution all over the world, it was impossible to know which institutions were at risk of insolvency. The safest thing for any bank to do in such a situation was to stop lending to any of its peers, a decision akin to cutting off the blood supply to the financial system. When banks and shadow banks are no longer able to borrow from one another, they might not be able to meet their obligations to depositors and other creditors; the payments system could cease to function; and economic activity around the world could face severe disruption. Carmen Reinhart and Kenneth Rogoff (2009, 208) are not quite as precise in their dating of the triggering event, but they concur with the BIS that, 'By mid-2007, a sharp rise in default rates on low-income housing mortgages in the United States eventually sparked a full-blown global financial panic.'

Sensemaking and Decision Making

The severity of the threat to the global economy was not immediately obvious in the summer of 2007. Perhaps the injection of additional liquidity would succeed in calming financial markets, enabling a speedy return to normality. The US authorities, especially the Federal Reserve, had a reputation for quelling episodes of instability before they turned into financial and macroeconomic disaster. But instead of stabilizing, the situation worsened on both sides of the Atlantic.

In September 2007, Britain faced its first run on a bank for 150 years. Northern Rock was the lender in trouble. A medium-sized bank that specialized in mortgage lending, Northern Rock relied heavily on funds borrowed short-term on wholesale financial markets. Those markets dried up in the summer of 2007, leaving Northern Rock in a desperate position. Fearing that there was no money left, depositors panicked, forcing the authorities to intervene and restore calm (Shin 2009). During 2008, a number of major US financial institutions slid towards the abyss, including the shadow or investment banks Bear Stearns and Lehman Brothers, the insurance company American International Group (AIG), and two large government-sponsored businesses involved in the mortgage market, Fannie Mae and Freddie Mac (Ferguson and Johnson 2009). In Britain, the Northern Rock episode was followed by the revelation of existential threats to two much bigger institutions, namely the Royal Bank of Scotland (RBS) and Halifax Bank of Scotland (HBOS) (Hall 2009). Economic activity in the USA began to fall in the spring of 2008, suggesting that problems in the financial arena were spilling over into the macroeconomy. Parallels with the early 1930s were becoming more compelling.

The most perceptive discussion of sensemaking by US policy makers in the early stages of the GFC is provided by Barry Eichengreen, albeit without actually using that term. Human beings, he argues, are pro-grammed to think analogically. In order to assess the threat facing the economy and select an appropriate response, policy makers in 2007–09 turned to the experience of the 1930s. Although economists are trained to think deductively and inductively, even they fall back on analogical reasoning in an emergency. When there is little time to digest the rapid flow of information, and no theoretical consensus on what should be done, historical precedent can provide a useful short-cut (Eichengreen 2012). Greenspan, for example, persisted with loose monetary policy in 2003 because of an analogy: he imagined that without continued stimulus the USA risked following the example of Japan, which had experienced a decade of lost growth in the 1990s (Greenspan 2008, 228–9).

The analogy that everyone in 2007–09 knew at least something about was the depression of the 1930s. Although the financial crashes of 1873 and 1907 were also relevant, they were much more obscure. Of course, the similarities between the early stages of the depression and the GFC can be taken too far (Bordo 2013). Whereas the stock market was the scene of the opening act of the depression in 1929, the derivatives and wholesale money markets were the starting points in 2007. Nonetheless, the adoption of the depression analogy was both inevitable and useful. The dominant retrospective assessment of US economic policy in the early 1930s emphasizes the passivity of those in power, especially at the Federal Reserve. The policy lesson usually drawn from the work of Milton Friedman and Anna Schwartz (1963) is that in times of peril the authorities must take decisive action to prevent any repetition of the downward spiral of the early 1930s, and that they should do so by cranking up the money supply and acting as an effective lender of last resort. Somewhat more controversial, but equally valuable in the context of 2007–09, was Keynes's message that remedial action by the central bank must be accompanied by expansionary fiscal policy (Keynes 1936; Skidelsky 2010).

Bernanke's knowledge of the 1930s was exceptional, as was that of another economic historian, Christina Romer, who chaired the President's Council of Economic Advisors in 2009–10 (Bernanke 2010; Romer 2009). Few other policy makers in Washington or London had studied the depression in detail. The diagnoses and prescriptions of Friedman and Schwartz and Keynes were easy enough for non-specialists to grasp; the challenge was to apply them creatively in day-to-day decision making. The pressure on elected and appointed officials was acute when faced by the impending failure of an important financial institution such as RBS or Lehman Brothers or AIG. It was doubly awkward that some of the institutions in difficulty were not actually banks, but rather other types of financial firm such as shadow banks or insurance companies. Orthodox lender-of-last-resort doctrine suggested that the central bank should lend freely to the banking system as a whole, but refrain from bailing out individual banks and other types of financial institution. However, there were no hard-and-fast rules in practice. In the past, central banks and governments had often stepped in to prevent the disorderly collapse of an individual bank or other financial institution that was deemed too big or too important to fail (Mishkin and White 2014). Policy makers had to muddle through, taking each case on its merits.

The decision by the Federal Reserve and the Treasury to bail out and then sell Bear Stearns to J.P. Morgan Chase in March 2008 is said to have been taken in an atmosphere of 'religious crisis'. Policy makers struggled to reconcile a pragmatic decision over Bear Stearns with their liberal economic principles (Ferguson and Johnson 2009, 15). Rescues of individual financial firms might be necessary to calm financial markets in the short run, but moral hazard was generated by any demonstration that failure or recklessness would be compensated by the authorities. Bernanke had difficulty justifying the Bear Stearns bailout to other central bankers and academics at the annual Jackson Hole conference in August

2008. Less than a month later, Bernanke and other top policy makers were required to decide the fate of Lehman Brothers and AIG. Lehman Brothers was abandoned to burn, but AIG was saved, choices that proved as controversial as the Bear Stearns rescue. Lehman Brothers was judged expendable on 15 September. The serious impact on international financial markets of Lehman's collapse called into question that judgement (Ferguson and Johnson 2009, 23; Bernanke 2008). The stakes were high, and decisions on the future of individual firms were contestable, but nonetheless American and British policy makers succeeded in averting a catastrophe on the scale of the 1930s.

Meryvn King, the Governor of the Bank of England between 2003 and 2013, interviewed Bernanke on BBC radio in 2014 concerning their experiences as central bankers between 2007 and 2009. Although the GFC had been a time of 'enormous pressure', said King, he had found it 'great fun and fascinating' to work with the Federal Reserve. Bernanke was more circumspect: 2007–09 had not been fun, but rather a 'challenging' period with 'complicated' problems and 'a lot of stress'. There were times when Bernanke had felt like the driver of a car spinning on an icy road and trying to regain control. Those moments had required immense concentration (King 2014).

Policy makers in the USA and the UK were not as confused in 2007–09 as they had been in 1929–31, for they had at their command a persuasive narrative of the role of policy in causing or preventing a depression. Although they were unable to avoid economic disaster, that disaster would have been far worse had they repeated the policy errors of the early 1930s. In short, the Anglo-American response to the threat of a new depression was relatively creative.

The Disaster Unfolds

The years between 2007 and 2009 saw widespread panic on world credit markets. The US subprime sector was not particularly large in itself, but there was great uncertainty over which institutions would ultimately bear the losses derived from subprime mortgages. The credit crunch was severe, with firms and households in many countries finding it difficult or even impossible to borrow. Stock markets crashed, investment spending plummeted, and businesses were forced to lay off workers or shut down.

Barry Eichengreen and Kevin O'Rourke (2010) show that world industrial production fell more rapidly in the year beginning April 2008 than in the year beginning June 1929. The volume of world trade and the level of world equity prices also dropped more steeply during the 2008–09 contraction than at the start of the interwar depression. But signs of recovery were already visible by mid-2009, whereas in the early 1930s the economic situation continued to deteriorate (Eichengreen and O'Rourke 2010; Almunia et al. 2010). Declining tax revenue and higher welfare expenditure worsened the fiscal outlook for most governments in 2008–09. Although some financial institutions collapsed, ordinary depositors were bailed out, albeit at taxpayers' expense. By contrast, depositors were abandoned in the 1930s, intensifying downward pressure on the money supply and economic activity. Overall, the world experienced a financial and economic disaster in 2007–09 that was second only to that of the 1930s.

The real costs of the downturn in 2008 are shown in Figures 7.1 and 7.2. GDP – and GDP per capita – fell in each of the selected countries between 2008 and 2009, typically by between 3 and 6 per cent; thereafter there was a slow recovery in the USA, Germany, France and the UK, but not in Greece, Ireland or Italy, the three distressed Eurozone states depicted. The economic performance of Greece in particular was spectacularly bad. The difficulties of peripheral Eurozone states are addressed

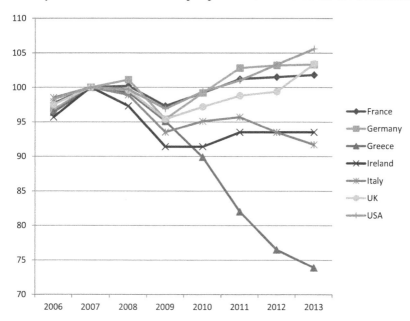

Source: www.stats.oecd.org.

Figure 7.1   *Index of real GDP at purchasing power parity, selected countries, 2006–13 (2007 = 100)*

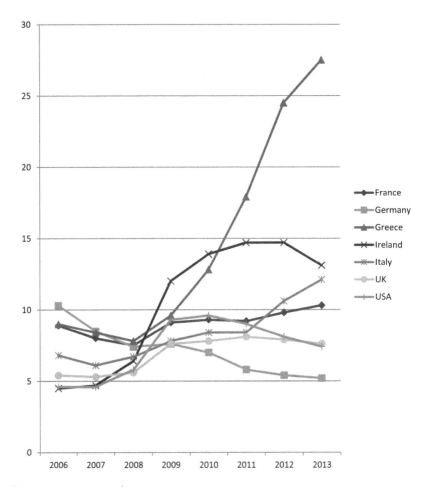

Source: www.stats.oecd.org.

*Figure 7.2   Harmonized unemployment rates (%), selected countries,
              2006–13*

later in the chapter, but it is worth drawing attention here to the stark
contrast between their experience and that of more resilient economies,
including the USA, the UK and Germany. Unemployment rates rose
significantly during the GFC, Germany being an exception to the rule.
Unemployment in Britain and the USA remained below 10 per cent,
however, and started to tail off from 2010. By contrast, the trend in
unemployment in the group of Eurozone countries (excepting Germany)

was resolutely upwards, reaching horrifying proportions especially in Greece. The failure of the Eurozone periphery – which after 2010 extended to Italy – to recover from the initial international downturn constitutes a second disaster. In comparison with the interwar depression, the economic disaster of 2007–09 was relatively mild in the USA and UK, not least because of the radical policy interventions applied by the authorities. The Eurozone disaster, however, has yet to run its course, and for some countries is already far more serious than 2007–09 and verging on the hopelessness of the 1930s. Germany was insulated from events elsewhere in the Eurozone by the competitiveness of its industries and its success in controlling labour costs within the framework of the single currency.

Rescue and Relief

Whereas the response of policy makers during the early stages of the depression was weak and often misdirected, policy makers in 2007–09 reacted with speed and decisiveness. Many (but not all) failing banks and shadow banks were saved, admittedly at huge cost to taxpayers, by means of nationalization either in whole or in part, and/or recapitaliz-ation, or the offer of an inducement to a competitor to effect a takeover. If more big banks and shadow banks had been allowed to cease trading, the payments system would have come under enormous strain. When Lehman Brothers closed in September 2008, the shock to financial confidence was enormous, ushering in the most dangerous period of the GFC. In the short term, individuals and households were cushioned to a greater degree than in the 1930s. Small depositors were assured by the authorities that their savings and transaction accounts would be protected even if their bank failed. Workers thrown out of their jobs had access to far more generous welfare benefits than had been available in the depression. Rising welfare payments acted as an automatic stabilizer, cushioning the fall in aggregate demand. As well as participating in the salvage of individual banks and shadow banks, the Federal Reserve, the Bank of England and some other central banks flooded financial markets with liquidity. They lent liberally and cheaply; short-term interest rates were reduced almost to zero. The classic lender-of-last-resort policy was to lend liberally but at a penalty rate, but in 2007–09 very low interest rates were considered necessary to assist the macroeconomy. Central banks paid less attention than previously to the quality of collateral offered by counterparties. The British and American governments and their central banks undertook breathtakingly large (and controversial) purchases of 'toxic' assets from banks and other financial institutions.

Those assets, and the risks lurking within them, were transferred to the national balance sheet. The Federal Reserve and the Bank of England also accommodated deficit spending by purchasing large amounts of official debt, an option not available within the Eurozone (Mishkin 2011; Reinhart 2011; Hall 2009).

At the international level, there was a greater spirit of cooperation than there had been in the early 1930s. A series of currency swap agreements was negotiated between the Federal Reserve and other central banks. At Washington, in November 2008, the leaders of the G20 group of economically important nations assumed responsibility for responding to the economic crash. At the London meeting of the G20 in April 2009, Gordon Brown, the British Prime Minister, encouraged governments around the world to embark on a coordinated round of fiscal and monetary expansion, and secured agreement to channel $1.1 trillion in new funding through the International Monetary Fund (IMF). Emergency measures were to be accompanied by longer-term reforms overseen by a Financial Stability Board. Some countries were already attempting to reflate their economies. The situation in the Eurozone, however, was more problematical because the structure and rules of the monetary union were so rigid. Nevertheless, Brown's initiative provided further evidence that the downturn would be dealt with differently than the depression in the 1930s (Keegan 2012; London Summit – Leaders' Statement 2009).

Allocating Blame

Writing of the financial and economic disaster of 2007 to 2009, Robert Skidelsky (2010, 22–3) remarks that: 'Whenever anything goes badly wrong our first instinct is to blame those in charge – in this case, bankers, credit agencies, regulators, central bankers and governments.' Banks and bankers were portrayed routinely in the media as either corrupt or incompetent. In *Rolling Stone*, Matt Taibbi (2009) accused Goldman Sachs, the leading US shadow bank, of being the 'great vampire squid' that had both created the bubble and rigged the bailout, manipulating the markets and the government to its own advantage. Sir Fred Goodwin, the Chief Executive of RBS, was described in *Newsweek* as 'the world's worst banker', whose poor decisions had effectively ruined his bank (Gross 2008). That the financial collapse was about more than the failings of individuals was grasped by at least some members of the public (Leiser et al. 2010), but it was difficult enough for specialists, let alone non-specialists, to understand the processes that had ruptured the system. Anyone connected with finance was liable to be branded a 'banker' and used as a convenient target.

Joseph Stiglitz (2009), a former Chief Economist of the World Bank, wrote an article for a non-specialist audience in which he sought to identify 'who killed America's economy'. He explained that his task was not only to find the culprit who had pulled the trigger, but also to identify the individuals and groups that had prepared the way for the crime. Most of the blame, Stiglitz concluded, attached to banks, other financial institutions and investors. They had underestimated or ignored risk in the scramble for quick profits. But their recklessness had been facilitated by various accessories. Greenspan and his allies in government, inspired by free market economics, were responsible for lax financial regulation. Irresponsible ratings agencies had given AAA ratings to securities that turned out to be highly risky. The Federal Reserve had kept interest rates low for too long in the early 2000s. Mainstream economists were also at fault for developing unrealistic financial models and questioning the need for regulation.

After any disaster, politicians insist on having their say, and rightly so, but their statements must be treated with caution, not only because they have an axe to grind, but also because they may lack experience of the field under investigation. In the USA the Financial Crisis Inquiry Commission (FCIC) was established in 2009 and reported in 2011. Membership consisted of six Democrat and four Republican nominees who possessed varying levels of financial expertise. The chair of the FCIC was a Democrat politician, Phil Angelides. Financial industry leaders were interrogated, but not savaged in the way that Ferdinand Pecora had savaged his victims in the 1930s. Although the FCIC was unable to reach a consensus, the majority of commissioners blamed the financial disaster on a combination of lax regulation, excessive risk taking and low ethical standards. The FCIC was not asked to make specific recommendations; its main purpose appears to have been to convince the public that the authorities were taking the events of 2007–09 seriously. It was a fantasy to expect that the underlying causes of the disaster could be identified so rapidly, let alone that politicians from rival parties could reach a common interpretation (Reveley and Singleton 2015; Financial Crisis Inquiry Commission 2011). The Levin–Coburn report of the Senate reached broadly similar conclusions, and called for regulatory reform (United States Senate Permanent Subcommittee on Investigations 2011).

In the UK, the former Chairmen and Chief Executives of RBS and HBOS were grilled by MPs during hearings of the Treasury Committee. Bankers and politicians participated in an elaborate blame game. The bankers acknowledged some errors, but insisted that they were first and foremost the victims of circumstance, and that the sudden tightening of global credit markets could not have been foreseen. The politicians, however, insisted that the reckless behaviour of senior bankers was the main cause of their institutions' failure. Andy Hornby, the former Chief Executive of HBOS, attracted as much criticism as Sir Fred Goodwin. It might not have helped that Hornby had a background in supermarket management with ASDA and was not a life-long banker. Banks, the Select Committee appeared to be suggesting, had lost their direction and values, and had become no different from other types of businesses such as retailers (Whittle and Mueller 2012; House of Commons Treasury Committee 2009). Almost inevitably, the politicians had the better of the argument: they had found their scapegoats.

Recovery and Reconstruction

As shown in Figures 7.1 and 7.2, the pace of revival in the USA, and even more so in the UK, was lacklustre. Output began to pick up in 2009, but it took longer for unemployment to recede. The aggressive interventions between mid-2007 and early 2009 had borne fruit. In Britain and the USA, the recovery was sustained by a new policy called Quantitative Easing (QE) and, to some extent, by fiscal stimulus. Although some of the Eurozone also shared in the early stages of recovery, several Eurozone countries were unable to sustain that revival.

QE evolved out of the emergency asset purchasing programmes at the height of the financial crunch in 2008. Under the terms of QE, financial asset purchases were continued by the Federal Reserve and the Bank of England with a view to assisting macroeconomic recovery. Short-term interest rates had fallen almost to zero, and no longer afforded any further leverage as a policy tool. Through the purchase of longer-term bonds, however, central banks could pump still more money into the financial system, replenish bank reserves and influence long-term interest rates. The aim was to boost lending and the flow of spending on real goods and services. Between November 2008 and December 2012, the Federal Reserve implemented, in full or in part, three rounds of QE, purchasing $3152 billion of securities, an amount equivalent to 22 per cent of gross domestic product (GDP) in 2008. By the end of 2012, the Bank of England had conducted QE to the tune of £379 billion, which was equivalent to 26 per cent of 2008 GDP. The Bank of Japan, which had pioneered QE in the early 2000s, also made extensive use of this tool between 2008 and 2012, but the European Central Bank (ECB) was more cautious (Fawley and Neely 2013). QE did have a positive impact on economic activity, but its effectiveness was tempered by the preference of banks for replenishing reserves, and of households and firms for repaying old debts before taking on new ones. In the UK, the exchange rate depreciated during bouts of QE, providing some additional help to export industries (Goodhart and Ashworth 2012).

Chairman Bernanke, speaking in November 2012, discussed the reasons for the gradual nature of the emergence of the USA from recession. Firstly, the housing market, which usually played an important role in the process, remained subdued. Secondly, lenders continued to be very cautious, in part because of the uncertainty surrounding the Eurozone. Thirdly, fiscal policy, while accommodating during the early stages of the recovery, had subsequently tightened somewhat, not least because of concerns, which were understandable, about the high level of public sector debt (Bernanke 2012). Politicians in Britain also evinced fears over rising government debt in the wake of the 2007–09 financial and economic disaster. The 2010–15 Conservative–Liberal Democrat coalition pursued a policy of austerity, albeit a mild one by the standards of the Eurozone, but one that nonetheless threw more of the burden of macroeconomic stimulus on the Bank of England, and dampened the pace of recovery (Summers 2014).

Mitigation and Regulatory Change

Given that the social impact of the GFC, especially in the USA, was less devastating than the social impact of the depression, the clamour for drastic reform was more subdued. Unemployment rates in the USA and the UK were substantially lower than in the early 1930s, and access to welfare payments was greater. Depositors in failing banks were saved from ruin by the US and British authorities. Populist reactions to the 2007–09 disaster, such as the Occupy movement in New York and London, were short-lived and posed no serious threat to the financial establishment (Calhoun 2013).

Financial institutions and their leaders lost face during 2007–09, but not their capacity to influence the content of subsequent reform legislation. Financial reform in the USA since 2008 has bolstered capital buffers, improved transparency, banned some types of speculation, subjected more types of institution to regulation, improved coordination between different regulatory agencies, and established procedures for dealing with the failure of large financial institutions. Although incredibly detailed, however, the Dodd–Frank Act of 2010 was a much more limited piece of legislation than its New Deal equivalents (Richardson 2012; Evanoff and Moeller 2012). In the UK, the thrust of reform, as recommended by the Vickers Commission, was in the direction of the 'ring-fencing' of retail banking from riskier activities. The Vickers proposals amount to a very watered-down version of Glass–Steagall

(Independent Commission on Banking 2011). No urgency appears to be attached to the ring-fencing, and it has been suggested that its purpose is less to guard against a further crash than to insulate taxpayers from future bailout costs (Goodhart 2012). A third generation of the Basel Accord was unveiled in an effort to enhance the capital adequacy, and improve the monitoring and supervision of international banks. Other attempts at coordinated financial reform were undertaken, or at least promised, after discussions in the G20 (Basel Committee on Banking Supervision 2011; Nolle 2015). More promising, perhaps, has been the growing interest of central banks in macroprudential policy, which is based on recognition that some types of instability operate at the systemic level as opposed to that of the individual financial business (Galati and Moessner 2013).

According to Barry Eichengreen (2015, 385–7), the insipid nature of post-disaster financial reform in the USA and the UK is explained by the relative success of policy makers in averting a calamity on the scale of the early 1930s. Such modest reforms do not, in his opinion, offer much of a bulwark against future instability. Moreover, the pressure for reform will diminish gradually as memories of Lehman Brothers and RBS recede; as was the case with flood defences after Hurricane Katrina. The financial reform process is simply another stage in the financial disaster cycle, and not an end point. The reforms adopted after 2008 were those deemed practical and expedient at the time, and no more.

THE EUROZONE DISASTER

A second financial and economic disaster followed closely on the heels of 2007–09. At the time of writing, in August 2015, the end of the Eurozone disaster is not yet in sight. Some Eurozone members seem destined to experience a barren decade of economic decline, revisiting the traumas of the 1930s. The structural limitations of the Eurozone have been compared to those of the European Gold Bloc in the 1930s (Eichengreen and Temin 2010). It has also been suggested that the Eurozone is even more inflexible than the pre-1914 Gold Standard because of the absence of any provision for a temporary suspension of membership (Bordo and James 2014). Struggling members of the Gold Bloc and the Eurozone were compelled to persist with severe austerity measures, despite sustaining enormous costs in terms of lost GDP, higher unemployment and reduced living standards. Recovery in the 1930s did not commence until the gold parities were abandoned. Essentially, the Anglo-American financial and economic disaster of 2007–09 exposed the underlying contradictions of the Eurozone.

Mitigation and Regulatory Change

Individual member states of the European Economic Community (EEC) participated in the global movement towards financial liberalization in the 1970s and 1980s. But systems of prudential supervision were developed at the national rather than the European level. Supervisors in EEC member states looked to Basel rather than to Brussels when attempting to coordinate their activities.

The prevention or mitigation of financial and economic disaster was not a primary objective of the promoters of monetary union within the European Union (EU), as it came to be known, although certain economic benefits were anticipated. Monetary union was essentially a political aspiration, part of European federalists' project of ever closer integration. Jacques Delors, the former French Prime Minister, set in motion the quest for monetary union in the 1980s. German reunification made the matter more urgent after 1990: monetary union was now regarded by some as a means of tying an enlarged Germany permanently into the EU, whilst restraining the dominance of the German Bundesbank over monetary and exchange rate policy. Under monetary union national central banks would become agents of a supranational central bank. Monetary union was expected to confer several economic benefits. Transaction costs for businesses and consumers inside the monetary union would be reduced. The periodic upsets that had frustrated efforts to coordinate exchange rates within Western Europe would be eliminated. Intra-European exchange rate adjustments had led to uncomfortable shifts in competitiveness between member states between the 1970s and 1990s. Businesses operating within the EU would benefit from the reduced uncertainty accompanying the disappearance of separate national currencies. Monetary union was achieved in 1999, albeit with several EU member states, most significantly Britain, declining to participate (Marsh 2011; James 2012).

The Eurozone possessed several design faults as a mechanism for preventing or mitigating disaster. As was often noted during the 1990s, the Eurozone would not be an optimal currency area. The German economy was very different from the Greek, as was the Finnish from the Portuguese. The most suitable interest rate and exchange rate for each member state would differ from those desired by its partners, especially at different points on their by no means synchronized business cycles. Within the Eurozone, however, one central bank, the ECB, would set an interest rate for the whole area, and there would be no nominal intra-Eurozone exchange rates, merely exchange rates between the euro and external currencies. Whereas tax revenues from prosperous states are redistributed to poorer states within the USA, which is both a monetary and a fiscal union, there is no appetite in EU member countries for a fiscal union. As for the ECB, it was designed, in classic 1990s style, to uphold price stability above all other macroeconomic objectives. The ECB's constitution insulated it from political interference and, at least in theory, outlawed any central bank lending to Eurozone governments (De Grauwe 1997; Eichengreen 1997; Jonung and Drea 2010).

What options would be open to a Eurozone member state on the edge of economic disaster? Nothing could be done by the domestic authorities to influence the nominal exchange rate, the interest rate or the money supply. The ECB could offer no accommodation to the government, although if necessary it could act as lender of last resort to the banking system. Other Eurozone states were prohibited by EU treaty from providing an intergovernmental bailout, and under no obligation to make emergency transfer payments. The assumption was that such a situation would never arise because membership of the Eurozone would hasten convergence between the zone's initially diverse economies. According to Otmar Issing, a member of the ECB Executive Board, monetary union was unstoppable because it was a 'symbol of a shared future and destiny' and everyone must trust the central bankers to make it work (Issing 2000). Delors later admitted, however, that monetary union was marred by the absence of any mechanism to assist member countries in distressed circumstances (Kirkup 2011).

Warnings

The transition from national currencies to the euro went smoothly. A dramatic fall in the rates at which firms, banks and governments on the periphery of the Eurozone could borrow in Europe's financial centres occurred in the late 1990s and early 2000s. This development reflected growing confidence, either that there would be convergence in the economies and institutions of the periphery and core, or that whatever the rules might say, in practice the core – principally Germany – would bail out the periphery in an emergency.

Until the onset of the GFC in 2007–09, the Eurozone appeared to be thriving. To commemorate the ECB's tenth anniversary, a group of leading central bankers and monetary experts, many of whom were European, was interviewed in 2007–08. Interviewees expressed concern about the admittance of some weaker countries into the Eurozone, and wondered how the system would cope in a period of financial instability, given that banks were supervised at the national level. But the overall mood of respondents was upbeat. Most importantly, they felt that the emergence of a situation that could result in demands for inter-governmental bailouts was only a 'remote possibility' (Cecchetti and Schoenholtz 2008, 37). ECB interviewees were proud of the Eurozone's achievements, especially in maintaining low and stable inflation without sacrificing economic growth (Cecchetti and Schoenholtz 2008, 41). There was an element of complacency, perhaps even of euphoria, in some responses.

Not enough weight was given to the serious imbalances that had accumulated within the Eurozone since 1999. These imbalances suggested that trouble might be brewing, regardless of events elsewhere in the global economy. Convergence was not taking place within the Eurozone. Real unit labour costs (RULC) in other Eurozone countries were actually rising relative to those in Germany. The relative increase in RULCs was greatest in the periphery: Ireland, Greece, Portugal, Spain and Italy (Lilico 2013, 109). Essentially, the rest of the Eurozone was becoming less competitive vis-à-vis Germany. Private – and to some extent public – sector entities on the periphery took advantage of low interest rates to borrow externally; in the Irish and Spanish cases to fuel a property boom. Many Eurozone governments struggled and failed to meet the fiscal and public debt targets stipulated in the EU's Stability and Growth Pact. Greece was the worst offender, combining lavish public spending with ineffective revenue collection, and borrowing abroad to fill the gap (Dannhauser 2013, 61–75; Featherstone 2011, 193–8).

The global recession of 2007–09 exacerbated fiscal imbalances within the Eurozone, prompted bank rescues at the national level, and encouraged further official external borrowing. Bank bailouts during this period often involved the substitution of official external debt for private external debt. The announcement by the new Greek socialist government in October 2009 that the previous government had cooked the books, and that official borrowing in 2009 would be much higher than expected, was alarming (Featherstone 2011, 199). Yet, even as late as March 2010, the ECB's position, as explained in the annual report by the President, Jean Claude Trichet, was that the Eurozone was in recovery from the recession, and that conditions in financial markets were improving. Fiscal deficits had risen during the recession, and must now be tackled as a priority, but the worst was over; at least that was Trichet's message (European Central Bank 2010, 10–13). Much of the Eurozone's leadership was in denial and would remain there.

The Triggering Event

Greece triggered the Eurozone financial and economic disaster. While Trichet was writing his reassuring foreword to the ECB annual report, intensive discussions were taking place over Greece's fiscal and debt problems. On 26 March 2010 the European Council agreed in principle to a joint rescue operation financed by the IMF and EU member states should the Greek situation deteriorate further. The rescue would involve bending the EU's rules against intergovernmental bailouts, but the circumstances would be exceptional. On 23 April the Greek Prime Minister, George Papandreou, formally requested a bailout. Papandreou had in effect issued a challenge to the EU to prevent a crisis from turning into a disaster. Accordingly, 23 April 2010 will be taken as the triggering point (Featherstone 2011, 202–3). At the end of 2009, Greece's official external debt was equal to 79 per cent of GDP (Cabral 2010). The bloated level of Greek debt and impending repayment deadlines placed a heavy burden on the budget, and on Greece's shy taxpayers. The historical record suggests that governments often default at lower ratios of official external debt to GDP than 79 per cent. Default essentially occurs when the political will to meet economic obligations is lost. Mexico, for example, defaulted in 1982 when debt was a mere 47 per cent of GDP (Reinhart and Rogoff 2009, 21–33).

Sensemaking and Decision Making

Greece's request for assistance posed several problems for EU leaders. If the Greeks were bailed out, who would be next in the queue? Would the Greeks demand even more later on? In other words, any bailout would have implications for moral hazard. But if the Greeks were allowed to default, would other peripheral states follow suit, and would the Eurozone collapse? Moreover, would those financial institutions that had lent to Greece fail or have to be bailed out? An existential threat to monetary union had been brought into the open.

The Greek emergency was interpreted first and foremost as a threat to the integrity of the monetary regime in the Eurozone, and perhaps even to the stability of the wider EU. That Greece was now in a desperate economic situation, with rapidly rising unemployment and worsening poverty, was not the main concern of some EU leaders. On 28 April 2010, the German Chancellor Angela Merkel and Dominique Strauss-Kahn, the Managing Director of the IMF, the global agency responsible for sorting out countries experiencing temporary financial difficulty, gave a joint press briefing in Berlin. Merkel described the Greek crisis as 'a matter of the stability of the Eurozone as a whole'. Strauss-Kahn concurred: 'the situation is serious, not only for Greece but for all the Euro-zone now. And the stability of the Euro-zone is really the point which is at stake.' Both leaders pointed out that any assistance programme must be accompanied by a 'strong commitment' from the Greeks to implement internal reforms (Merkel and Strauss-Kahn 2010). In other words, the Greeks had mismanaged their affairs very badly; so badly that without remedial action the Eurozone as a whole would be in jeopardy. Merkel and Strauss-Kahn plainly were not thinking about the plight of people in Greece. The German press also tended to portray Greece as an example of national policy failure, albeit one facilitated by weak Eurozone rules, that must be solved by the imposition by the Eurozone leadership of strict institutional reforms on Athens (Kutter 2014).

A rescue package worth €110 billion, combined with harsh austerity measures, was agreed by Greece, the EU and the IMF on 2 May 2010. The programme was to be ratified by EU leaders meeting at Brussels over the weekend of 7–9 May. David Marsh (2011, 250) describes this as 'the most traumatic weekend [so far] in the Euro's history'. The package won approval, but the preceding debate revealed deep-seated differences within the EU leadership. Trichet chastised those governments that had failed to control their budgets. International financial markets were in turmoil, as they tried to predict which of the peripheral countries, or PIIGS (Portugal, Ireland, Italy, Greece, Spain) as they were known, would be the next to require a bailout. Nicolas Sarkozy, the French President, supported by other southern EU representatives, wanted the ECB to start buying sovereign bonds on a grand scale to avert disaster. Trichet and Merkel, however, insisted that the ECB's independence must not be sacrificed. The German position was that an extensive rescue programme to assist other members would breach the Eurozone's no-bailout rule, and would not be acceptable to the German Constitutional Court (Marsh 2011, 250–53).

Essentially, a gap was emerging between a Southern or Latin group, which sympathized with heavily indebted and uncompetitive countries whilst remaining strongly committed to monetary union, and a more legalistic Northern group, marshalled by Germany, whose members were unlikely to require bailing out. Understanding of the situation facing the Eurozone, and of how it might be managed, differed markedly between the two groups. Sensemaking failed to produce a consensus over the best policies to sustain monetary union.

The Disaster Unfolds

Figures 7.1 and 7.2 reveal that the economies of Ireland and Italy experienced a prolonged recession or depression. They did not share in the recovery experienced by the USA, the UK or Germany. Even the French and German recoveries appeared to stall after 2010, and French unemployment crept upwards. The performance of the Greek economy was particularly abysmal. The Eurozone disaster was three-sided: troubled banking systems, dangerous levels of sovereign debt and the absence of economic growth. What is more, those problems were mutually reinforcing. For example, failing banks required official bail-outs, which increased sovereign debt, which in turn undermined confidence in sovereign debt as a bank asset (Shambaugh 2012).

All peripheral Eurozone countries faced a credit crunch, as banks tightened their lending criteria. All experienced severe cuts in government spending. The intensity of the disaster reflected the structure of the Eurozone, and the drastic measures taken to preserve the status quo. The parallels with Europe under the Gold Standard in the 1930s are striking. Perhaps the most shocking statistics of all were those for youth unemployment. In 2012, 23 per cent of young people (aged under 25), in the EU as a whole were unemployed, but the rates on the periphery were far higher: 55 per cent in Greece, 53 per cent in Spain, 38 per cent in Portugal, and even 35 per cent in Italy (European Commission 2013, 5). The cost of the Eurozone disaster in terms of long-term social cohesion could be very high indeed.

Rescue and Relief

The goal of Eurozone leaders was to uphold the monetary union at all costs. Relief and rescue measures were directed towards saving the Eurozone. The citizens of troubled Eurozone countries, particularly those on the periphery, would have to make sacrifices for the sake of the monetary regime. It was a clear case of back to the 1930s.

The key difference between the monetary policy approaches of the Federal Reserve and the ECB after 2008 was the inability of the latter to engage in genuine QE until 2015. Although the ECB devised creative ways of lending to troubled governments prior to 2015, it was with the proviso that those operations were 'sterilized' in order to prevent any increase in Eurozone money supply. Sterilization weakened the effectiveness of ECB lending as a macroeconomic as opposed to financial tool. The ECB also provided emergency liquidity to stressed banking systems in Eurozone countries. The Greek rescue package of 2010 was followed by bailouts for Ireland, Portugal, Cyprus, and then Greece again. Bailouts involved loans from EU governments, led by Germany, and the IMF. Spain received separate assistance to help resolve its banking problems. As part of the second Greek rescue in 2012, private sector creditors were bullied into accepting a 'haircut', and lost half of their money, which was better than losing it all. In return for bailout loans, recipient governments were required to make large cuts in their fiscal deficits and introduce measures to improve the flexibility of their economies. Some funds were used for bank recapitalization. Progress was monitored by the Troika, consisting of the European Commission, the IMF and the ECB. Although portrayed as decisive, the Eurozone rescue packages were compromise measures designed to reassure worried financial markets, and buy time in the hope that the economic situation on the periphery would improve (Lane 2012; O'Rourke and Taylor 2013).

At the time of writing, in August 2015, the Eurozone remained intact, and Greece had just agreed to further austerity measures in return for a third bailout. The primary objective of the rescue programme – protecting the Eurozone regime – was still being achieved. However, the conditions accompanying the bailouts tended to worsen the plight of recipient countries. Austerity and reform were supposed to facilitate internal devaluation, or large reductions in wages and prices that would restore competitiveness. In a world of sticky wages and prices internal, devaluation was a long and painful process, involving higher unemployment and business closures for an indeterminate period. Price deflation, moreover, increased the burden of existing debt, whether held domestically or externally, a phenomenon known as debt deflation. The more severe the austerity, the harder it was for peripheral countries to service and repay sovereign debt. It was a vicious cycle. Austerity was not restricted to countries with bailouts, and was implemented to a greater or lesser extent throughout the Eurozone. Unlike the authorities in the USA and the UK, the Eurozone's leaders stubbornly refused to accept the parallels between the 1930s and their own situation, largely because their commitment to the project of monetary union outweighed all other considerations (De Grauwe and Ji 2013; Eichengreen and Temin 2010). The extent of their denial could be breathtaking, and in June 2013 the French President, François Hollande, declared the Eurozone debt crisis at an end (Neate and agencies 2013).

Allocating Blame

Financial disaster raises all sorts of political ghosts. Reflecting on the terms of Ireland's bailout, and the seeming occupation of Dublin by representatives of the Troika, the *Irish Times* wondered aloud in November 2010: 'Was this what the men of 1916 [who revolted against British rule] died for? ... Having obtained our political independence from Britain ... we have now surrendered our sovereignty to the European Commission, the International Monetary Fund, and the European Central Bank' (quoted in Marsh 2011, 260).

Bitterness between Germany and the nations of Southern Europe rose to levels of intensity not witnessed since the aftermath of the Second World War. Elements of the media in Mediterranean countries were inclined to portray Angela Merkel as a new Hitler, bent on subjugating poorer European countries. Instead of fostering European solidarity, monetary union has sharpened divisions, especially between the relatively rich North and the poorer South. The Greek Finance Ministry announced in December 2014 that Germany still owed Greece €341 billion in reparations for the wars of 1914–18 and 1939–45. In 2015 the radical Syriza-led coalition in Athens stepped up the rhetorical war with Germany. The Justice Minister warned that it might be necessary to seize German property in order to recover reparations. But Germany refused to accept any connection between the legacy of the Second World War and Greece's current obligations to its creditors (Connolly and Smith 2015). During renewed negotiations with the EU and IMF in the summer of 2015, the Greek Finance Minister, Yanis Varoufakis, accused his country's creditors of pursuing a policy of 'terrorism' (Sehmer 2015). In Northern Europe, especially in Germany and Finland, the 'Club Med' countries were often portrayed as scroungers. Eurozone politics descended into a running brawl, partly because the underlying issues were so complex and intractable.

Quantitative historical research suggests that the countries that stayed in depression the longest in the 1930s also experienced the largest growth in support for extremist parties, especially of the right. By analogy, a prolonged depression in the Eurozone today could pose a threat to EU political institutions (de Bromhead et al. 2013). The continued legitimacy of the EU cannot be taken for granted. Far right parties, such as Marine Le Pen's National Front in France and New Dawn in Greece, have attacked both the Eurozone and the EU. Radical left-wing parties, including Syriza in Greece and Podemos in Spain, have made the struggle against austerity central to their political strategy. The Eurozone leadership faces challenges to its dominance from both left and right.

Recovery and Reconstruction

Internal devaluation and institutional reform are the official recipes for recovery in the Eurozone. Even in the most favourable of circumstances, however, such remedies work slowly. It is harder to achieve internal devaluation in a world of stable price levels or deflation than in a world of inflation, where it is enough to restrict the growth of wages and prices to levels below those in competitor countries. Actual as opposed to relative cuts in wages and prices are more difficult to engineer (Shambaugh 2012). Current policies may take a decade or more to succeed, but the Eurozone may not have a decade to spare if austerity leads to political revolt. In the 1930s, recovery was normally preceded by the abandonment of the Gold Standard. The Eurozone, however, is a stronger regime than the Gold Standard was in the 1930s because it is the centrepiece of a drive for European unity. Abandoning the Gold Standard was thought to pose serious economic risks, but defecting from the euro would signify retreat from the European project.

Other than continued austerity, what are the options for the Eurozone? The first would be to introduce a fiscal union in support of the monetary union. Better-off Northern members could then be taxed on a regular basis to subsidize poorer Southern members. The political objections to sharing fiscal sovereignty might be difficult to overcome. A second option would be to transform the Eurozone from a deflationary bloc into a reflationary one. This would involve the redesign of the ECB to facilitate a more aggressive monetary policy, and the adoption of a coordinated policy of fiscal reflation. But it would be awkward to reconcile such an approach with Germany's aversion to inflation. Even more unlikely is the proposal of George Soros (2013) that Germany should leave the Eurozone unless it is prepared to play a more constructive part in making the current regime work. A new German currency would soar in value, restoring some of the lost competitiveness of the rest of the Eurozone.

One or more weaker countries could withdraw from the monetary union, although the costs of doing so would be considerable. Whether the exit of Greece, for example, would initiate a domino effect on the periphery is uncertain, but cannot be excluded (Eichengreen 2010). Any country that left the Eurozone might also choose to default on official external debt. The burden of debt denominated in foreign currency would become even more onerous for a country with a depreciating currency. But sovereign defaults, whilst not to be taken lightly, are commonplace in financial history (Reinhart and Rogoff 2009). A new currency on the periphery would depreciate rapidly, fuelling inflation, although the central bank and Finance Ministry would regain macroeconomic control over time. A further banking crash would be almost inevitable. But competitiveness would be enhanced, unless wages were allowed to increase rapidly enough to nullify the effects of depreciation. After an interval, foreign lenders would return. Of course, an unruly end to monetary union would be extremely destabilizing in the short term for all EU states, and measures would be necessary to protect the banking systems in EU financial centres from collapse. It need not, however, be the end of the world.

Mitigation and Regulatory Change

Since the onset of the Eurozone disaster there have been some adjustments to the monetary and financial regime, albeit without changing it fundamentally. The utility of finding ways, however imperfect, around the prohibition on intergovernmental bailouts resulted in the formation of the European Financial Stability Forum in 2010, which then evolved into the European Stability Mechanism in 2011. These were the organs through which loans were directed to Greece and other supplicants (Gocaj and Meunier 2013). The ECB also tried to wriggle out of some of its treaty constraints, despite encountering stiff German resistance. In 2015 the ECB at last adopted a genuine programme of QE, although on a more limited scale than practised by the US, UK or Japanese central banks (Annunziata 2015). As part of the project to create a European banking union to reinforce the monetary union, a Single Supervisory Mechanism, overseen by the ECB, was set up in 2014, with overall responsibility for supervising 120 important banks and banking groups (Deutsche Bundesbank 2014). Such reforms are unlikely to be sufficient to offer effective disaster mitigation in the future; that is, assuming the Eurozone survives the current conflagration. Thomas Sargent (2012), in his Nobel Prize lecture, makes an analogy between the Eurozone today and the USA in its infancy. He concludes that the Eurozone requires a fiscal union to complement the monetary union. Fiscal union in the USA entailed the transfer of state debts and key powers of taxation to the federal government. Yet it is unclear whether the members of the Eurozone have as much in common today as the US states did in the early years of independence from Britain. Proposals for Eurobonds have been treated with suspicion. The richer Eurozone members are wary of taking on any lasting responsibility for subsidizing their poorer partners, which is what would have to happen in a fiscal union.

CONCLUSION

The 2007–09 Anglo-American financial and economic disaster, and the Eurozone disaster that began in 2010, are closely related. The Anglo-American smash helped to destabilize the Eurozone, a regime that was already fragile because of its inflexibility. Seen from a longer-term perspective, the Anglo-American events followed a typical Minskian trajectory of rising euphoria and reckless lending and borrowing, followed by panic when lenders and borrowers realized that assets were grotesquely overvalued. This time was not different, except perhaps in two respects: namely the scale of the boom and bust, and the rapid reaction of policy makers to the triggering event in financial markets. Sensemaking in New York and London was driven by a determination not to repeat the 1930s, and owed much to the intellectual legacy of Keynes and Friedman and Schwartz. That an economic historian of the 1930s, Ben Bernanke, was Chairman of the Federal Reserve was an unexpected bonus. Because the disaster in the Anglo-American world was contained by prompt remedial action there was less pressure than in the 1930s for the reform of banks and the financial system. For better or worse, little was done to mitigate future financial disasters.

In the Eurozone the situation was far more serious. Monetary union was fashioned in a way that in some respects outdid the most dangerous features of the Gold Standard. Nominal exchange rates within the Eurozone were irrevocably fixed, and national central banks deprived of any influence over monetary conditions. Misperceptions of risk on the part of foreign lenders resulted in a flood of capital into weaker Eurozone economies, much of which was used unproductively in activities such as property speculation. Eurozone banking systems and the budgets of peripheral governments incurred substantial damage in 2007–09, from which some did not fully recover. By 2010, several Eurozone states required bailouts, in return for which they were subjected to harsh austerity programmes. Austerity delayed economic revival, and pushed some countries, including Greece, into a deeper recession, provoking a heartfelt backlash against the inequity of European governance. By promoting an inflexible monetary union, the leaders of the EU in the 1990s were in effect saying 'This time is different' in the institutional realm. When the crunch came in 2010, they failed to recognize that the key challenge was to avoid depression, and not to preserve the integrity of the ECB and the rules of monetary union. That failure of sensemaking led to a repetition of the dysfunctional economic strategies applied within the Gold Bloc in the 1930s. By viewing the twin economic disasters of the early twenty-first century through the lens of the disaster cycle, we are able to come to a better understanding of the dilemmas faced by decision makers and their responses whether good or bad.

8. Conclusion

On 12 August 2015 a warehouse containing hazardous substances blew up in the city of Tianjin, China. Many buildings in the area surrounding the warehouse were destroyed and others were damaged. The preliminary death toll was 44, a number anticipated to rise because 66 critically injured people were in hospital (BBC 2015a). By 20 August, the number of fatalities had risen to 114. Quarrelling over who was to blame, how victims and their families should be compensated, and what should be done to protect the city in the future, was already in full swing (BBC 2015b). Although not as lethal as the Halifax explosion during the First World War, an event that prompted one of the earliest forays into disaster studies (Prince 1920), the Tianjin explosion in principle may be analysed using similar tools.

The disaster cycle framework was developed in the 1970s, largely as a guide for those involved in disaster mitigation and response. In the hands of practitioners and disaster management scholars it became known as the disaster management cycle. The disaster cycle is used here with somewhat different ends in mind. In this book the primary goal is to show that disasters in widely different spheres of activity pass through comparable stages. To that end, each chapter after the introduction to the disaster cycle (Chapter 1) examines a different sort of disaster: a natural disaster (Hurricane Katrina), a World War (1914–18), an economic disaster (the Great Depression of the early 1930s), two industrial disasters (Senghenydd and Aberfan), a health disaster (the effects of tobacco), and finally the Global Financial 'Crisis' and Eurozone disaster of the early twenty-first century.

As an economic and business historian I am particularly interested in exploring the extent to which economic and financial disasters pass through the same stages as natural and industrial disasters. Although the needs of policy makers, practitioners and businesses are not my primary concern, the cases discussed above show that there is unexploited potential for those operating in different spheres of activity to learn from one another's experience of disaster. There already has been a limited degree of cross-fertilization. For example, the US Government Account-ability Office opted to structure its account of four financial 'crises' in the

1980s with the assistance of a version of the disaster cycle (Government Accountability Office 1997). Robert Peckham (2013) shows how policy makers in the financial and public health arenas have exchanged ideas about how to manage contagion. The US National Transportation Safety Board has been proposed as a model for mitigating and managing disaster risk in the financial services industry (Fielding et al. 2011). In the main, however, there is a marked reluctance to grasp the similarities in how disasters occur in the financial and other spheres. No doubt this has something to do with differing terminology, especially the preference of economists and economic policy makers for referring to a 'crisis' when describing an event that in any other field might be considered a disaster.

The variant of the disaster cycle that is used in this volume has some distinctive features. It begins with a stage termed 'mitigation and regulatory change'. Previous disasters are likely to induce changes in regulation, as well as efforts to strengthen defences and prepare to meet new threats. This stage of the cycle (like the others) is highly politicized. The nature and extent of mitigation and regulatory change are products of bargaining between interested parties, some of which are more concerned with cost minimization than with protecting the public. The public themselves are liable to lose interest in mitigation as the last disaster slips from the collective memory to be replaced by different concerns. The next stage is marked by the arrival of new danger warnings. In a climate of complacency or euphoria those warnings may not be heeded.

The following stage, the triggering point, is possibly the most problematic. An event occurs that, if not dealt with effectively, will lead to disaster. In an extreme case, such as the Senghenydd Colliery explosion, the time available for an effective response before the disaster unfolds may be negligible or zero. Policy makers and other actors may or may not grasp the significance of the triggering event. In fact it may be obvious only in retrospect, and even then there may be some uncertainty over which in a chain of events was actually the trigger. A sequence of incidents preceded the depression of the 1930s, and it is only in hindsight that some scholars have identified the Wall Street Crash as the trigger, or challenge demanding a creative response. Historians cannot avoid making decisions about how to organize the past, and this involves selecting the key events for analysis. That the identification of the triggering point involves a degree of subjective judgement is an inconvenience but not a fatal objection.[1] The triggering point ushers in a critical period – a time of crisis defined as threat or challenge – that lasts until rescue and relief work are accomplished.

Sensemaking and decision making comprise the next, and in some respects most important, phase of the cycle. In many, but not all cases a disaster may still be avoidable if appropriate remedial action is taken. A diplomatic solution to the European tensions of 1914, for example, could have prevented war. An effective response by monetary policy makers to the downward spiral in the US economy at the start of the 1930s could have avoided depression. Even in a situation where human action cannot prevent disaster, as in the case of an advancing hurricane, it may be possible to cushion the impact by evacuating the population. Sensemaking is a term taken from the work of Karl Weick (1993), and in particular his account of the Mann Gulch disaster of 1949. In a situation of great threat and uncertainty, policy makers may be overwhelmed and either panic or make the wrong decisions. Even when there is no apparent urgency to respond, which might be the case with slow-moving disasters such as smoking, policy makers and other relevant actors, including the public, may prevaricate because they are comfortable with the status quo. Practitioners may learn a great deal from comparing the sensemaking and decision making processes of their counterparts across a range of types of disaster. This is an area that calls out for further research. Mark Stein's (2004) comparison of sensemaking during the Three Mile Island and Apollo 13 incidents goes some way in that direction. The episodes selected for examination in this book are ones in which sensemaking and decision making failed; the aim is to analyse disasters rather than near misses.

When sensemaking and decision making fail, the disaster will unfold, generating large physical and/or financial costs. Human and other capital may be destroyed, output may be lost, and large financial burdens may be imposed on the government and the taxpayers. Such costs are difficult to quantify, and do not fall evenly. In addition there could be significant psychological costs that are not quantifiable.

In practice, some of the stages of the disaster cycle are likely to overlap. The rescue and relief stage could actually begin before the disaster has struck, as response teams and assets are deployed and people evacuated in anticipation of an adverse event. This stage is probably the most familiar to anyone who has watched reporting of disasters on television or read about them in newspapers. With the conclusion of the rescue and relief phase, the critical period of the disaster comes to an end.

As soon as the disaster unfolds the thoughts of those affected and of observers will turn to the question of 'Who is to blame?' That this is always the case is proof that even apparently natural disasters have some social causes. Why were the building regulations not tightened in order to increase resistance to earthquakes? Why were the authorities unable to evacuate everyone before the hurricane struck? Why was there a failure to regulate financial markets more thoroughly, or to design them in such a way as to increase resilience? By introducing the allocation of blame as a distinct phase of the cycle it becomes possible to examine the ways in which the authorities attempt to manage blame and assure the public that disaster will not recur. These are rarely even-handed exercises; they could even involve an element of fantasy. The blame stage also overlaps with other post-disaster stages.

Reconstruction is also a political as a well as a practical stage. The nature and extent of rebuilding and the allocation of reconstruction costs are matters for public discussion. This is obvious, for example, in the debate over reparations after the First World War. Finally, the cycle returns to the beginning with a new round of mitigation and regulatory change, the enthusiasm for which will diminish over time.

Disasters are not all the same. They can happen quickly (a hurricane) or slowly (the effects of smoking). During certain disasters some stages of the cycle will be compressed almost to the point of disappearance. After the initial explosion at Senghenydd, there was effectively nothing that colliery management (the sensemakers and decision makers) could do to stop the carnage, although some argued that they would have been able to do something if a different type of ventilator fan had been in place. By contrast, in the case of smoking the authorities and the public devoted more than a decade to sensemaking after the publication in 1950 of studies linking tobacco to lung cancer. Nevertheless even those two disasters followed a broadly similar path at the conceptual level.

The disaster cycle is driven, or in the case of natural disasters strongly influenced, by human and organizational behaviour. Human beings decide to live on flood plains and put the attendant risks to the back of their minds. Human beings are prone to emotions that cloud their rationality and their capacity to assess risk in all sorts of situations, including the period of tension leading to war and the period of euphoria preceding a financial crash. Once a disaster has occurred they compete to assign or escape blame. It is difficult to imagine this ever changing, although greater awareness of past mistakes could have a limited dampening effect. Disasters will recur, although not necessarily in the same place or in quite the same way. Something is learned from each revolution of the cycle, and the next one will not be quite the same.[2] US policy makers looked to the depression when responding to the financial collapse of 2007–09. On the other hand, Eurozone policy makers were not able to absorb the lessons of the 1930s.

It would have been possible to devote each chapter to a certain stage of the disaster cycle rather than to a particular type of disaster. There are several possible ways of dividing up the material. Such an alternative approach could have been disorienting for readers unfamiliar with the range of cases considered. In the event it proved difficult to put individuals and groups neatly into the crisis manager categories – collectivists, integrators, reactives and paralytics – developed by Amanda Olejarski and James Garnett (2010). Perhaps this too merits further research.

In this concluding chapter I have pointed out several ways in which the contents of the book could be useful to those interested in mitigating and responding to disasters in various fields. There is always something to be learned from comparative studies, not least when the comparisons made are not the most obvious ones. Nevertheless, I am not persuaded that better knowledge of disasters will enable their prevention in the future. Whatever the sphere of operations – financial, diplomatic, industrial, public health or traditional natural disaster management – the best intentions of people and organizations will continue to be overridden by self-interested, careless, myopic and sometime febrile human behaviour.

NOTES

1. I am particularly grateful to Simon Mollan of the University of York for making me think more carefully about such matters.
2. This point was made in discussion by Professor Guo of China Foreign Affairs University.

References

N.B. The References section is organized by chapter because the case studies differ considerably and each relies on a largely distinct literature.

CHAPTER 1

Abolafia, Mitchel Y. (2010), 'Narrative construction as sensemaking: how a central bank thinks', *Organization Studies*, **31**, 349–67.

Ahamed, Liaquat (2010), *Lords of Finance*, London: Windmill.

Akerlof, George A. and Robert J. Shiller (2009), *Animal Spirits: How Human Psychology Drives the Economy, and Why it Matters for Global Capitalism*, Princeton, NJ: Princeton University Press.

Aldrich, Daniel P. (2010), 'Separate and unequal: post-tsunami aid distribution in southern India', *Social Science Quarterly*, **91** (5), 1369–89.

Anderson, Charles, D., Dennis R. Capozza and Robert Van Order (2011), 'Deconstructing a mortgage meltdown: a methodology for decomposing underwriting quality', *Journal of Money, Credit and Banking*, **43** (4), 609–31.

Ashdown, John (2015), '"We'll have to look at the data": England's World Cup disaster deconstructed', *Guardian* (online edition), 9 March, accessed 27 March 2015 at www.theguardian.com/sport/2015/mar/09/england-world-cup-distaster-peter-moores.

Baird, A., P. O'Keefe, K.N. Westgate and B. Wisner (1975), 'Towards an explanation and reduction of disaster proneness', Occasional Paper no.11, University of Bradford, Disaster Research Unit.

Barro, Robert J. (2006), 'Rare disasters and asset markets in the twentieth century', *Quarterly Journal of Economics*, **121** (3), 823–66.

Bartrip, Peter (2013), 'Tarred roads or tobacco? Debates on the cause of lung cancer, nineteen-twenties to nineteen-fifties', *Historical Research*, **86** (231), 138–57.

Birkland, Thomas A. (2009), 'Disasters, lessons learned, and fantasy documents', *Journal of Contingencies and Crisis Management*, **17** (3), 146–56.

Boin, Arjen (2009), 'The new world of crises and crisis management: implications for policymaking and research', *Review of Policy Research*, **26** (4), 367–77.

Carr, Lowell J. (1932), 'Disaster and the sequence-pattern concept of social change', *American Journal of Sociology*, **38** (2), 207–18.

Cavallo, Eduardo and Ilan Noy (2011), 'The economics of natural disasters: a survey', *International Review of Environmental and Resource Economics*, **5**, 63–102.

Cavallo, Eduardo, Michael Treadway and Rita Funaro (2010), 'The economic toll in Haiti – and its implications', *IDEAS: Ideas for Development in the Americas*, **22** (May–August), 4.

Clarke, Lee (1999), *Mission Improbable: Using Fantasy Documents to Tame Disaster*, Chicago, IL: University of Chicago Press.

Coetzee, Christo and Dewald van Niekerk (2012), 'Tracking the evolution of the disaster management cycle: a general system theory approach', *Jàmbá: Journal of Disaster Risk Studies*, **4** (1), 1–9.

Coppola, Damon P. (2011), *Introduction to International Disaster Management*, 2nd edn, Burlington, MA: Butterworth-Heinemann.

de Groot, Bert and Philip Hanses Franses (2012), 'Common socio-economic cycle periods', *Technological Forecasting and Social Change*, **79**, 59–68.

Dynes, Russell R. (1998), 'Coming to terms with community disaster', in Enrico L. Quarantelli (ed.), *What is a Disaster?*, London and New York: Routledge, pp. 109–26.

Eichengreen, Barry J. (2012), 'Economic history and economic policy', *Journal of Economic History*, **72** (2), 289–307.

Financial Crisis Inquiry Commission (2010), *The Official Transcript of the First Public Hearing of the Financial Crisis Inquiry Commission*, 13 January, accessed 27 September 2013 at http://fcic-static. law.stanford.edu/cdn_media/fcic-testimony/2010-0113-Transcript.pdf.

Flandreau, Marc, Juan H. Flores, Norbert Gaillard and Sebastián Nieto-Parra (2009), 'The end of gatekeeping: underwriters and the quality of sovereign bond markets, 1815–2007', *NBER International Seminar on Macroeconomics*, **6** (1), 53–92.

Gawronski, Vincent T. and Richard Scott Olson (2013), 'Disasters as crisis triggers for critical junctures: the 1976 Guatemala case', *Latin American Politics and Society*, **55** (2), 133–49.

Gilbert, Claude (1998), 'Studying disaster: changes in the main conceptual tools', in Enrico L. Quarantelli (ed.), *What is a Disaster?*, London and New York: Routledge, pp. 11–18.

Government Accountability Office (1997), *Financial Crisis Management: Four Financial Crises in the 1980s*, GAO/GGD-97-96, Washington, DC: GAO.

Greenspan, Alan (2008), *The Age of Turbulence*, London: Penguin.

Grossman, Richard (2013), *Wrong: Nine Economic Policy Disasters and What We Can Learn From Them*, Oxford: Oxford University Press.

Haldane, Andrew G. and Robert M. May (2011), 'Systemic risk in financial ecosystems', *Nature*, **469**, 351–5.

Hallegatte, Stephane and Valentin Przyluski (2010), 'The economics of natural disasters', *CESifo Forum*, **2**, 14–24.

Healy, Andrew and Neil Malhotra (2009), 'Myopic voters and natural disaster policy', *American Political Science Review*, **103** (3), 387–406.

Hooper, John (2014), 'L'Aquila earthquake scientists win appeal', *Guardian*, online edition, 10 November, accessed 7 April 2015 at www.theguardian.com/world/2014/nov/10/laquila-earthquake-scientists-win-appeal-seismologists.

Horwich, George (1990), 'Disasters and market response', *Cato Journal*, **9** (3), 531–55.

House of Commons Treasury Committee (2009), *Banking Crisis*, Vol. 1, *Oral Evidence*, HC 144-I, London: Stationery Office.

Hutter, Bridget M. (2001), *Regulation and Risk: Occupational Health and Safety on the Railways*, Oxford: Oxford University Press.

Jacks, David S. (2008), 'Review of *Economic Disasters of the Twentieth Century*', *Australian Economic History Review*, **48** (3), 321–2.

Jackson, Jeffrey H. (2011), 'Envisioning disaster in the 1910 Paris flood', *Journal of Urban History*, **37** (2), 176–207.

Janis, Irving L. (1972), *Victims of Groupthink: A Psychological Study of Foreign Policy Decisions and Fiascoes*, Boston, MA: Houghton Mifflin.

Johnson, Suzanne Nora (2010), 'A financial malignancy', in Howard Kunreuther and Michael Useem (eds), *Learning from Catastrophes: Strategies for Reaction and Response*, Upper Saddle River, NY: Wharton School Publishing, pp. 156–69.

Kindleberger, Charles P. and Robert Z. Aliber (2011), *Manias, Panics, and Crashes: A History of Financial Crises*, 6th edn, Basingstoke: Palgrave Macmillan.

Kreps, Gary A. (1998), 'Disaster as systemic event and social catalyst', in Enrico L. Quarantelli (ed.), *What is a Disaster?*, London and New York: Routledge, pp. 31–55.

Kunreuther, Howard and Michael Useem (eds) (2010), *Learning from Catastrophes: Strategies for Reaction and Response*, Upper Saddle River, NY: Wharton School Publishing.

Laeven, Luc and Fabián Valencia (2012), 'Systemic banking crises database: an update', IMF Working Paper 12/163.

Lewis, W. Arthur (1978), *Growth and Fluctuations 1870–1913*, London: George Allen & Unwin.

Maitlis, Sally and Scott Sonenschein (2010), 'Sensemaking in crisis and change: inspiration and insights from Weick (1988)', *Journal of Management Studies*, **47** (3), 551–80.

May, Robert (2013), 'Financial ecosystems can be vulnerable too', *Financial Times*, online edition, 19 October, accessed 1 April 2015 at www.ft.com/cms/s/0/a6ee48b4-0d63-11e2-99a1-00144feabdc0.html#ax zz3W2wvlF46.

May, Robert M., Simon A. Levin and George Sugihara (2008), 'Complex systems: ecology for bankers', *Nature*, **451**, 893–5.

Michel-Kerjan, Erwann (2010), 'Haven't you switched to risk management 2.0 yet?', in Erwann Michel-Kerjan and Paul Slovic (eds), *The Irrational Economist: Making Decisions in a Dangerous World*, New York: Public Affairs, pp. 41–50.

Michel-Kerjan, Erwann and Paul Slovic (eds) (2010), *The Irrational Economist: Making Decisions in a Dangerous World*, New York: Public Affairs.

Minsky, Hyman P. (1982), 'The financial-instability hypothesis: capitalist processes and the behaviour of the economy', in Charles P. Kindleberger and Jean-Pierre Laffargue (eds), *Financial Crises: Theory, History and Policy*, Cambridge: Cambridge University Press, pp. 13–39.

Minsky, Hyman P. (2008), *John Maynard Keynes*, New York: McGraw-Hill.

National Governors' Association (1978), *Emergency Preparedness Project Final Report*, Washington, DC: Government Printing Office.

Neal, David M. (1997), 'Reconsidering the phases of disaster', *International Journal of Mass Emergencies and Disasters*, **15** (2), 239–64.

Neal, David M. (2013), 'Social time and disaster', *International Journal of Mass Emergencies and Disasters*, **31** (2), 247–70.

Neal, Larry (2000), 'A shocking view of economic history', *Journal of Economic History*, **60** (2), 317–34.

Odell, Kerry A. and Marc D. Weidenmier (2004), 'Real shock, monetary aftershock: the 1906 San Francisco earthquake and the panic of 1907', *Journal of Economic History*, **64** (4), 1002–27.

O'Gráda, Cormac (2009), *Famine: A Short History,* Princeton, NJ: Princeton University Press,

Olejarski, Amanda M. and James L. Garnett (2010), 'Coping with Katrina: assessing crisis management behaviours in the Big One', *Journal of Contingencies and Crisis Management*, **18** (1), 26–38.

Oliver, Michael J. (2007), 'Financial crises', in Michael J. Oliver and Derek H. Aldcroft (eds), *Economic Disasters of the Twentieth Century*, Cheltenham, UK and Northampton, MA, USA: Edward Elgar Publishing, pp. 182–235.

Oliver, Michael J. and Derek H. Aldcroft (eds) (2007), *Economic Disasters of the Twentieth Century*, Cheltenham, UK and Northampton, MA, USA: Edward Elgar Publishing.

Peckham, Robert (2013), 'Economies of contagion: financial crisis and pandemic', *Economy and Society*, **42** (2), 226–48.

Pereira, Alvaro S. (2009), 'The opportunity of a disaster: the economic impact of the 1755 Lisbon earthquake', *Journal of Economic History*, **69** (2), 466–99.

Perrow, Charles (1984), *Normal Accidents: Living with High-Risk Technologies*, New York: Basic Books.

Pigou, Arthur C. (1921), *The Political Economy of War*, London: Macmillan.

Platz, Stephanie (2000), 'The shape of national time: daily life, history, and identity during Armenia's transition to independence, 1991–1994', in Daphne Berdahl, Matti Bunzl and Martha Lampland (eds), *Ethnographies of Transition in Eastern Europe and the Former Soviet Union*, Ann Arbor, MI: University of Michigan Press, pp. 114–38.

Prince, Samuel Henry (1920), *Catastrophe and Social Change*, New York: Columbia University Press.

Quarantelli, Enrico L. (ed.) (1998), *What is a Disaster?*, London and New York: Routledge.

Reinhart, Carmen M. and Kenneth S. Rogoff (2009), *This Time is Different: Eight Centuries of Financial Folly*, Princeton, NJ: Princeton University Press.

Rohrer, Tim and Mary Jean Vignone (2012), 'The bankers go to Washington: theory and method in conceptual metaphor analysis', *Nouveaux cahiers de linguistique française*, **30**, 5–38.

Rostow, Walt W. (1960), *The Stages of Economic Growth: A Non-Communist Manifesto*, Cambridge: Cambridge University Press.

Rostow, Walt W. (1978), *The World Economy: History and Prospect*, London: Macmillan.

Shaluf, Ibrahim M., Fakharu'-l Razi Ahmadun and Aini Mat Said (2003), 'A review of disaster and crisis', *Disaster Prevention and Management*, **12** (1), 24–32.

Singleton, John (2011), *Central Banking in the Twentieth Century*, Cambridge: Cambridge University Press.

Singleton, John (2015), 'Using the disaster cycle in economic and social history', in A.T. Brown, Andy Burn and Rob Doherty (eds), *Crises in Economic and Social History: A Comparative Perspective*, Woodbridge: Boydell & Brewer, pp. 53–78.

Singleton, John (2016), 'Financial crises and disaster management', in Matthew Hollow, Folarin Akinbami and Ranald Michie (eds), *Complexity, Crisis and the Evolution of the Financial System: Critical*

Perspectives on American and British Banking, Cheltenham, UK and Northampton, MA, USA: Edward Elgar Publishing, pp. 306–28.

Singleton, John, with Arthur Grimes, Gary Hawke and Sir Frank Holmes (2006), *Innovation and independence: The Reserve Bank of New Zealand, 1973–2002*, Auckland: Auckland University Press.

Skoufias, Emmanuel (2003), 'Economic crises and natural disasters: coping strategies and policy implications', *World Development*, **31** (7), 1087–102.

Stein, Mark (2004), 'The critical period of disasters: insights from sense-making and psychoanalytic theory', *Human Relations*, **57** (10), 1243–61.

Stein, Mark (2011), 'A culture of mania: a psychoanalytic view of the incubation of the 2008 credit crisis', *Organization*, **18** (2), 173–86.

Stultz, René M. and Luigi Zingales (2009), 'The financial crisis: an inside view. Comments and discussion', *Brookings Papers on Economic Activity*, **2009**, 64–78.

Times Higher Education Reporters (2013), 'Lessons from the L'Aquila earthquake', *Times Higher Education* (online edition), 3 October, accessed 21 October 2013 at www.timeshighereducation.co.uk/features/lessons-from-the-laquila-earthquake/2007742.fullarticle.

Tooze, Adam (2007), *The Wages of Destruction: The Making and Breaking of the Nazi Economy*, London: Penguin.

Tuckett, David and Richard Taffler (2008), 'Phantastic objects and the financial market's sense of reality: a psychoanalytic contribution to the understanding of stock market instability', *International Journal of Psychoanalysis*, **89**, 389–412.

Turner, Barry A. (1976), 'The organizational and interorganizational development of disasters', *Administrative Science Quarterly*, **21** (3), 378–97.

Viscusi, W. Kip (2008), 'How to value a life', *Journal of Economics and Finance*, **32** (4), 311–23.

Warren, G.F. and F.A. Pearson (1932), 'The future of the general price level', *Journal of Farm Economics*, **14** (1), 23–46.

Watkins, Myron W. (1933), 'The literature of the crisis', *Quarterly Journal of Economics*, **47** (3), 504–32.

Weick, Karl E. (1993), 'The collapse of sensemaking in organizations: the Mann Gulch disaster', *Administrative Science Quarterly*, **38** (4), 628–52.

Weick, Karl E. (1995), *Sensemaking in Organizations*, Thousand Oaks, CA: Sage.

Wirtz, James J. (2013), 'Indications and warning in an age of uncertainty', *International Journal of Intelligence and Counter Intelligence*, **26** (3), 550–62.

Withers, Hartley (1917), *War and Lombard Street*, London: John Murray.

CHAPTER 2

Allemeyer, Marie Luisa (2012), 'The struggle against the sea: an early modern coastal society between metaphysical and physical attempts to control nature', in Andrea Janku, Gerrit J. Schenk and Franz Mauelshagen (eds), *Historical Disasters in Context: Science, Religion, and Politics*, London: Routledge, pp. 75–93.

Athukorala, Prema-Chandra and Budy P. Resosudarmo (2006), 'The Indian Ocean tsunami: economic impact, disaster management, and lessons', *Asian Economic Papers*, **4** (1), 1–39.

Barry, John M. (1997), *Rising Tide: The Great Mississippi Flood of 1927 and How It Changed America*, New York: Simon & Schuster.

Bea, Keith (2007), 'Federal emergency management policy changes after Hurricane Katrina: a summary of statutory provisions', Congressional Research Service Report for Congress, RL33729.

Bijker, Wiebe E. (2007), 'American and Dutch coastal engineering: differences in risk conception and differences in technological culture', *Social Studies of Science*, **37**, 143–51.

Boettke, Peter, Emily Chamlee-Wright, Peter Gordon, Sanford Ikeda, Peter T. Leeson and Russell Sobel (2007), 'The political, economic, and social aspects of Katrina', *Southern Economic Journal*, **74** (2), 363–76.

Cigler, Beverly A. (2009), 'Post-Katrina hazard mitigation on the Gulf Coast', *Public Organization Review*, **9**, 325–41.

Comfort, Louise K., Thomas A. Birkland, Beverly A. Cigler and Earthea Nance (2010), 'Retrospectives and prospectives on Hurricane Katrina: five years and counting', *Public Administration Review*, **70** (5), 669–78.

Congleton, Roger D. (2006), 'The story of Katrina: New Orleans and the political economy of catastrophe', *Public Choice*, **127**, 5–30.

Davis, Donald R. and David E. Weinstein (2002), 'Bones, bombs, and break points: the geography of economic activity', *American Economic Review*, **92** (5), 1269–89.

Delano, Frederic A. (1928), 'The Report of the Committee on Mississippi Flood Control appointed by the United States Chamber of Commerce', *Annals of the American Academy of Political and Social Science*, **135**, 25–33.

Eggler, Bruce (2012), 'New Orleans reached 81 percent of pre-Katrina population in 2012, census figures show', *Times-Picayune* (online edition), 14 March, accessed 25 May 2013 at www.nola.com/politics/index.ssf/2013/03/new_orleans_reached_81_percent.html.

Garnett, James L. and Alexander Kouzmin (2007), 'Communicating throughout Katrina: competing and complementary conceptual lenses on crisis', *Public Administration Review*, **67**, Special Issue on Administrative Failure in the Wake of Hurricane Katrina, 171–88.

Gerritsen, Herman (2005), 'What happened in 1953? The big flood in the Netherlands in retrospect', *Philosophical Transactions of the Royal Society A*, **363**, 1271–91.

Goldenberg, Stanley B., Christopher W. Landsea, Alberto M. Mestas-Nuñez and William M. Gray (2001), 'The recent increase in Atlantic hurricane activity: causes and implications', *Science*, **293**, 474–9.

Gotham, Kevin Fox (2014), 'Racialization and rescaling: post-Katrina rebuilding and the Louisiana Road Home Program', *International Journal of Urban and Regional Research*, **38** (3), 773–90.

Government Accountability Office (2008), 'Actions taken to implement the Post-Katrina Emergency Management Reform of 2006', GAO-09-59R.

Gros, Jean-Germain (2011), 'Anatomy of a Haitian tragedy: when the fury of nature meets the debility of the state', *Journal of Black Studies*, **42** (2), 131–57.

Healy, Andrew and Neil Malhotra (2009), 'Myopic voters and natural disaster policy', *American Political Science Review*, **103** (3), 387–406.

Henry, A.J. (1927), 'Frankenfield on the 1927 floods in the Mississippi Valley', *Monthly Weather Review*, **55** (10), 437–52.

Hofmann, Mark A. (2014), 'Reinsurers re-evaluate private market after rollback of NFIP reforms', *Business Insurance*, **48** (10), 31.

Horwich, George (2000), 'Economic lessons of the Kobe earthquake', *Economic Development and Cultural Change*, **48** (3), 521–42.

Horwitz, Steven (2009), 'Wal-Mart to the rescue: private enterprise's response to Hurricane Katrina', *Independent Review*, **13** (4), 511–28.

Irons, Larry (2005), 'Hurricane Katrina as a predictable surprise', *Homeland Security Affairs*, **1** (2), 1–19.

Kirlik, Alex (2007), 'Lessons learned from the design of the decision support system used in the Hurricane Katrina evacuation decision', *Proceedings of the Human Factors and Ergonomics Society 51st Annual Meeting*, Thousand Oaks, CA: Sage, pp. 253–7.

Klein, Naomi (2007), *The Shock Doctrine: The Rise of Disaster Capitalism*, London: Penguin.

Knabb, Richard D., Jamie R. Rhome and Daniel P. Brown (2011), *Tropical Cyclone Report: Hurricane Katrina 23–30 August 2005*, Miami: National Hurricane Center, accessed 22 May 2013 at www.nhc.noaa.gov/pdf/TCR-AL122005_Katrina.pdf.

Knowles, Scott Gabriel and Howard C. Kunreuther (2014), 'Troubled waters: the National Flood Insurance Program in historical perspective', *Journal of Policy History*, **26** (3), 327–53.

Krupa, Michelle (2011), 'Ray Nagin casts himself as hero of Hurricane Katrina in memoir', Nola Blog, accessed 19 August 2014 at http://blog.nola.com/politics/print.html?entry=/2011/06/ray_nagin_casts_himself_as_her.html.

Kunreuther, Howard and Mark Pauly (2006), 'Rules rather than discretion: lessons from Hurricane Katrina', *Journal of Risk and Uncertainty*, **33**, 101–16.

Lehrer, Eli (2013), 'Strange bedfellows: SmarterSafe.Org and the Biggert-Waters Act of 2012', *Duke Environmental Law & Policy Forum*, **23**, 351–61.

Lipton, Eric (2006), '"Breathtaking" waste and fraud in Hurricane aid', *New York Times* (online edition), 27 June, accessed 25 August 2014 at www.nytimes.com/2006/06/27/washington/27katrina.html?pagewanted=all&_r=0.

Lohof, Bruce (1970), 'Herbert Hoover, spokesman of humane efficiency: the Mississippi flood of 1927', *American Quarterly*, **22** (3), 690–700.

Malhotra, Neil and Alexander G. Kuo (2008), 'Attributing blame: the public's response to Hurricane Katrina', *Journal of Politics*, **70** (1), 120–35.

Mann, Michael E. and Kerry A. Emanuel (2006), 'Atlantic hurricane trends linked to climate change', *Eos, Transactions American Geophysical Union*, **87** (24), 233–41.

Martinko, Mark J., Denise M. Breaux, Arthur D. Martinez, James Summers and Paul Harvey (2009), 'Hurricane Katrina and attributions of responsibility', *Organizational Dynamics*, **38** (1), 52–63.

Meier, Mischa (2012), 'Roman emperors and "natural disasters" in the first century AD', in Andrea Janku, Gerrit J. Schenk and Franz Mauelshagen (eds), *Historical Disasters in Context: Science, Religion, and Politics*, London: Routledge, pp. 15–30.

Meyer, Robert (2010), 'Why we still fail to learn from disasters', in Erwann Michel-Kerjan and Paul Slovic (eds), *The Irrational Economist: Making Decisions in a Dangerous World*, New York: Public Affairs, pp. 124–31.

Michel-Kerjan, Erwann (2010), 'Catastrophe economics: the National Flood Insurance Program', *Journal of Economic Perspectives*, **24** (4), 165–86.

Mittal, Anu (2005), 'Army Corps of Engineers, Lake Pontchartrain and Vicinity Hurricane Protection Project: testimony of Anu Mittal on behalf of the United States Government Accountability Office before the Subcommittee on Energy and Water Development, Committee on

Appropriations, House of Representatives, on September 28, 2005', accessed 14 April 2015 at www.gao.gov/new.items/d051050t.pdf.

Neal, David M. (2013), 'Social time and disaster', *International Journal of Mass Emergencies and Disasters*, **31** (2), 247–70.

Nicolson, Peter (2005), 'Hurricane Katrina: why did the levees fail? Testimony of Peter Nicolson on behalf of the American Society of Civil Engineers before the Committee on Homeland Security and Governmental Affairs, US Senate, on November 2, 2006', accessed 19 August 2014 at www.hsgac.senate.gov/download/2005-11-02-nicholson-testimony.

Norberg, Johan (2008), 'The Klein doctrine: the rise of disaster polemics', Cato Institute Briefing Papers, No. 102, Washington, DC.

Nordhaus, William (2010), 'The economics of hurricanes and implications of global warming', *Climate Change Economics*, **1** (1), 1–20.

Olejarski, Amanda M. and James L. Garnett (2010), 'Coping with Katrina: assessing crisis management behaviours in the Big One', *Journal of Contingencies and Crisis Management*, **18** (1), 26–38.

Organisation for Economic Co-operation and Development (OECD) (2014), *National Accounts at a Glance 2014*, Paris: OECD.

Parker, Charles F., Erik K. Stern, Eric Paglia and Christer Brown (2009), 'Preventable catastrophe? The Hurricane Katrina disaster revisited', *Journal of Contingencies and Crisis Management*, **17** (4), 206–20.

Pearcy, Matthew T. (2002), 'After the flood: a history of the 1928 Flood Control Act', *Journal of the Illinois State Historical Society*, **95** (2), 172–201.

Perrow, Charles (2007), *The Next Catastrophe: Reducing Our Vulnerabilities to Natural, Industrial, and Terrorist Disasters*, Princeton, NJ: Princeton University Press.

Picou, J. Steven and Kenneth Hudson (2010), 'Hurricane Katrina and mental health: a research note on Mississippi Gulf Coast residents', *Sociological Inquiry*, **80** (3), 513–24.

Pietruska, Jamie L. (2011), 'US Weather Bureau Chief Willis Moore and the reimagination of uncertainty in long-range forecasting', *Environment and History*, **17**, 79–105.

Rappaport, Edward N., et al. (2009), 'Advances and challenges at the National Hurricane Center', *Weather and Forecasting*, **24**, 395–419.

Regnier, Eva (2008), 'Public evacuation decisions and hurricane track uncertainty', *Management Science*, **54** (1), 16–28.

Rockwell, Llewellyn H. and Walter E. Block (2010), 'The economics and ethics of Hurricane Katrina', *American Journal of Economics and Sociology*, **69** (4), 1294–320.

Rogers, J. (2008), 'Development of the New Orleans flood protection system prior to Hurricane Katrina', *Journal of Geotechnical and Geoenvironmental Engineering*, **134**, 602–17.

Rojecki, Andrew (2009), 'Political culture and disaster response: the great floods of 1927 and 2005', *Media, Culture and Society*, **31** (6), 957–76.

Rooney, Peggy (1989), 'Louisiana's wetlands calamity', *EPA Journal*, **15** (5), 37–9.

Schleifstein, Mark (2013), 'With New Orleans' new levee system complete, local officials worry about paying for its upkeep', *Times-Picayune*, online edition, 17 August, accessed 6 October 2014 at www.nola.com/hurricane/index.ssf/2013/08/with_new_orleans_new_levee_sys.html.

Schultz, Jessica and James R. Elliott (2013), 'Natural disasters and local demographic change in the United States', *Population and Environment*, **34**, 293–312.

Shrum, Wesley (2014), 'What caused the flood? Controversy and closure in the Hurricane Katrina disaster', *Social Studies of Science*, **44** (1), 3–33.

Shughart, William (2006), 'Katrinanomics: the politics and economics of disaster relief', *Public Choice*, **127** (1), 31–53.

Sisk, Blake and Carl L. Bankston III (2014), 'Hurricane Katrina, a construction boom, and a new labour force: Latino immigrants and the New Orleans construction industry, 2000 and 2006–2010', *Population Research and Policy Review*, **33** (3), 309–34.

Spencer, Robyn (1994), 'Contested terrain: the Mississippi flood of 1927 and the struggle to control black labor', *Journal of Negro History*, **79** (2), 170–81.

Thiede, Brian C. and David L. Brown (2013), 'Hurricane Katrina: who stayed and why?', *Population Research and Policy Review*, **32** (6), 803–24.

Trumbo, Craig, Michell A. Meyer, Holly Marlatt, Lori Peek and Bridget Morrissey (2014), 'An assessment of change in risk perception and optimistic bias for hurricanes among Gulf Coast residents', *Risk Analysis*, **34** (6), 1013–24.

United States House of Representatives (2006), *A Failure of Initiative: Final Report of the Select Bipartisan Committee to Investigate the Preparation for and Response to Hurricane Katrina*, Washington, DC: US Government Printing Office.

United States Senate, Committee on Homeland Security and Governmental Affairs (2006), *Hurricane Katrina: A Nation Still Unprepared*, Washington, DC: US Government Printing Office.

Vigdor, Jacob (2008), 'The economic aftermath of Hurricane Katrina', *Journal of Economic Perspectives*, **22** (4), 135–54.

Welky, David (2011), *The Thousand Year Flood: The Ohio-Mississippi Disaster of 1937*, Chicago, IL: University of Chicago Press.

Zolkos, Rodd (2012), 'New Orleans passes flooding test; insurers unmoved by Isaac's failure to breach defenses', *Business Insurance*, **46** (36), 1.

Zucchino, David (2014), 'C. Ray Nagin, former New Orleans mayor, sentenced to 10 years in prison', *Los Angeles Times*, online edition, 9 July, accessed 22 August 2014 at www.latimes.com/nation/nationnow/la-na-nn-ray-nagin-new-orleans-sentenced-20140709-story.html.

CHAPTER 3

Aldcroft, Derek H. (1977), *From Versailles to Wall Street*, London: Allen Lane.

Aldcroft, Derek H. and Stephen Morewood (1995), *Economic Change in Eastern Europe since 1918*, Aldershot, UK and Brookfield, VT, USA: Edward Elgar Publishing.

Angell, Norman (1913), *The Great Illusion: A Study of the Relation of Military Power to National Advantage*, 4th edn, New York and London: G.P. Putnam's Sons.

Balderston, Theo (1989), 'War finance and inflation in Britain and Germany, 1914–1918', *Economic History Review*, **42** (2), 222–44.

Barber, William J. (1991), 'British and American economists and attempts to comprehend the nature of war, 1910–20', *History of Political Economy*, **23** (supplement), 61–88.

Berghahn, Volker R. (2014), 'Origins', in Jay Winter (ed.), *The Cambridge History of the First World War*, Vol. I, *Global War*, Cambridge: Cambridge University Press, pp. 16–38.

Best, Geoffrey (1983), *Humanity in Warfare: The Modern History of the International Law of Armed Conflicts*, London: Methuen.

Blum, Matthias (2011), 'Government decisions before and during the First World War and the living standards in Germany during a drastic natural experiment', *Explorations in Economic History*, **48**, 556–67.

Boemeke, Manfred F., Gerald D. Feldman and Elisabeth Glaser (eds) (1998), *The Treaty of Versailles: A Reassessment After 75 Years*, Cambridge: Cambridge University Press.

Bogart, Ernest L. (1920), *Direct and Indirect Costs of the Great World War*, New York: Oxford University Press.

Boltho, Andrea (2001), 'Reconstruction after two world wars: why the differences?', *Journal of European Economic History*, **30** (2), 429–56.

Bonzon, Thierry and Belinda Davis (1997), 'Feeding the cities', in Jay Winter and Jean-Louis Robert (eds), *Capital Cities at War: Paris, London, Berlin 1914–1919*, Cambridge: Cambridge University Press, pp. 305–41.

Broadberry, Stephen and Mark Harrison (2005), 'The economics of World War I: an overview', in Stephen Broadberry and Mark Harrison (eds), *The Economics of World War I*, Cambridge: Cambridge University Press, pp. 3–40.

Childers, Erskine (1903), *The Riddle of the Sands*, London: Smith, Elder.

Clark, Christopher (2013), *The Sleepwalkers: How Europe Went to War in 1914*, London: Penguin.

Clout, Hugh (1989), 'The reconstruction of Reims, 1919–30', *Planning Outlook*, **32** (1), 23–34.

Clout, Hugh (1993), 'The revival of rural Lorraine after the Great War', *Geografiska Annaler Series B, Human Geography*, **75** (2), 73–91.

Clout, Hugh (2005), 'The great reconstruction of towns and cities in France, 1918–35', *Planning Perspectives*, **20**, 1–33.

Commission of Responsibilities (1919), *Violation of the Laws and Customs of War: Reports of Majority and Dissenting Reports of American and Japanese Members of Commission of Responsibilities*, Oxford: Clarendon Press.

Davis, Belinda (2000), *Home Fires Burning: Food, Politics, and Everyday Life in World War I Berlin*, Chapel Hill, NC: University of North Carolina Press.

Dawson, Grant (2002), 'Preventing "a great moral evil": Jean de Bloch's "The Future of War" as anti-revolutionary pacifism', *Journal of Contemporary History*, **37** (1), 5–19.

de Bloch, Jean (1899), *The Future of War in its Technical, Economic and Political Relations*, Boston, MA: Doubleday & McClure.

Delaporte, Sophie (2010), 'Military medicine', in John Horne (ed.), *A Companion to World War I*, Chichester: Wiley-Blackwell, pp. 295–306.

den Hertog, Johan (2010), 'The Commission for Relief in Belgium and the First World War', *Diplomacy and Statecraft*, **21** (4), 593–613.

Deperchin, Annie (2014), 'The laws of war', in Jay Winter (ed.), *The Cambridge History of the First World War*, Vol. I, *Global War*, Cambridge: Cambridge University Press, pp. 615–38.

Dunbabin, J.P. (1993), 'The League of Nations' place in the international system', *History*, **78** (254), 421–42.

Eichengreen, Barry (1998), *Globalizing Capital: A History of the International Monetary System*, Princeton, NJ: Princeton University Press.

Eloranta, Jari (2002), 'European states in the international arms trade, 1920–1937: the impact of external threats, market forces, and domestic constraints', *Scandinavian Economic History Review*, **50** (1), 44–67.

Eloranta, Jari (2007), 'From the great illusion to the Great War: military spending behaviour of the Great Powers, 1870–1913', *European Review of Economic History*, **11** (2), 255–83.

Eloranta, Jari (2011), 'Why did the League of Nations fail?', *Cliometrica*, **5** (1), 27–52.

Ferguson, Niall (1998), 'The balance of payments question', in Manfred F. Boemeke, Gerald D. Feldman and Elisabeth Glaser (eds), *The Treaty of Versailles: A Reassessment After 75 Years*, Cambridge: Cambridge University Press, pp. 401–40

Ferguson, Niall (1999), *The Pity of War*, New York: Basic Books.

Frankel, Jeffrey A. (1997), *Regional Trading Blocs in the World Economic System*, Washington, DC: Institute for International Economics.

Gatrell, Peter (2005), 'Poor Russia, poor show: mobilising a backward economy for war, 1917–1918', in Stephen Broadberry and Mark Harrison (eds), *The Economics of World War I*, Cambridge: Cambridge University Press, pp. 235–75

Gatrell, Peter (2008), 'Refugees and forced migrants during the First World War', *Immigrants and Minorities*, **26** (1–2), 82–100.

Hamilton, Richard F. (2010), 'War planning: obvious needs, not so obvious solutions', in Richard F. Hamilton and Holger H. Herwig (eds), *War Planning 1914*, Cambridge: Cambridge University Press, pp. 1–23.

Hamilton, Richard F. and Holger H. Herwig (2004), *Decisions for War 1914–1917*, Cambridge: Cambridge University Press.

Hamilton, Richard F. and Holger H. Herwig (eds) (2008), *The Origins of World War I*, Cambridge: Cambridge University Press.

Hantke, Max and Mark Spoerer (2010), 'The imposed gift of Versailles: the fiscal effects of restricting the size of Germany's armed forces, 1924–9', *Economic History Review*, **63** (4), 849–64.

Harrison, Mark (2010), *The Medical War: British Military Medicine in the First World War*, Oxford: Oxford University Press.

Héran, François (2014), 'Lost generations: the demographic impact of the Great War', *Population and Societies*, **510**, 1–4.

Hobson, John A. (1902), *Imperialism: A Study*, London: George Allen & Unwin.

Horn, Martin and Talbot Imlay (2005), 'Money in wartime: France's financial preparations for the two world wars', *International History Review*, **27** (4), 709–53.

Huebner, S.S. (1917), 'Life insurance and the war', *Scientific Monthly*, **4** (4), 342–54.

Humphries, Mark Osborne (2014), 'Pandemic paths of infection: the First World War and the origins of the 1918 influenza', *War in History*, **21** (1), 55–81.

Hutchinson, John F. (1996), *Champions of Charity: War and the Rise of the Red Cross*, Boulder, CO: Westview.

Jones, Heather (2009), 'International or transnational? Humanitarian action during the First World War', *European Review of History*, **16** (5), 697–713.

Jones, Heather (2014), 'Prisoners of war', in Jay Winter (ed.), *The Cambridge History of the First World War*, Vol. II, *The State*, Cambridge: Cambridge University Press, pp. 266–90.

Kampmark, Binoy (2007), 'Sacred sovereigns and punishable war crimes: the ambivalence of the Wilson administration towards a trial of Kaiser Wilhelm II', *Australian Journal of Politics and History*, **53** (4), 519–37.

Keynes, John Maynard (1919), *The Economic Consequences of the Peace*, London: Macmillan.

Kieser, Han-Lukas and Donald Bloxham (2014), 'Genocide', in Jay Winter (ed.), *The Cambridge History of the First World War*, Vol. I, *Global War*, Cambridge: Cambridge University Press, pp. 585–614.

Komlos, John (1983), *The Habsburg Monarchy as a Customs Union*, Princeton, NJ: Princeton University Press.

Kramer, Alan (2008), *Dynamic of Destruction: Culture and Mass Killing in the First World War*, Oxford: Oxford University Press.

Kramer, Alan (2014), 'Blockade and economic warfare', in Jay Winter (ed.), *The Cambridge History of the First World War*, Vol. II, *The State*, Cambridge: Cambridge University Press, pp. 460–89.

Lambert, Nicolas (2012), *Planning for Armageddon: British Economic Warfare and the First World War*, Cambridge, MA: Harvard University Press.

MacMillan, Margaret (2003), *Paris 1919*, New York: Random House.

MacMillan, Margaret (2013), *The War that Ended Peace: How Europe Abandoned Peace for the First World War*, London: Profile.

Maddison, Angus (1991), *Dynamic Forces in Capitalist Development*, Oxford: Oxford University Press.

Maddison, Angus (1995), *Monitoring the World Economy 1820–1992*, Paris: OECD.

Maddison, Angus (2006), 'Western Europe 1500–2001', in Angus Maddison, *The World Economy: Volume 1: A Millennial Perspective and Volume 2: Historical Statistics*, Paris: OECD.

Mahan, Alfred T. (2012), 'The great illusion', *North American Review*, **195**, 319–32.

Markevich, Andrei and Mark Harrison (2011), 'Great War, civil war, and recovery: Russia's national income, 1913 to 1928', *Journal of Economic History*, **71** (3), 672–703.

Marks, Sally (1998), 'Smoke and mirrors: in smoke-filled rooms and the Galerie des Glaces', in Manfred F. Boemeke, Gerald D. Feldman and Elisabeth Glaser (eds), *The Treaty of Versailles: A Reassessment After 75 Years*, Cambridge: Cambridge University Press, pp. 337–70.

Marks, Sally (2013), 'Mistakes and myths: the Allies, Germany, and the Versailles Treaty, 1918–1921', *Journal of Modern History*, **85** (3), 632–59.

Maurer, John H. (1997), 'Arms control and the Anglo-German naval race before World War I: lessons for today?', *Political Science Quarterly*, **112** (2), 285–306.

Mises, L. von (1983), *Nation, State, and Economy*, New York: New York University Press.

Moggridge, Donald E. (1992), *Maynard Keynes: An Economist's Biography*, London: Routledge.

Mombauer, Annika (1999), 'A reluctant military leader? Helmuth von Moltke and the July crisis of 1914', *War in History*, **6** (4), 417–46.

Mombauer, Annika (2010), 'German war plans', in Richard F. Hamilton and Holger H. Herwig (eds), *War Planning 1914*, Cambridge: Cambridge University Press, pp. 48–79.

Morris, A.J.A. (1971), 'The English radicals' campaign for disarmament and the Hague Conference of 1907', *Journal of Modern History*, **43** (3), 367–93.

Mottram, Ralph Hale (1929), 'A personal record', in R.H. Mottram, John Easton and Eric Partridge, *Three Personal Experiences of the War*, London: Scholartis.

Offer, Avner (1988), 'Morality and Admiralty: "Jacky" Fisher, economic warfare and the laws of war', *Journal of Contemporary History*, **23** (1), 99–118.

Offer, Avner (1995), 'Going to war in 1914: a matter of honor?', *Politics and Society*, **23** (2), 213–41.

Peden, George (1979), *British Rearmament and the Treasury, 1932–1939*, Edinburgh: Scottish Academic Press.

Roberts, Richard (2013), *Saving the City: The Great Financial Crisis of 1914*, Oxford: Oxford University Press.

Robertson, Emily (2014), 'Propaganda and "manufactured hatred": a reappraisal of the ethics of First World War British and Australian atrocity propaganda', *Public Relations Inquiry*, **3** (2), 245–66.

Roses, Joan R. and Nikolaus Wolf (2010), 'Aggregate growth, 1913–1950', in Stephen Broadberry and Kevin H. O'Rourke (eds), *The Cambridge Economic History of Modern Europe*, Vol. 2, *1870 to the Present*, Cambridge: Cambridge University Press, pp. 181–207.

Rotte, Ralph (1997), 'Economics and peace-theory on the eve of World War I', in Jurgen Brauer and William G. Gissy (eds), *Economics of Conflict and Peace*, Aldershot: Avebury, pp. 7–30.

Singleton, John (2007), '"Destruction and misery" … the First World War', in Michael J. Oliver and Derek H. Aldcroft (eds), *Economic Disasters of the Twentieth Century*, Cheltenham, UK and Northampton, MA, USA: Edward Elgar Publishing, pp. 9–50.

Stevenson, David (1996), *Armaments and the Coming of War: Europe 1904–1914*, Oxford: Clarendon Press.

Stevenson, David (2004), *1914–1918: The History of the First World War*, London: Penguin.

Stevenson, David (2012), 'Fortifications and the European military balance before 1914', *Journal of Strategic Studies*, **35** (6), 829–59.

Strachan, Hew (2003), *The First World War*, Vol. 1, *To Arms*, Oxford: Oxford University Press.

Strachan, Hew (2014), 'The origins of the First World War', *International Affairs*, **90** (2), 429–39.

Tessaris, Chiara (2010), 'The war relief work of the American Joint Distribution Committee in Poland and Lithuania, 1915–18', *East European Jewish Affairs*, **40** (2), 127–44.

Travers, T.H.E. (1979), 'Technology, tactics, and morale: Jean de Bloch, the Boer War, and British military theory, 1900–1914', *Journal of Modern History*, **51** (2), 264–86.

Vasquez, John A. (2014), 'The First World War and international relations theory: a review of books on the 100th anniversary', *International Studies Review*, **16** (4), 623–44.

Waldman, Thomas (2010), 'Politics and war: Clausewitz's paradoxical equation', *Parameters*, **40** (3), 1–13.

Webster, Andrew (2005), 'Making disarmament work: the implementation of the international disarmament provisions in the League of Nations Covenant, 1919–1925', *Diplomacy and Statecraft*, **16** (3), 551–69.

Wells, H.G. (1908), *The War in the Air*, London: Bell.

Wertheim, Stephen (2012), 'The League of Nations: a retreat from international law?', *Journal of Global History*, **7** (2), 210–32.

Winter, Jay (1985), *The Great War and the British People*, Basingstoke: Macmillan.

Winter, Jay (1998), *Sites of Memory, Sites of Mourning: The Great War in European Cultural History*, London: Canto.

Wolf, Nikolaus, Max-Stephan Schulze and Hans-Christian Heinemeyer (2011), 'On the economic consequences of the peace: trade and borders after Versailles', *Economic History Review*, **71** (4), 915–49.

Zagare, Frank C. (2009a), 'After Sarajevo: explaining the blank check', *International Interactions: Empirical and Theoretical Research in International Relations*, **35** (1), 106–27.

Zagare, Frank C. (2009b), 'Explaining the 1914 war in Europe: an analytic narrative', *Journal of Theoretical Politics*, **21** (1), 63–95.

Zagare, Frank C. and D. Marc Kigour (2006), 'The deterrence-versus-restraint dilemma in extended deterrence: explaining British policy in 1914', *International Studies Review*, **8** (4), 623–41.

CHAPTER 4

Adam, Arthur, Carter Goodrich, Joseph Demmery, Willard L. Thorp and Alvin H. Hansen (1931), 'The business depression of nineteen hundred thirty – discussion', *American Economic Review*, **21** (1), Supplement, 183–201.

Akerlof, George A. and Robert L. Shiller (2009), *Animal Spirits: How Human Psychology Drives the Economy, and Why it Matters for Global Capitalism*, Princeton, NJ: Princeton University Press.

Almunia, Miguel, Agustín Bénétrix, Barry Eichengreen, Kevin O'Rourke and Gisela Rua (2010), 'From Great Depression to great credit crisis: similarities, differences, and lessons', *Economic Policy*, **25** (62), 219–65.

Balderston, Theo (2002), *Economics and Politics in the Weimar Republic*, Cambridge: Cambridge University Press.

Barber, William J. (1985), *From New Era to New Deal: Herbert Hoover, the Economists, and American Economic Policy, 1921–1933*, Cambridge: Cambridge University Press.

Bernanke, Benjamin S. (1983), 'Nonmonetary effects of the financial crisis in the propagation of the Great Depression', *American Economic Review*, **73** (3), 257–76.

Bernanke, Benjamin S. (1995), 'The macroeconomics of the Great Depression: a comparative approach', *Journal of Money, Credit, and Banking*, **27** (1), 1–28.

Bernanke, Benjamin S. (2000), *Essays on the Great Depression*, Princeton, NJ: Princeton University Press.

Bernanke, Benjamin S. (2004), 'Money, gold, and the Great Depression', H. Parker Willis Lecture in Economic Policy at Washington and Lee University, Lexington, VA, accessed 6 June 2015 at www.federalreserve.gov/boarddocs/speeches/2004/200403022/default.htm.

Billings, Mark and Forrest Capie (2011), 'Financial crisis, contagion, and the British banking system between the world wars', *Business History*, **53** (2), 193–215.

Board of Governors of the Federal Reserve System (1994), *The Federal Reserve System: Purposes and Functions*, 8th edn, Washington, DC: Board of Governors of the Federal Reserve System.

Bordo, Michael, Barry Eichengreen, Daniela Klingebiel, Maria Soledad Martinez-Peria and Andrew K. Rose (2001), 'Is the crisis problem growing more severe?', *Economic Policy*, **16** (32), 51–82.

Bordo, Michael D., Owen Humpage and Anna J. Schwartz (2007), 'The historical origins of US exchange market intervention policy', *International Journal of Finance and Economics*, **12** (2), 109–32.

Brinkley, Alan (1983), *Voices of Protest: Huey Long, Father Coughlin and the Great Depression*, New York: Vintage.

Brown, Ian (1997), *Economic Change in South East Asia, c. 1830–1980*, Kuala Lumpur: Oxford University Press.

Carosso, Vincent P. (1970a), *Investment Banking in America: A History*, Cambridge, MA: Harvard University Press.

Carosso, Vincent P. (1970b), 'Washington and Wall Street: the New Deal and investment bankers, 1933–1940', *Business History Review*, **44** (4), 425–45.

Clavin, Patricia (1992), '"The fetishes of so-called international bankers": central bank co-operation for the World Economic Conference, 1932–3', *Contemporary European History*, **1** (3), 281–311.

Cole, Harold L. and Lee E. Ohanian (2004), 'New Deal policies and the persistence of the Great Depression: a general equilibrium analysis', *Journal of Political Economy*, **112** (4), 779–816.

Crafts, N.F.R. (1987), 'Long-term unemployment in Britain in the 1930s', *Economic History Review*, **40** (3), 418–32.

Crafts, N.F.R. and Peter Fearon (2010), 'Lessons from the 1930s Great Depression', *Oxford Review of Economic Policy*, **26** (3), 285–317.

Davis, J.S. (1920), 'World currency and banking: the first Brussels financial conference', *Review of Economic Statistics*, **2** (12), 349–60.

de Bromhead, Alan, Barry Eichengreen and Kevin H. O'Rourke (2013), 'Right-wing political extremism in the 1920s and 1930s: do German lessons generalize?', *Journal of Economic History*, **63** (2), 371–406.

Dominguez, Kathryn M., Ray C. Fair and Matthew D. Shapiro (1988), 'Forecasting the depression: Harvard versus Yale', *American Economic Review*, **78** (4), 595–612.

Eggertsson, Gauti B. (2008), 'Great expectations and the end of the depression', *American Economic Review*, **98** (4), 1476–516.

Eichengreen, Barry J. (1992), *Golden Fetters: The Gold Standard and the Great Depression, 1919–1939*, Oxford: Oxford University Press.

Eichengreen, Barry J. (1996), *Globalizing Capital*, Princeton, NJ: Princeton University Press.

Eichengreen, Barry J. and Marc Flandreau (1997), 'Editors' introduction', in Barry J. Eichengreen and Marc Flandreau (eds), *The Gold Standard in Theory and History*, 2nd edn, London: Routledge, pp. 1–21.

Eichengreen, Barry and T.J. Hatton (1988), 'Interwar unemployment in international perspective: an overview', in Barry Eichengreen and T.J. Hatton (eds), *Interwar Unemployment in International Perspective*, Dordrecht: Kluwer, pp. 1–60.

Eichengreen, Barry and Richard Portes (1990), 'The interwar debt crisis and its aftermath', *World Bank Research Observer*, **5** (1), 69–94.

Eichengreen, Barry J. and Peter Temin (2000), 'The gold standard and the Great Depression', *Contemporary European History*, **9** (2), 183–207.

Einzig, Paul (1931), *Behind the Scenes of International Finance*, London: Macmillan.

Federal Reserve System (1930), 'Minutes of the meeting of the Executive Committee of the Open Market Policy Conference, September 25, 1930', Open Market Policy Conference for the Federal Reserve System, Open Market Operations: Final Minutes, Open Market Policy Conference Meetings (May 1930–July 1933) , Box 1438, Folder 1, Records of the Federal Reserve System, 1878–1996 , Record Group 82, United States National Archives and Records Administration, accessed 28 May 2015 at https://fraser.stlouisfed.org/scribd/?item_id=469292&filepath=/docs/historical/nara/nara_rg082_e01_b1438_01.pdf.

Flood, Mark D. (1992), 'The great deposit insurance debate', *Federal Reserve Bank of St. Louis Review*, **74** (4), 51–77.

Friedman, Milton and Anna J. Schwartz (1963), *A Monetary History of the United States, 1870–1960*, Princeton, NJ: Princeton University Press.

Friedman, Walter A. (2013), *Fortune Tellers: The Story of America's First Economic Forecasters*, Princeton, NJ: Princeton University Press.

Grossman, Richard S. (1994), 'The shoe that didn't drop: explaining banking instability during the Great Depression', *Journal of Economic History*, **54** (3), 654–82.

Hamilton, James D. (1987), 'Monetary factors in the Great Depression', *Journal of Monetary Economics*, **19**, 145–69.

Hatton, Timothy J. (2004), 'Unemployment and the labour market, 1870–1939', in Roderick Floud and Paul Johnson (eds), *The Cambridge Economic History of Modern Britain*, Vol. 2, Cambridge: Cambridge University Press, pp. 344–73.

Hendrickson, Jill M. (2001), 'The long and bumpy road to Glass–Steagall reform: a historical and evolutionary analysis of banking legislation', *American Journal of Economics and Sociology*, **60** (4), 849–79.

Hoover, Herbert (1952), *The Memoirs of Herbert Hoover: The Great Depression 1929–1941*, New York: Macmillan.

Howson, Susan (2011), *Lionel Robbins*, Oxford: Oxford University Press.

Huertas, Thomas F. and Joan L. Silverman (1986), 'Charles E. Mitchell: scapegoat of the crash?', *Business History Review*, **60** (1), 81–103.

James, Harold (1984), 'The causes of the German banking crisis of 1931', *Economic History Review*, **38** (1), 68–87.

James, Harold (1986), *The German Slump: Politics and Economics 1924–1936*, Oxford: Clarendon Press.

James, Harold (1999), 'The Reichsbank 1876–1945', in Deutsche Bundesbank (ed.), *Fifty Years of the Deutsche Mark*, Oxford: Oxford University Press, pp. 3–53.

James, Harold (2001), *The Deutsche Bank and the Nazi Economic War Against the Jews*, Cambridge: Cambridge University Press.

James, Harold (2004), *The Nazi Dictatorship and the Deutsche Bank*, Cambridge: Cambridge University Press.

James, Harold (2010), '1929: the New York stock market crash', *Representations*, **110** (1), 129–44.

Keynes, John Maynard (1924), *A Tract on Monetary Reform*, London: Macmillan.

Keynes, John Maynard (1931), 'Keynes celebrates the end of the Gold Standard', accessed 24 April 2013 at www.youtube.com/watch?v=U1S9F3agsUA.

Keynes, John Maynard (1936), *The General Theory of Employment, Interest, and Money*, London: Macmillan.

Keynes, John Maynard (1978), 'The great slump', in *The Collected Writings of John Maynard Keynes*, ed. Elizabeth Johnson and Donald Moggridge, Cambridge: Cambridge University Press, pp. 126–34.

Kindleberger, Charles P. (1987), *The World in Depression 1929–1939*, London: Penguin.

Kopper, Christopher (2011), 'New perspectives on the 1931 banking crisis in Germany and Central Europe', *Business History*, **53** (2), 216–29.

Kroszner, Randall S. and Raghuram G. Rajan (1994), 'Is the Glass–Steagall Act justified? A study of the US experience with universal banking before 1933', *American Economic Review*, **84**, 810–32.

Landis, Michele L. (1999), 'Fate, responsibility, and "natural" disaster relief: narrating the American welfare state', *Law and Society Review*, **33** (2), 257–318.

League of Nations (1920), 'Report of the International Financial Conference', in World Peace Foundation, *League of Nations 1920*, Vol. 3, Boston, MA: World Peace Foundation, pp. 221–54.

League of Nations (1934), *Commercial Banks, 1925–1933*, Geneva: League of Nations.

League of Nations (1935), *Commercial Banks, 1929–1934*, Geneva: League of Nations.

League of Nations (annually, 1935–40), *Money and Banking*, Geneva: League of Nations.

League of Nations (1944), *International Currency Experience*, Geneva: League of Nations.

Maddison, Angus (1995), *Monitoring the World Economy 1820–1992*, Paris: OECD.

Maddison, Angus (2006), *The World Economy*, Paris: OECD.

Meltzer, Allan H. (2003), *A History of the Federal Reserve*, Vol. 1, *1913–1951*, Chicago, IL: University of Chicago Press.

Morgan, Kevin (2006), *Ramsay MacDonald*, London: Haus.

Parker, Randall E. (ed.) (2002), *Reflections on the Great Depression*, Cheltenham, UK and Northampton, MA, USA: Edward Elgar Publishing.

Parker, Randall E. (ed.) (2007), *The Economics of the Great Depression: A Twenty-First Century Look Back at the Economics of the Interwar Period*, Cheltenham, UK and Northampton, MA, USA: Edward Elgar Publishing.

Perino, Michael A. (2010), *The Hellhound of Wall Street: How Ferdinand Pecora's Investigation of the Great Crash Forever Changed American Finance*, New York: Penguin.

Plotnick, Robert D., Eugene Smolensky, Eireik Evenhouse and Siobhan Reilly (2000), 'The twentieth century record of inequality and poverty in the United States', in Stanley L. Engerman and Robert E. Gallman (eds), *The Cambridge Economic History of the United States*, Vol. 3, Cambridge: Cambridge University Press, pp. 249–99.

Reinhart, Carmen M. and Kenneth S. Rogoff (2009), *This Time is Different: Eight Centuries of Financial Folly*, Princeton, NJ: Princeton University Press.

Reinhart, Carmen M. and Kenneth S. Rogoff (2013), 'Financial and sovereign debt crises: some lessons learned and those forgotten', IMF Working Paper WP/13/266.

Reveley, James and John Singleton (2013), 'Re-storying bankers: historical antecedents of banker bashing in Britain and America', *Management and Organizational History*, **8** (4), 329–44.

Ritschl, Albrecht (2003), '"Dancing on a volcano": the economic recovery and collapse of Weimar Germany, 1924–33', in Theo Balderston (ed.), *The World Economy and National Economies in the Interwar Slump*, Basingstoke: Palgrave, pp. 105–42.

Ritschl, Albrecht and Samad Sarferaz (2014), 'Currency versus banking in the financial crisis of 1931', *International Economic Review*, **55** (2), 349–73.

Romer, Christina D. (1992), 'What ended the Great Depression?', *Journal of Economic History*, **52** (4), 757–84.

Romer, Christina D. (1993), 'The nation in depression', *Journal of Economic Perspectives*, **7** (2), 9–39.

Roosevelt, Franklin D. (1933), 'Inaugural address of the President, March 4 1933', accessed 7 February 2014 at http://www.archives.gov/education/lessons/fdr-inaugural/.

Ryan, Halford R. (1988), *Franklin D. Roosevelt's Rhetorical Presidency*, Westport, CT: Greenwood.

Salais, Robert (1988), 'Why was unemployment so low in France during the 1930s?', in Barry Eichengreen and T.J. Hatton (eds), *Interwar Unemployment in International Perspective*, Dordrecht: Kluwer, pp. 247–88.

Schumpeter, Josef (1931), 'The present world depression: a tentative diagnosis', *American Economic Review*, **21** (1), Supplement, 179–82.

Singleton, John (2011), *Central Banking in the Twentieth Century*, Cambridge: Cambridge University Press.

Skidelsky, Robert (1970), *Politicians and the Slump: The Labour Government of 1929–1931*, Harmondsworth: Pelican.

Snyder, Carl (1931), 'The world-wide depression of 1930', *American Economic Review*, **21** (1), Supplement, 172–8.

Straumann, Tobias (2009), 'Rule rather than exception: Brüning's fear of devaluation in comparative perspective', *Journal of Contemporary History*, **44** (4), 603–17.

Tooze, Adam (2007), *The Wages of Destruction: The Making and Breaking of the Nazi Economy*, London: Penguin.

United States Senate (1934), *Stock Exchange Practices: Report of the Committee on Banking and Finance*, Washington, DC: Government Printing Office.

Webb, Beatrice (1956), *Beatrice Webb's Diaries, 1924–1932*, ed. Margaret Cole, London: Longmans, Green.

Weitz, John (1997), *Hitler's Banker: Hjalmar Horace Greeley Schacht*, New York: Little, Brown.

Wheatcroft, S.G. (2004), 'Towards explaining Soviet famine of 1931–3: political and natural factors in perspective', *Food and Foodways*, **12** (2), 107–36.

Wheatcroft, S.G. (2009), 'The first 35 years of Soviet living standards: secular growth and conjunctural crises in a time of famines', *Explorations in Economic History*, **46**, 24–52.

Wheelock, David C. (1990), 'Member bank borrowing and the Fed's contractionary monetary policy during the Great Depression', *Journal of Money, Credit and Banking*, **22** (4), 409–26.

White, Eugene (1986), 'Before the Glass–Steagall Act: an analysis of the investment banking activities of national banks', *Explorations in Economic History*, **23**, 33–55.

White, Lawrence H. (2008), 'Did Hayek and Robbins deepen the Great Depression?', *Journal of Money, Credit and Banking*, **40** (4), 751–68.

Williamson, Phillip (1984), 'A "bankers' ramp"? Financiers and the British political crisis of August 1931', *English Historical Review*, **99** (393), 770–806.

Wolf, Nikolaus (2008), 'Scylla and Charybdis: explaining Europe's exit from gold, January 1928 – December 1936', *Explorations in Economic History*, **45**, 383–401.

CHAPTER 5

Aldrich, Mark (1995), '"The needless peril of the coal mine": the Bureau of Mines and the campaign against coal mine explosions, 1910–1940', *Technology and Culture*, **36** (3), 483–518.

Ashworth, William (1986), *The History of the British Coal Industry*, Vol. 5, *1946–1982: The Nationalized Industry*, Oxford: Clarendon Press.

Benson, John (1975), 'English coal-miners' trade-union accident funds, 1850–1900', *Economic History Review*, **28** (3), 401–12.

Birkland, Thomas A. (2009), 'Disasters, lessons learned, and fantasy documents', *Journal of Contingencies and Crisis Management*, **17** (3), 146–56.

Bogart, Ernest L. (1920), *Direct and Indirect Costs of the Great World War*, New York: Oxford University Press

Boyns, Trevor (1985), 'Work and death in the South Wales coalfield, 1870–1914', *Welsh History Review*, **12** (4), 514–37.

Boyns, Trevor (1986), 'Technical change and colliery explosions in the South Wales coalfield, c. 1870–1914', *Welsh History Review*, **13** (2), 155–77.

Broadcasters' Audience Research Board (2014), 'Television ownership in private domestic households 1956–2014 (millions)', accessed 7 January 2015 at www.barb.co.uk/resources/tv-facts/tv-ownership.

Bryan, Andrew (1975), *The Evolution of Health and Safety in Mines*, Letchworth: Mine & Quarry.

Bryan, Andrew (2004), 'Redmayne, Sir Richard Augustine Studdert (1865–1955)', rev. Robert Brown, *Oxford Dictionary of National Biography*, Oxford: Oxford University Press, accessed 17 November 2014 at www.oxforddnb.com/view/article/35701.

Chief Inspector of Mines (1920), *Mines and Quarries: General Report, with Statistics for 1919*, Vol. 1, Cmd. 925, London: HMSO.

Clwyd, Ann (1973),'Reclamation plan "caused tip flood"', *Guardian*, 29 September, p. 4.

Couto, Richard A. (1989), 'Economics, experts, and risk: lessons from the catastrophe at Aberfan', *Political Psychology*, **10** (2), 309–24

Daily Mail (1913a), '£55,000 Senghenydd fund', *Daily Mail*, 28 October, p. 5.

Daily Mail (1913b), 'Royal £2,350 for miners', *Daily Mail*, 8 November, p. 5.

Daily Mail (1913c), '£100,000 in 32 days', *Daily Mail*, 17 November, p. 5.

Daily Mail (1913d), 'Blackburn Rovers at Cardiff', *Daily Mail*, 18 November, p. 10.

Davies, Edmund (1967), *Report of the Tribunal Appointed to Inquire into the Disaster at Aberfan on October 21st, 1966*, HL 316 and HC 553, London: HMSO.

Davies, Ivor J. (1914), 'Carbon monoxide poisoning in the Senghenydd explosion', *Proceedings of the Royal Society of Medicine*, **7** (Neurological Section), 49–68.

Davies, M.C.R., A.G. Johnston and K.P. Williams (1998), 'Stabilised mixed colliery spoil in land reclamation', *International Journal of Surface Mining, Reclamation and Environment*, **12** (1), 1–4.

Department of Scientific and Industrial Research Advisory Council (1918), *First Report of the Mine Rescue Apparatus Research Committee*, London: DSIR.

Duckham, Baron F. (1976), 'The Oaks disaster, 1866', in John Benson and Robert G. Neville (eds), *Studies in the Yorkshire Coal Industry*, Manchester: Manchester University Press, pp. 66–91.

Feickert, David Gordon (2007), 'Tensions of transition: the safety problems of the Chinese coal industry', MA thesis, Victoria University of Wellington.

Foregger, Richard (1974), 'Development of mine rescue and underwater breathing apparatus: appliances of Henry Fleuss', *Journal of the History of Medicine*, **29** (3), 317–30.

Galloway, W., S.T. Evans and J.T. Robson (1902), *Reports to His Majesty's Secretary of State for the Home Department on the Causes Attending an Explosion at the Universal Colliery, Glamorganshire on May 24th, 1901*, Cd. 947, London: HMSO.

Glyn, Andrew and Stephen Machin (1997), 'Colliery closures and the decline of the UK coal industry', *British Journal of Industrial Relations*, **35** (2), 197–214.

Gowers, Sir Ernest (1927), 'Commissions and committees and legislation in the coal industry, 1867–1926', *Iron and Coal Trades Review Diamond Jubilee Edition*, **115**, 112–19.

Griffiths, Trevor (2001), *The Lancashire Working Classes, c. 1880–1930*, Oxford: Clarendon Press.

Holmes, Richard (2004), *Tommy: The British Soldier on the Western Front, 1914–1918*, London: HarperCollins.

Hoyland, Peter (1989), 'An offer that Merthyr's miners could not refuse', *Guardian*, 25 August, p. 2.

Hudspeth, H.M. (1937), *Explosions in Coal Mines: A Comparison Between Britain and France: Report*, Cmd. 5566, London: HMSO.

Hutter, Bridget M. (1992), 'Public accident inquiries: the case of the Railway Inspectorate', *Public Administration*, **70**, 177–92.

James, Brian (1991), 'Was this the best we could do for Aberfan?', *Daily Mail*, 15 October, p. 6.

Johnes, Martin (2000), 'Aberfan and the management of trauma', *Disasters*, **24** (1), 1–17.

Jones, Alan Victor (2006), 'Towards safer working: the hazards and the risks of introducing electrical equipment in British coal mines up to about 1930', *Transactions of the Newcomen Society*, **76**, 115–26.

Jones, Dot (1980), 'Workmen's compensation and the South Wales miner, 1898–1914', *Bulletin of the Board of Celtic Studies*, **29** (1), 133–55.

Kennedy, Ray (1966), 'Coal Board killed them, say parents', *Daily Mail*, 25 October, p. 6.

Lane Fox, G.R. (1925), *Colliery Accident Funds (Great Britain): Return to an Order of the Honourable the House of Commons, dated July 22, 1925*, Cmd. 155, London: HMSO.

Lewis-Beck, Michael S. and John R. Alford (1980), 'Can government regulate safety? The coal mine example', *American Political Science Review*, **74** (3), 745–56.

Lieven, Michael (1989), 'Representations of the working class community: the Senghenydd mining disaster, 1913', *Llafur*, **5** (2), 17–29.

Lieven, Michael (1999), 'Senghenydd and the historiography of the South Wales coalfield', *Morgannwg: Transactions of the Glamorgan Local History Society*, **43**, 8–35.

Man, C.K. and K.A. Teacoach (2009), 'How does limestone rock dust prevent coal dust explosions in coal mines?', *Mining Engineering*, **61** (9), 69–73.

Manchester Guardian (1913a), 'Pit disaster: no more news of missing men', *Manchester Guardian*, 17 October, p. 8.

Manchester Guardian (1913b), 'Senghenydd disaster: Home Office and the miners' demand', *Manchester Guardian*, 12 November, p. 5.

Manchester Guardian (1913c), 'Senghenydd inquiry: representatives of owners and miners as assessors', *Manchester Guardian*, 20 December, p. 10.

Manchester Guardian (1914a), 'The Senghenydd verdict', *Manchester Guardian*, 15 January, p. 1.

Manchester Guardian (1914b), 'Senghenydd disaster: result of Home-Office prosecution', *Manchester Guardian*, 20 July, p. 12.

Manchester Guardian (1914c), 'Miners and Senghenydd magistrates: Federation's protest', *Manchester Guardian*, 23 July, p. 10.

Manchester Guardian (1914d), 'The Senghenydd colliery prosecutions', *Manchester Guardian*, 20 October, p. 10.

McLean, Iain and Martin Johnes (1997), 'On moles and the habits of birds: the unpolitics of Aberfan', *Twentieth Century British History*, **8** (3), 285–309.

McLean, Iain and Martin Johnes (1999), 'Regulating gifts of generosity: Aberfan and the Charity Commission', *Legal Studies*, **19** (3), 380–96.

McLean, Iain and Martin Johnes (2000), *Aberfan: Government and Disasters*, Cardiff: Welsh Academic Press.

Mills, Catherine (2005), 'A hazardous bargain: occupational risk in Cornish mining 1875–1914', *Labour History Review*, **70** (1), 53–71.

Murray, John E. and Javier Silvestre (2015), 'Small-scale technologies and European coal mine safety, 1850–1900', *Economic History Review*, **68** (3), 887–910.

Neville, Robert G. (1978), 'The Courrières colliery disaster, 1906', *Journal of Contemporary History*, **13**, 33–52.

Pantti, Mervi Katriina and Karin Wahl-Jorgensen (2011), '"Not an act of God": anger and citizenship in press coverage of British man-made disasters', *Media, Culture, Society*, **33** (1), 105–22.

Redmayne, Richard A.S. and Samuel Pope (1911a), *Report on the Causes of and Circumstances Attending and Explosion and Underground Fire which Occurred at the Wellington Pit, Whitehaven Colliery on the 11th May 1910*, Cd. 5524, London: HMSO.

Redmayne, Richard A.S. and Samuel Pope (1911b), *Reports on the Explosion which Occurred at the No. 3 Pit, Hulton Colliery, on the 21st December 1910*, Cd. 5692, London: HMSO.

Redmayne, Richard A.S., Evan Williams and Robert Smillie (1914), *Reports to the Right Honourable the Secretary of State for the Home Department on the Causes and Circumstances Attending the Explosion which Occurred at the Senghenydd Colliery on Tuesday, 14th October 1913*, Cd. 7346, London: HMSO.

Rockley, Baron Evelyn (1938), *Royal Commission on Safety in Coal Mines: Report*, Cmd. 5890, London: HMSO.

Routh, Guy (1980), *Occupation and Pay in Great Britain 1906–79*, London: Macmillan.

Saleh, Joseph H. and Amy M. Cummings (2011), 'Safety in the mining industry and the unfinished legacy of mining accidents: safety levers and defense-in-depth for addressing mining hazards', *Safety Science*, **49**, 764–77.

Stern, Gerald M. (1976), 'Disaster', *New York Times*, 27 February, p. 31.

Stone, Richard (2002), 'Counting the cost of London's killer smog', *Science*, **298**, 2106–7.

Supple, Barry (1987), *The History of the British Coal Industry*, Vol. 4, *1913–1946: The Political Economy of Decline*, Oxford: Clarendon Press.

Tawney, R.H. (1920), 'The British coal industry and the question of nationalization', *Quarterly Journal of Economics*, **35** (1), 61–107.

Thomson, G.M. and S. Rodin (1972), 'Colliery spoil tips – after Aberfan', Institution of Civil Engineers, Paper No. 7522, London: ICE.

Thomson, G.M. et al. (1973), 'Discussion: colliery spoil tips – after Aberfan', *Institution of Civil Engineers Proceedings*, **55** (3), 677–712.

The Times (1913), 'Work resumed at Senghenydd', *The Times*, 27 November, p. 21.

The Times (1914), 'Miner soldiers', *The Times*, 6 October, p. 3.

The Times (1997), 'Aberfan fund repaid', *The Times*, 1 August, p. 2.

Turner, Barry A. (1976), 'The organizational and interorganizational development of disasters', *Administrative Science Quarterly*, **21** (3), 378–97.

Tweedale, Geoffrey (2004 [2008]), 'Robens, Alfred, Baron Robens of Woldingham (1910–1999)', *Oxford Dictionary of National Biography*, Oxford: Oxford University Press; online edn, January 2008, accessed 8 January 2015 at www.oxforddnb.com/view/article/72445.

Welsby, Catherine (1995), '"Warning her as to her future behaviour": the lives of the widows of the Senghenydd Mining Disaster of 1913', *Llafur*, **6** (4), 93–109.

Wicks, David (2001), 'Institutionalized mindsets of invulnerability: differentiated institutional fields and the antecedents of organisational crisis', *Organization Studies*, **22** (4), 659–92.

Williamson, Stanley (1999), *Gresford: The Anatomy of a Disaster*, Liverpool: Liverpool University Press.

Winter, M.G. and C. Henderson (2003), 'Estimates of the quantities of recycled aggregates in Scotland', *Engineering Geology*, **70** (3–4), 205–15.

Wright, Tim (2012), *The Political Economy of the Chinese Coal Industry: Black Gold and Blood-Stained Coal*, London: Routledge.

Young, Audrey (2012), 'Pike River: "unrelenting picture of failure"', *New Zealand Herald*, accessed 5 November 2014 at www.nzherald.co.nz/business/news/article.cfm?c_id=3&objectid=10845310.

CHAPTER 6

Alderman, Jess and Richard A. Daynard (2006), 'Applying lessons from tobacco litigation to obesity lawsuits', *American Journal of Preventive Medicine*, **30** (1), 82–8.

Allender, S., R. Balakrishnan, P. Scarborough, P. Webster and M. Rayner (2009), 'The burden of smoking-related ill health in the UK', *Tobacco Control*, **18** (4), 262–7.

Alston, Lee J., Ruth Dupré and Tomas Nonnenmacher (2002), 'Social reformers and legislation: the prohibition of cigarettes in the United States and Canada', *Explorations in Economic History*, **39**, 425–45.

Associated Press (1935), 'Smokers warned of stomach ulcers', *New York Times*, 29 October, p. 1.

Bachinger, Eleonore, Martin McKee and Anna Gilmore (2008), 'Tobacco policies in Nazi Germany: not as simple as it seems', *Public Health*, **122**, 497–505.

Bailey, Christopher J. (2004), 'From "informed choice" to "social hygiene": government control of cigarette smoking in the US', *Journal of American Studies*, **38** (1), 41–65.

Bartrip, Peter (2013), 'Tarred roads or tobacco? Debates on the cause of lung cancer, nineteen-twenties to nineteen-fifties', *Historical Research*, **86** (231), 138–57.

Becker, Gary S. and Kevin M. Murphy (1988), 'A theory of rational addiction', *Journal of Political Economy*, **96** (4), 675–700.

Bedard, Kelly and Olivier Deschênes (2006), 'The long-term impact of military service on health: evidence from World War II and Korean War veterans', *American Economic Review*, **96** (1), 176–94.

Bell, Kirsten and Helen Keane (2012), 'Nicotine control: e-cigarettes, smoking and addiction', *International Journal of Drug Policy*, **23** (3), 242–7.

Berridge, Virginia (2003), 'Post-war smoking policy in the UK and the redefinition of public health', *Twentieth Century British History*, **14** (1), 61–82.

Berridge, Virginia (2006), 'The policy response to the smoking and lung cancer connection in the 1950s and 1960s', *Historical Journal*, **49** (4), 1185–209.

Berridge, Virginia (2007), 'Medicine and the public: the 1962 Report of the Royal College of Physicians and the new public health', *Bulletin of the History of Medicine*, **81** (1), 286–311.

British American Tobacco (n.d.), 'The health risks of smoking: a cause of serious disease', accessed 22 January 2015 at www.bat.com/group/sites/UK__9D9KCY.nsf/vwPagesWebLive/DO52AMG6?opendocument &SKN=1.

Brody, Jane E. (1984), 'The growing militancy of the nation's non-smokers', *New York Times*, 15 January, p. E6.

Burnham, John C. (1989), 'American physicians and tobacco use: two surgeons general, 1929 and 1964', *Bulletin of the History of Medicine*, **63** (1), 1–31.

Cairncross, Alec (1985), *Years of Recovery: British Economic Policy 1945–51*, London: Methuen.

Cantor, David (2006), 'Cancer, quackery and the vernacular meanings of hope in 1950s America', *Journal of the History of Medicine and Allied Sciences*, **61** (3), 324–68.

Cater, Percy (1946), 'Tobacco, films not cut', *Daily Mail*, 15 February, p. 1.

Clancy, Luke (2009), 'Progress in tobacco control', *Health Policy*, **91** (Supplement 1), S3–S14.

Comis, Robert L. (2003), 'A brief history of the research and treatment of lung cancer from 1970 to 2003', *International Journal of Clinical Oncology*, **8**, 230–33.

Communicable Disease Centre (2014), 'Nicotine: systemic agent', accessed 26 January 2015 at www.cdc.gov/niosh/ershdb/emergency responsecard_29750028.html.

Connor, Steve (2012), 'Smoking will "kill up to a billion people worldwide this century"', *Independent*, online edition, 28 October, accessed 20 January 2015 at www.independent.co.uk/life-style/health-and-families/health-news/smoking-will-kill-up-to-a-billion-people-world wide-this-century-8229907.html.

Courtwright, David T. (2005), '"Carry on smoking": public relations and advertising strategies of American and British tobacco companies since 1950', *Business History*, **47** (3), 421–32.

Daily Mail Reporter (1951), 'Doctors blame smoking', *Daily Mail*, 29 June, p. 5.

DeVita, Vincent T. and Edward Chu (2008), 'A history of cancer chemotherapy', *Cancer Research*, **68** (21), 8643–53.

Diamond, Jared (2005), *Collapse: How Societies Choose to Fail or Survive*, London: Penguin.

Dillon, Patrick (2002), *The Much-Lamented Death of Madam Geneva*, London: Review.

Dinan, John and Jac C. Heckelman (2005), 'The anti-tobacco movement in the Progressive Era: a case study of direct democracy in Oregon', *Explorations in Economic History*, **42**, 529–46.

Doll, Richard (1998), 'Uncovering the effects of smoking: historical perspective', *Statistical Methods in Medical Research*, **7**, 87–117.

Doll, Richard and A. Bradford Hill (1950), 'Smoking and carcinoma of the lung: preliminary report', *British Medical Journal*, **2** (4286), 739–48.

Doll, Richard and A. Bradford Hill (1954), 'The mortality of doctors in relation to their smoking habits: a preliminary report', *British Medical Journal*, **1** (4877), 1451–5.

Doll, Richard and A. Bradford Hill (1956), 'Lung cancer and other causes of death in relation to smoking: a second report on the mortality of British doctors', *British Medical Journal*, **2** (5001), 1071–6.

Elliot, Rosemary (2012), 'Smoking for taxes: the triumph of fiscal policy over health in postwar West Germany, 1945–55', *Economic History Review*, **65** (4), 1450–74.

Eriksen, Michael, Judith Mackay and Hana Ross (2012), *The Tobacco Atlas*, 4th edn, Atlanta, GA: American Cancer Society.

Forey, Barbara, Jan Hamling, John Hamling, Alison Thornton and Peter Lee (2011), *International Smoking Statistics (Web Edition): A Collection of Worldwide Historical Data: Germany*, Sutton: P.N. Lee Statistics & Computing.

Forey, Barbara, Jan Hamling, John Hamling, Alison Thornton and Peter Lee (2012a), *International Smoking Statistics (Web Edition): A Collection of Worldwide Historical Data: United Kingdom*, Sutton: P.N. Lee Statistics & Computing.

Forey, Barbara, Jan Hamling, John Hamling, Alison Thornton and Peter Lee (2012b), *International Smoking Statistics (Web Edition): A Collection of Worldwide Historical Data: USA*, Sutton: P.N. Lee Statistics & Computing.

Gallus, S., A. Schiaffino, C. La Vecchia, J. Townsend and E. Fernandez (2006), 'Price and cigarette consumption in Europe', *Tobacco Control*, **15** (2), 114–19.

Glantz, Stanton A., John Slade, Lisa A. Bero, Peter Hanauer and Deborah E. Barnes (eds) (1996), *The Cigarette Papers*, Berkeley, CA: University of California Press.

Goodman, Jordan (1993), *Tobacco in History: The Cultures of Dependence*, London: Routledge.

Gruber, Jonathan (2001), 'Tobacco at the crossroads: the past and future of smoking regulation in the United States', *Journal of Economic Perspectives*, **15** (2), 193–212.

Hammond, E. Culyer and Daniel Horn (1954), 'The relationship between human smoking habits and death rates: a follow-up study of 187,766 men', *Journal of the American Medical Association*, **155** (15), 1316–28.

Hannah, Leslie (2006), 'The Whig fable of American Tobacco, 1895–1913', *Journal of Economic History*, **66** (1), 42–73.

Hedrick, James L. (1971), 'The economic costs of cigarette smoking', *HSMHA Health Reports*, **86** (2), 179–82.

Hu, Teh-wei, Hai-Yen Sung, and Theodore E. Keeler (1995), 'Reducing cigarette consumption in California: tobacco taxes vs an anti-smoking media campaign', *American Journal of Public Health*, **85** (9), 1218–22.

Huisman, Martijn, Johannes Brug and Johan Machenbach (2007), 'Absinthe – is its history relevant for current public health?', *International Journal of Epidemiology*, **36** (4), 738–44.

Jacobson, Peter D., Jeffrey Wasserman and John R. Anderson (1997), 'Historical overview of tobacco legislation and regulation', *Journal of Social Issues*, **53** (1), 75–95.

James I (1885 [1604]), *A Counter-Blaste to Tobacco*, Edinburgh: E. &. G. Goldsmid.

Jha, Prabhat and Frank J. Chaloupka (1999), *Curbing the Epidemic: Governments and the Economics of Tobacco Control*, Washington, DC: World Bank.

Klein, Jonathan D. and William Dietz (2010), 'Childhood obesity: the new tobacco', *Health Affairs*, **29** (3), 388–92.

Laurence, William L. (1940), 'Lung cancer rise laid to cigarettes', *New York Times*, 26 October, p. 17.

Levin, Morton L., Hyman Goldstein and Paul R. Gerhardt (1950), 'Cancer and tobacco smoking', *Journal of the American Medical Association*, **143** (4), 336–8.

Lombard, Herbert L. and Carl R. Doering (1928), 'Cancer studies in Massachusetts. 2. Habits, characteristics and environment of individuals with and without cancer', *New England Journal of Medicine*, **198**, 481–7.

McCulloch, Jock and Geoffrey Tweedale (2008), *Defending the Indefensible: The Global Asbestos Industry and its Fight for Survival*, Oxford: Oxford University Press.

Medical Research Council (1957), 'Tobacco smoking and cancer of the lung: statement by the Medical Research Council', *British Medical Journal*, **1** (5034), 1523–4.

Milićević, Nataša (2002), 'The hospice movement: history and current worldwide situation', *Archive of Oncology*, **10** (1), 29–32.

Miller, Karen S. (1999), *The Voice of Business: Hill & Knowlton and Postwar Public Relations*, Chapel Hill, NC: University of North Carolina Press.

Mills, Clarence A. and Marjorie Mills Porter (1950), 'Tobacco smoking habits and cancer of the mouth and respiratory system', *Cancer Research*, **10** (9), 539–42.

Monahan, David T. (1957), 'Cancer of the lung', *Annals of Surgery*, **145** (4), 583–90.

New York Times (1941), '"Smokers' cancer" laid to sunburn', *New York Times*, 8 April, p. 30.

New York Times (1950), 'Smoking found tied to cancer of the lungs; 94.1% of males studied used cigarettes', *New York Times*, 27 May, p. 22.

Novotny, Thomas E. and Hadii Mamudu (2008), 'Progression of tobacco control policies: lessons from the United States and implications for global action', World Bank Health, Nutrition and Population (HNP) Discussion Paper, Washington, DC: World Bank.

Oreskes, Naomi and Erik M. Conway (2011), *Merchants of Doubt*, London: Bloomsbury.

Our Medical Correspondent (1950), 'Smoking and cancer: results of expert study', *The Times*, 29 September, p. 2.

Palazzo, Albert (2000), *Seeking Victory on the Western Front: The British Army and Chemical Warfare in World War I*, Lincoln: University of Nebraska Press.

Parascandola, Mark (2001), 'Cigarettes and the US Public Health Service in the 1950s', *American Journal of Public Health*, **91** (2), 196–205.

Patel, Preeti, Cassandra A. Okechukwu, Jeff Collin and Belinda Hughes (2009), 'Bringing "Light, Life and Happiness": British American Tobacco and music sponsorship in sub-Saharan Africa', *Third World Quarterly*, **30** (4), 685–700.

Peters, C. Brooks (1939), 'Nazis censoring private morals', *New York Times*, 12 March, p. 66.

Peto, Richard, Alan D. Lopez, Jillian Boreham and Michael Thun (2006), *Mortality from Smoking in Developed Countries 1950–2000*, 2nd edn, Geneva: International Union Against Cancer, accessed 4 February 2015 at www.ctsu.ox.ac.uk/deathsfromsmoking/.

Plumb, Robert K. (1954), 'Cancer unit asks a smoking parley', *New York Times*, 23 October, p. 17.

Proctor, Robert N. (1999), 'Bitter pill', *Sciences*, **39** (3), 14–19.

Proctor, Robert N. (2012), 'The history of the discovery of the cigarette–lung cancer link: evidentiary traditions, corporate denial, global toll', *Tobacco Control*, **21**, 87–91.

Ramin, Brodie (2006), 'Science, politics, and tobacco in the developing world', *Canadian Journal of Development Studies*, **27** (3), 383–401.

Rasmussen, Susanne R., Eva Prescott, Thorkild I.A. Sorensen and Jes Sogaard (2004), 'The total life-time costs of smoking', *European Journal of Public Health*, **14**, 95–100.

Rosenblatt, Milton B. (1964), 'Lung cancer in the 19th century', *Bulletin of the History of Medicine*, **38** (5), 395–425.

Royal College of Physicians (1962), *Smoking and Health: A Report of the Royal College of Physicians of London on Smoking in Relation to Cancer of the Lung and Other Diseases*, London: Pitman Medical.

Schrek, Robert, Lyle A. Baker, George P. Ballard and Sidney Dolgoff (1950), 'Tobacco smoking as an etiologic factor in disease. I. Cancer', *Cancer Research*, **10** (1), 49–58.

Sirabionian, Andrei (2005), 'Why tobacco litigation has not been successful in the United Kingdom: a comparative analysis of tobacco litigation in the United States and the United Kingdom', *Northwestern Journal of International Law and Business*, **25** (2), 485–507.

Siu, Wanda (2009), 'Social construction of reality: the tobacco issue', *Critical Public Health*, **19** (1), 23–44.

Slovic, Paul (2001), 'Cigarette smokers: rational actors or rational fools?', in Paul Slovic (ed.), *Smoking: Risk, Perception and Policy*, Thousand Oaks, CA: Sage, pp. 97–124.

Surgeon General's Advisory Committee on Smoking and Health (1964), *Smoking and Health: Report of the Advisory Committee to the Surgeon General of the Public Health Service*, Washington, DC: Public Health Service.

Sussman, Steve, Pallav Pokhrel, David Black, Matthew Kohrman, Stephen Hamann, Prakit Vateesatokit and Stephen E.D. Nsimba (2007), 'Tobacco control in developing countries: Tanzania, Nepal, China, and Thailand as examples', *Nicotine and Tobacco Research*, **9** (Supplement 3), S447–S457.

Talley, Colin Lee, Howard I. Kushner and Claire E. Sterk (2004), 'Lung cancer, chronic disease epidemiology, and medicine, 1948–1964', *Journal of the History of Medicine and Allied Sciences*, **59** (3), 329–74.

Tate, Cassandra (1999), *Cigarette Wars: The Triumph of 'The Little White Slaver'*, New York: Oxford University Press.

Tinkler, Penny (2001), '"Red tips for hot lips": advertising cigarettes for young women in Britain, 1920–70', *Women's History Review*, **10** (2), 249–72.

Tobacco Manufacturers' Association (n.d.), 'Tax revenue from tobacco', accessed 4 February 2015 at www.the-tma.org.uk/tma-publications-research/facts-figures/tax-revenue-from-tobacco/.

Tobacco Tax Council (1975), *The Tax Burden on Tobacco: Historical Compilation*, Vol. 10, Tobacco Tax Council.

Tobin, Richard J. and Walter I. Knausenberger (1998), 'Dilemmas of development: burley tobacco, the environment and economic growth in Malawi', *Journal of Southern African Studies*, **24** (2), 405–24.

Tweedale, Geoffrey (2000), *Magic Mineral to Killer Dust*, Oxford: Oxford University Press.

US Treasury (1998), 'The economic costs of smoking in the United States and the benefits of comprehensive tobacco legislation', Treasury Report 3113, accessed 4 February 2015 at www.treasury.gov/press-center/press-releases/Documents/tobacco.pdf.

Verellen, Dirk, Mark De Ridder and Guy Storme (2008), 'A (short) history of image-guided radiotherapy', *Radiotherapy and Oncology*, **86**, 4–13.

Viscusi, W. Kip and Joni Hersch (2008), 'The mortality cost to smokers', *Journal of Health Economics*, **27**, 943–58.

Walker, R.B. (1980), 'Medical aspects of tobacco smoking and the anti-tobacco movement in Britain in the nineteenth century', *Medical History*, **24**, 391–402.

Washington Post (1929), 'Jeff Davis' niece bobs hair at 90', *Washington Post*, 17 March, p. M7.

Weber, Bruce (2009), 'H.A. Engle, tobacco plaintiff, dies at 89', *New York Times*, 24 July, accessed 6 February 2015 at www.nytimes.com/2009/07/24/us/24engle.html?_r=0.

Webster, Charles (1984), 'Tobacco smoking addiction: a challenge to the National Health Service', *British Journal of Addiction*, **79**, 7–16.

Witschi, Hanspeter (2001), 'A short history of lung cancer', *Toxicological Sciences*, **64**, 4–6.

Woods, Robert S. (2006), 'Tobacco's tipping point: the Master Settlement Agreement as a focusing event', *Policy Studies Journal*, **34** (3), 419–36.

World Health Organization (WHO) (2009), *History of the World Health Organization Framework Convention on Tobacco Control*, Geneva: WHO.

Wrigley, Chris (2014), 'Smoking for king and country', *History Today*, **64** (4), 24–30.

Wynder, Ernest L. and Evarts A. Graham (1950), 'Tobacco smoking as a possible etiologic factor in bronchiogenic carcinoma: a study of six hundred and eighty-four proved cases', *Journal of the American Association*, **143** (4), 329–36.

CHAPTER 7

Abiad, Abdul and Ashoka Mody (2005), 'Financial reform: what shakes it? What shapes it?', *American Economic Review*, **95** (1), 66–88.

Abiad, Abdul, Enrica Detragiache and Thierry Tressel (2010), 'A new database of financial reforms', *IMF Staff Papers*, **57** (2), 281–302.

Almunia, Miguel, Agustín Bénétrix, Barry Eichengreen, Kevin O'Rourke and Gisela Rua (2010), 'From Great Depression to great credit crisis: similarities, differences, and lessons', *Economic Policy*, **25**, 219–65.

Annunziata, Marco (2015), 'The ECB's QE decision', Vox, 23 January, accessed 19 March 2015 at www.voxeu.org/article/ecb-s-qe-decision.

Bank for International Settlements (2007), *77th Annual Report*, Basel: BIS.

Bank for International Settlements (2008), *78th Annual Report*, Basel: BIS.

Bank of England (2007), *Financial Stability Report April 2007*, London: Bank of England.

Barth, James R., R. Dan Brumbaugh and James A. Wilcox (2000), 'Glass–Steagall repealed: market forces compel a new bank legal structure', *Journal of Economic Perspectives*, 14 (2), 191–204.

Basel Committee on Banking Supervision (2011), *Basel III: A Global Regulatory Framework for More Resilient Banks and Banking Systems*, Basel: Bank for International Settlements.

Bernanke, Benjamin S. (2000), *Essays on the Great Depression*, Princeton, NJ: Princeton University Press.

Bernanke, Benjamin S. (2008), 'Reducing systemic risk', speech at the Federal Reserve Bank of Kansas City's Annual Economic Symposium, Jackson Hole, Wyoming, 22 August, accessed 3 March 2015 at www.federalreserve.gov/newsevents/speech/bernanke20080822a.htm.

Bernanke, Benjamin S. (2010), 'Economic policy: lessons from history', speech at the 43rd Annual Alexander Hamilton Awards Dinner, Center for the Study of the Presidency and Congress, Washington, DC, April, accessed 3 March 2015 at www.federalreserve.gov/newsevents/speech/bernanke20100408a.htm.

Bernanke, Benjamin S. (2012), 'The economic recovery and economic policy', speech at the Economic Club of New York, 20 November, accessed 10 March 2015 at www.federalreserve.gov/newsevents/speech/bernanke20121120a.htm.

Bordo, Michael D. (2013), 'The Federal Reserve's role: actions before, during, and after the 2008 panic in the historical context of the great contraction', Hoover Institution, Economics Working Paper 13111.

Bordo, Michael, Barry Eichengreen, Daniela Klingebiel, Maria Soledad Martinez-Peria and Andrew K. Rose (2001), 'Financial crises: lessons from the last 120 years', *Economic Policy*, **16** (32), 51–82.

Bordo, Michael D. and Harold James (2014), 'The European crisis in the context of the history of previous financial crises', *Journal of Macroeconomics*, **39**, 275–84.

Cabral, Ricardo (2010), 'The PIGS' external debt problem', Vox, 8 May, accessed 13 March 2015 at www.voxeu.org/article/gips-external-debt-problem.

Calhoun, Craig (2013), 'Occupy Wall Street in perspective', *British Journal of Sociology*, **64** (1), 26–38.

Calomiris, Charles W. (2006), 'The regulatory record of the Greenspan Fed', *American Economic Review*, **96** (2), 170–73.

Capie, Forrest (2010), *The Bank of England 1950s to 1979*, Cambridge: Cambridge University Press.

Cecchetti, Stephen G. and Kermit L. Schoenholtz (2008), 'How central bankers see it: the first decade of ECB policy and beyond', NBER Working Papers No. 14489.

Connolly, Kate and Helena Smith (2015), 'German anger over Greek demand for war reparations', *Guardian*, online edition, 12 March, accessed 17 March 2015 at www.theguardian.com/world/2015/mar/12/german-anger-over-greek-demand-for-war-reparations.

Dannhauser, Jamie (2013), 'The euro – the story of a suboptimal currency area', in Philip Booth (ed.), *The Euro: The Beginning, the Middle ... and the End?*, London: Institute of Economic Affairs, pp. 52–82.

de Bromhead, Alan, Barry Eichengreen and Kevin O'Rourke (2013), 'Right-wing political extremism in the 1920s and 1930s: do German lessons generalize?', *Journal of Economic History*, **63** (2), 371–406.

De Grauwe, Paul (1997), *The Economics of Monetary Integration*, 3rd edn, Oxford: Oxford University Press.

De Grauwe, Paul and Yuemei Ji (2013), 'Panic-driven austerity in the Eurozone and its implications', VoxEU, accessed 13 March 2014 at www.voxeu.org/article/panic-driven-austerity-eurozone-and-its-implications.

Demirgüç-Kunt, Asli and Tolga Sobaci (2001), 'Deposit insurance around the world: a database', *World Bank Economic Review*, **15** (3), 481–90.

Deutsche Bundesbank (2014), 'Launch of the banking union: the Single Supervisory Mechanism in Europe', *Monthly Report of the Deutsche Bundesbank*, **66** (10), 43–64.

Dowd, Kevin and Martin Hutchinson (2010), *Alchemists of Loss: How Modern Finance and Government Intervention Crashed the Financial System*, Chichester: John Wiley.

Eichengreen, Barry (1997), *European Monetary Unification: Theory, Practice, and Analysis*, Cambridge, MA: MIT Press.

Eichengreen, Barry (2010), 'The breakup of the euro area', in Alberto Alesina and Francesco Giavazzi (eds), *Europe and the Euro*, Chicago, IL: University of Chicago Press, pp. 11–51.

Eichengreen, Barry (2012), 'Economic history and economic policy', *Journal of Economic History*, **72** (2), 289–307.

Eichengreen, Barry (2015), *Hall of Mirrors: The Great Depression, the Great Recession and the Uses – and Misuses – of History*, Oxford: Oxford University Press.

Eichengreen, Barry and Kevin H. O'Rourke (2010), 'A tale of two depressions: what do the new data tell us?', Vox, accessed 4 March 2015 at www.voxeu.org/article/tale-two-depressions-what-do-new-data-tell-us-february-2010-update#jun09.

Eichengreen, Barry and Peter Temin (2010), 'Fetters of gold and paper', *Oxford Review of Economic Policy*, **26** (3), 370–84.

European Central Bank (2010), *Annual Report 2009*, Frankfurt: ECB.

European Commission (2013), 'Youth unemployment', accessed 16 March 2015 at http://ec.europa.eu/europe2020/pdf/themes/21_youth_unemployment.pdf.

Evanoff, Douglas D. and Willaim F. Moeller (2012), 'Dodd–Frank: content, purpose, implementation status, and issues', *Federal Reserve Bank of Chicago Economic Perspectives*, **115** (3), 85–97.

Fawley, Brett W. and Christopher J. Neely (2013), 'Four stories of quantitative easing', *Federal Reserve Bank of St Louis Review*, **95** (1), 51–88.

Featherstone, Kevin (2011), 'The Greek sovereign debt crisis and EMU – a failing state in a skewed regime', *Journal of Common Market Studies*, **49** (2), 193–217.

Ferguson, Thomas and Robert Johnson (2009), 'Too big to bail: the "Paulson Put", presidential politics, and the global financial meltdown, part II: fatal reversal – single payer and back', *International Journal of Political Economy*, **38** (2), 5–45.

Financial Crisis Inquiry Commission (2011), *The Financial Crisis Inquiry Report*. Washington, DC: US Government Printing Office.

Friedman, Milton and Anna Schwartz (1963), *A Monetary History of the United States, 1870–1960*, Princeton, NJ: Princeton University Press.

Galati, Gabriele and Richhild Moessner (2013), 'Macroprudential policy – a literature review', *Journal of Economic Surveys*, **27** (5), 846–78.

Gocaj, Ledina and Sophie Meunier (2013), 'Time will tell: the EFSF, the ESM, and the euro crisis', *European Integration*, **35** (3), 239–53.

Goodhart, Charles A.E. (2012), 'The Vickers report: an assessment', *Law and Financial Markets Review*, **6** (1), 32–7.

Goodhart, Charles A.E. and Jonathan P. Ashworth (2012), 'QE: a successful start may be running into diminishing returns', *Oxford Review of Economic Policy*, **28** (4), 640–70.

Greenspan, Alan (2008), *The Age of Turbulence*, London: Penguin.

Gross, Daniel (2008), 'The world's worst banker?', *Newsweek*, 2 December, accessed 6 February 2010 at www.newsweek.com/id/171688.

Hall, Maximilian J.B. (2009), 'The sub-prime crisis, the credit crunch and "bank failure": an assessment of the UK authorities' response', *Journal of Financial Regulation and Compliance*, **17** (4), 427–52.

House of Commons Treasury Committee (2009), *Banking Crisis*, Volume 1, *Oral Evidence*, HC 144-I, London: HMSO.

Independent Commission on Banking (2011), *Final Report Recommendations*, London: Independent Commission on Banking.

Issing, Otmar (2000), 'Should we have faith in central banks?', St Edmund's College Millennium Year Lecture, Cambridge, 26 October, accessed 11 July 2009 at www.ecb.int/press/key/date/2000/html/sp00 1026_2.en.html.

James, Harold (2012), *Making the European Monetary Union*, Cambridge MA: Belknap Press.

Jonung, Lars and Eoin Drea (2010), 'It can't happen, it's a bad idea, it won't last: US economists on the EMU and the euro, 1989–2002', *Economic Journal Watch*, **7** (1), 4–52.

Kahn, George A. (2005), 'The Greenspan era: lessons for the future – a summary of the Bank's 2005 economic symposium', *Federal Reserve Bank of Kansas City Economic Review*, **90** (4), 35–45.

Kaminsky, Graciela Laura and Sergio L. Schmukler (2008), 'Short-run pain, long-run gain: financial liberalization and stock market cycles', *Review of Finance*, **12**, 253–92.

Keegan, William (2012), *'Saving the World'? Gordon Brown Reconsidered*, London: Searching Finance.

Keynes, John Maynard (1936), *The General Theory of Employment, Interest, and Money*, London: Macmillan.

Kindleberger, Charles P. and Robert Z. Aliber (2011), *Manias, Panics, and Crashes: A History of Financial Crises*, 6th edn, Basingstoke: Palgrave Macmillan.

King, Mervyn (2014), 'Mervyn King and former chairman of Federal Reserve Ben Bernanke reflect on world financial crisis', *BBC Radio 4 Today Programme*, 29 December, accessed 4 March 2015 at www.bbc.co.uk/programmes/p02g1zmb.

Kirkup, James (2011), 'Euro doomed from the start, says Jacques Delors', *Daily Telegraph*, online edition, 2 December, accessed 9 April 2013 at www.telegraph.co.uk/finance/financialcrisis/8932647/Euro-doomed-from-start-says-Jacques-Delors.html.

Kutter, Amelie (2014), 'A catalytic moment: the Greek crisis in the German financial press', *Discourse and Society*, **25** (4), 446–66.

Lane, Philip R. (2012), 'The European sovereign debt crisis', *Journal of Economic Perspectives*, **26** (1), 49–67.

Lastra, Rosa M. (1996), *Central Banking and Banking Regulation*, London: LSE Financial Markets Group.

Leiser, David, Sacha Bourgeois-Gironde and Rinat Benita (2010), 'Human foibles or systemic failure – lay perceptions of the 2008–2009 financial crisis', *Journal of Socio-Economics*, **39** (2), 132–41.

Lilico, Andrew (2013), 'Better off in?', in Philip Booth (ed.), *The Euro: The Beginning, the Middle ... and the End?*, London: Institute of Economic Affairs, pp. 107–22.

London Summit – Leaders' Statement, 2 April 2009, accessed 6 March 2015 at www.imf.org/external/np/sec/pr/2009/pdf/g20_040209.pdf.

Marsh, David (2011), *The Euro*, New Haven: Yale University Press.

Mayer, Martin (1990), *The Greatest Ever Bank-Robbery: The Collapse of the Savings and Loan Industry*. New York: Charles Scribner's Sons.

Merkel, Angela and Dominique Strauss-Kahn (2010), 'Transcript of statements to the media by German Chancellor Angela Merkel and the managing director of the International Monetary Fund (IMF), Dominique Strauss-Kahn, on April 28, 2010 in Berlin', accessed 16 March 2015 at www.imf.org/external/np/tr/2010/tr042810.htm.

Mishkin, Frederic S. (2011), 'Over the cliff: from the subprime to the Global Financial Crisis', *Journal of Economic Perspectives*, **25** (1), 49–70.

Mishkin, Frederic S. and Eugene N. White (2014), 'Unprecedented actions: the Federal Reserve's response to the Global Financial Crisis in historical perspective', Federal Reserve Bank of Dallas, Globalization and Monetary Policy Institute, Working Paper 209.

Neate, Rupert and agencies (2013), 'François Hollande: the Eurozone crisis is over', *Guardian*, online edition, 9 June, accessed 17 March 2015 at www.theguardian.com/world/2013/jun/09/francois-holland-eurozone-crisis-over.

Noble, Gregory W. and John Ravenhill (eds) (2000), *The Asian Financial Crisis and the Architecture of International Finance*, Cambridge: Cambridge University Press.

Nolle, Daniel E. (2015), 'Who's in charge of fixing the world's financial system? The under-appreciated lead role of the G20 and the FSB', *Financial Markets, Institutions and Instruments*, **24** (1), 1–82.

O'Rourke, Kevin and Alan Taylor (2013), 'Cross of euros', *Journal of Economic Perspectives*, **27** (3), 167–91.

Pierce, Andrew (2008), 'The queen asks why no one saw the credit crunch coming', *Daily Telegraph*, online edition, 5 November,

accessed 26 February 2015 at www.telegraph.co.uk/news/uknews/the
royalfamily/3386353/The-Queen-asks-why-no-one-saw-the-credit-crunch-
coming.html.

Rajan, Raghuram G. (2010), *Fault Lines: How Hidden Fractures Still
Threaten the World Economy*, Princeton, NJ: Princeton University
Press.

Reinhart, Carmen and Kenneth Rogoff (2009), *This Time is Different*,
Princeton, NJ: Princeton University Press.

Reinhart, Vincent (2011), 'A year of living dangerously: the management
of the financial crisis in 2008', *Journal of Economic Perspectives*, **25**
(1), 71–90.

Reveley, James and John Singleton (2015), 'Financial fantasy documents
and public learning: the case of the US Financial Crisis Inquiry report',
in Michael A. Peters, João Paraskeva and Tina Besley (eds), *The
Global Financial Crisis and Educational Restructuring*, New York:
Peter Lang, pp. 165–76.

Richardson, Matthew (2012), 'Regulating Wall Street: the Dodd-Frank
Act', *Federal Reserve Bank of Chicago Economic Perspectives*, **115**
(3), 505–20.

Romer, Christina D. (2009), 'Back from the brink', speech at Federal
Reserve Bank of Chicago, 24 September, accessed 3 March 2015 at
http://eml.berkeley.edu/~cromer/Back_from_the_Brink2.pdf.

Sargent, Thomas J. (2012), 'Nobel lecture: United States then, Europe
now', *Journal of Political Economy*, **120** (1), 1–40.

Sehmer, Alexander (2015), 'Greece referendum: Varoufakis accuses EU
creditors of "terrorism" as Greeks go to the polls', *Independent*, online
edition, 5 July, accessed 29 July 2015 at www.independent.co.uk/news/
world/europe/greece-referendum-varoufakis-accuses-eu-creditors-of-
terrorism-as-greeks-go-to-the-polls-10366701.html.

Shambaugh, Jay C. (2012), 'The euro's three crises', *Brookings Papers
on Economic Activity*, **2012** (1), 157–211.

Shin, Hyun Song (2009), 'Reflections on Northern Rock: the bank run
that heralded the Global Financial Crisis', *Journal of Economic
Perspectives*, **23**, 101–20.

Siklos, Pierre L. (2002), *The Changing Face of Central Banking*,
Cambridge: Cambridge University Press.

Singleton, John (2011), *Central Banking in the Twentieth Century*,
Cambridge: Cambridge University Press.

Singleton, John, with Arthur Grimes, Gary Hawke and Sir Frank Holmes
(2006), *Innovation and Independence: The Reserve Bank of New
Zealand, 1973–2002*, Auckland: Auckland University Press.

Skidelsky, Robert (2010), *Keynes: The Return of the Master*, London:
Penguin.

Soros, George (2013), 'Eurobonds or Euro-exit: the choice is Germany's', *Guardian*, online edition, 30 April, accessed 8 June 2013 at www.guardian.co.uk/business/blog/2013/apr/30/eurobonds-euro-germany-george-soros.

Stiglitz, Joseph (2009), 'The anatomy of a murder: who killed America's economy?', *Critical Review*, **21** (2), 329–39.

Summers, Lawrence (2014), 'Britain's economic growth is not a sign that austerity works', *Washington Post*, online edition, 4 May, accessed 10 March 2015 at www.washingtonpost.com/opinions/britains-economic-growth-is-not-a-sign-that-austerity-works/2014/05/04/26b345e8-d204-11e3-937f-d3026234b51c_story.html.

Taibbi, Matt (2009), 'The great American bubble machine', *Rolling Stone*, online edition, 1082, 9 July, accessed 9 March 2015 at www.rollingstone.com/politics/news/the-great-american-bubble-machine-201 00405.

Taylor, John B. (2009), 'Economic policy and the financial crisis: an empirical analysis of what went wrong', *Critical Review: A Journal of Politics and Society*, **21** (2–3), 341–64.

United States Senate Permanent Subcommittee on Investigations (2011), *Wall Street and the Financial Crisis: Anatomy of a Financial Collapse*, Washington, DC: Permanent Subcommittee on Investigations.

Whittle, Andrea and Frank Mueller (2012), 'Bankers in the dock: moral storytelling in action', *Human Relations*, **65** (1), 111–39.

Wood, Duncan Robert (2005), *Governing Global Banking: The Basel Committee and the Politics of Financial Globalization*, Aldershot: Ashgate.

CHAPTER 8

BBC (2015a), 'China explosion: Tianjin delay toll rises in port blasts', 13 August, accessed 13 August 2015 at www.bbc.co.uk/news/world-Asia-33900268.

BBC (2015b), 'Tianjin explosions: UN expert says China "lacked transparency"', 20 August, accessed 21 August 2015 at www.bbc.co.uk/news/world-asia-china-33998655.

Fielding, Eric, Andrew W. Lo and Jian Helen Yang (2011), 'The National Transportation Safety Board: a model for systemic risk management', *Journal of Investment Management*, **9** (1), 17–49.

Government Accountability Office (1997), *Financial Crisis Management: Four Financial Crises in the 1980s*, GAO/GGD-97-96, Washington, DC: GAO.

Olejarski, Amanda M. and James L. Garnett (2010), 'Coping with Katrina: assessing crisis management behaviours in the Big One', *Journal of Contingencies and Crisis Management*, **18** (1), 26–38.

Peckham, Robert (2013), 'Economies of contagion: financial crisis and pandemic', *Economy and Society*, **42** (2), 226–48.

Prince, Samuel Henry (1920), *Catastrophe and Social Change*, New York: Columbia University Press.

Stein, Mark (2004), 'The critical period of disasters: insights from sense-making and psychoanalytic theory', *Human Relations*, **57** (10), 1243–61.

Weick, Karl E. (1993), 'The collapse of sensemaking in organizations: the Mann Gulch disaster', *Administrative Science Quarterly*, **38** (4), 628–52.

Index